MULTICULTURAL EDUCATION
THROUGH
COMPETENCY-BASED TEACHER EDUCATION

William A. Hunter
Editor

American Association of Colleges for Teacher Education
Washington, D.C.
1974

Acknowledgements and Disclaimers

U.S. Office of Education

The project presented or reported herein was performed pursuant to a Grant from the U.S. Office of Education, Department of Health, Education, and Welfare. However, the opinions expressed herein do not necessarily reflect the position or policy of the U.S. Office of Education, and no official endorsement by the U.S. Office of Education should be inferred.

The University of Toledo

The project presented or reported herein was performed pursuant to a Grant from The University of Toledo, through the Teacher Corps, and subcontracted to AACTE. However, the opinions expressed herein do not necessarily reflect the position or policy of The University of Toledo, and no official endorsement by the University should be inferred.

American Association of Colleges for Teacher Education

The papers included in this collection do not necessarily reflect the viewpoint of the American Association of Colleges for Teacher Education (AACTE). Rather, in accordance with permission granted by the U.S. Government, AACTE is reprinting herein the position papers to stimulate discussion, study, and experimentation among educators. AACTE expresses its heartfelt appreciation to those individuals, organizations, and agencies which have released publication rights to the Association.

ii

Published 1974 by
AMERICAN ASSOCIATION OF COLLEGES FOR TEACHER EDUCATION
Suite 610, One Dupont Circle, Washington, D.C. 20036

Printed in the United States of America

Library of Congress Catalog Card Number: 74-24858
Standard Book Number: 910052-85-9

FOREWORD

E Pluribus Unum. This national motto has been the basis and foundation from which not only our country has grown but from which our educational thrust has sprung. Examined in its proper syntactical sequence, the translation is "out of many, one." Yet history records a focus on the unifying aspect "one" to the exclusion of the pluralistic concept expressed with the words "out of many."

"America is God's crucible, the Great Melting Pot—God is making the American" *(The Melting Pot,* Act I, by Israel Zangwill). The optimism expressed by this turn-of-the-century playwright has not been ratified by history, and multiracial and multiethnic richness has been too long sacrificed at the altar of the melting pot. The creation of the "model American" is at best a quaint myth. Even during those years when the melting pot theory was an integral tenet of national faith, Americans' references to their fellow citizens were so consistently prefaced by a statement of ethnic origin that in 1918, *Metropolitan* magazine found it useful to coin the phrase "hyphenated Americans." That idiom still has meaning for us today, a fact which, in itself, is testimony that the melting pot theory never proved itself in the crucible of reality. Although in recent years that theory has fallen into disrepute, the message has not reached all segments of society and therefore has not reached all our schools. iii

The goal of education in contemporary society must be to develop individuals who are open to change and who are flexible, adaptive, and receptive. This of necessity means introducing students to the great diversity of lifestyles which our multicultural heritage embraces.

In the past, some weak starts have been made in the schools to introduce a multicultural approach. But often it was done for the wrong reasons—an expedient move to reduce tensions, to defuse protest, and to relieve anticipated community pressures. Since reasons for doing something subtly influence *how* we act, these attempts failed. They were stop-gap measures hastily decided upon and inadequately implemented. Often these programs brought kids, teachers, and materials together in a classroom in the hope that "something" would happen. However, no number of crossed fingers or lucky rabbits' feet or speeches at school boards can replace honest assessment of the problem and adequate program preparation.

The schools' ultimate objective is the design and implementation of a culturally pluralistic curriculum which will accurately represent our diverse society. These studies in cultural heritage must emerge from introspection on the part of curriculum designers, students, and teachers. Fusing this introspection with objective historical scholarship and the results of current research about the learning processes will provide a sound formulation. Curriculum materials of excellence and innovative teacher training can then be finally screened by having them subject to confirmation by members of the racial/ethnic group to which the materials refer.

On this foundation, teachers will be trained to emphasize the learning processes and human relationships, the affective realm, rather than just teaching processes and the cognitive realm. They will learn that the goal is not to placate cultural minorities, nor to aggrandize the cultural majority, but to bring about a new sense of being and a wholesomeness in the entire society through a strengthening of its parts.

The poet, Gerard Manley Hopkins, celebrated the great variety found in life with these words:

> Glory be to God for dappled things—
> For skies of couple-color as a brindled cow;
> For rose-moles in all stipple upon trout that swim;
> Fresh-firecoal chestnut-falls; finches' wings;
> Landscapes plotted and pieced—fold, fallow, and plow;
> And all trades, their gear and tackle and trim.
> All things counter, original, spare, strange;
> Whatever is fickle, freckled (who know how?)
> With swift, slow; sweet, sour; adazzle, dim;
> He fathers-forth whose beauty is past change:
> Praise Him.*

iv

It seems only proper to celebrate, with the same kind of gusto and joy, the richly diverse cultural heritage of America. There is no more noble way for educators to do this than to recognize the need to widen, rather than narrow, the range of human variability in our society and to help proliferate the creed that to be different is not to be inferior. We need to exert our efforts to make the school a place where differences, between and among people, are not merely tacitly accepted but are celebrated as a national blessing.

This document is an effort in that direction. The authors and AACTE have spent many hours, months, and years pondering the issues and the questions. This book reflects that deliberation. As we approach our bicentennial year and reflect on the heritage of this country, let us renew our confidence in the motto which honors the difference and diversity of "We the People" by showing it to be the source of our national unity.

E Pluribus Unum.

William L. Smith
Director, Teacher Corps
U.S. Office of Education
Washington, D.C.

---

*"Pied Beauty" originally appeared in *Poems of Gerard Manley Hopkins,* published by Oxford University Press (Fourth edition, 1967). This poem is now in the public domain.

FOREWORD

America is a culturally diverse society. As such, its educational system demands teachers and other education personnel who are trained to carry out professional tasks in a wide variety of settings and with full understanding of the significance of multiculturalism for meaningful education.

Inasmuch as over 90 percent of the education personnel in our nation are prepared in the more than 860 member colleges and universities of the American Association of Colleges for Teacher education, it is no accident that the Association has had a long and important leadership role in multicultural education. Through its Commission on Multicultural Education, established in 1970, AACTE has called for greater attention to the preservation and enhancement of cultural pluralism in education, and particularly in the preparation of education personnel.

In 1973 the members of the Commission on Multicultural Education, under the chairmanship of James Kelly, dean, University of Pittsburgh School of Education, and the Association's Committee on Performance-Based Teacher Education chaired by J.W. Maucker, vice president for academic affairs, Kansas State Teachers College, and with the active involvement of Karl Massanari, AACTE/PBTE's project director, conceived of a plan to explore the potential of competency-based teacher education with respect to the preparation of teachers in and for multicultural school settings. This proposal brought together two major interests of AACTE in a way that enhanced the Association resources available. Fortunately, the Teacher Corps, under the direction of William Smith and with the active support of James Steffensen and Preston Royster, was able to provide support for the project. The cooperation of The University of Toledo and George E. Dickson, dean of the College of Education, have been essential to the success of the undertaking.

The American Association of Colleges for Teacher Education is proud to publish this report of the Writing Conference which is the culmination of the Multicultural Education/Competency-Based Teacher Education Project. It is a pioneering effort to identify teacher competencies needed by all teachers who teach students in a culturally diverse society. The Association commends this document to all who are engaged in the improvement of teacher preparation, in the hope and expectation that the thoughts contained herein will enhance the quality of the dialogue concerning competency-based education, and thereby insure more effective teachers of young Americans for future multicultural generations.

As previously noted, the Teacher Corps and the University of Toledo have played important roles in making this activity possible.

On behalf of the Association and its officers, I want to express sincere thanks as well as congratulations to all who gave of their valuable time and professional insight as writers, editors, and consultants. Theirs was a difficult task and they did it well. We are grateful for the efforts and advice of the AACTE/PBTE Committee and the Association's Commission on Multicultural Education.

Especially, I wish to thank William A. Hunter, who served as principal investigator, and his assistant, Geneva F. Watkins. Without their professional commitment to the task, this document would not have been possible.

Finally, the AACTE publications staff should receive recognition for final copyediting, design coordination, and actual publication. Truly the total publication has been the product of excellent cooperation!

Edward C. Pomeroy
Executive Director
American Association of Colleges
   for Teacher Education
Washington, D.C.

October 1974

CONTENTS

vii

viii

ix

Participants at the Multicultural Writing Conference
Norman, Oklahoma, June 1974

These pictures capture in part the rich diversity of Americans who came to significant agreement on education needed by both minority Americans and the total cultural mix of our society.

PREFACE

Today, there exist wide variations in the extent and degree to which equal and adequate educational opportunities are available to children and youth in American society. Greater disparities and inadequacies attend educational provisions for the culturally diverse, in spite of implied consti- tutional guarantees for equal educational opportunity. There are many reasons for this, these having been variously identified, explored, investi- gated, and discussed by educators, sociologists, economists, political scientists, psychologists, anthropologists, and other specialists. There is agreement among many analysts that one cause of these conditions is the fact that there has not been adequate national commitment to education and the educational enterprise. Nor is there a real tangible, enduring sensi- tivity to the vicissitudes of multicultural education and its necessity for relevant learning, and to the integrity of contributing influencing factors in a pluralistic society.

The elimination of this undesirable, non-American condition requires an educational system prioritized and geared to accommodate cultural diversity. It will also require educators adequately prepared and favorably inclined to work effectively with children of different ethnic groups and/or other cultural identities.

Scattered and often uncoordinated efforts have been undertaken in cor- recting this situation. These include studies and work by the United States Office of Education (particularly through the Teacher Corps, by the National Center for the Improvement of Educational Systems (NCIES), Career Op- portunity Program), by colleges and universities (through multicultural- intracultural education programs), and by agencies and organizations giving special attention to special problems relating to the interests or special purposes of the agency or organization (such as AACTE, NEA). Additionally, special ethnic or cultural study groups (such as the Multicultural Education Task Force of the National Institute of Education (NIE) of the U.S. Office of Education (USOE), the National Association for the Advancement of Colored People (NAACP), and the U.S. Commission on Civil Rights) have made significant studies also.

This publication, *Multicultural Education through Competency-Based Teacher Education,* is the result of a Multicultural Education/Competency- Based Teacher Education Project (M/CBTE) which, among other objectives, sought to bring together the findings of separate studies, projects, and re- search efforts. The Project proposed to take a broader approach to the overall problem of quality education by seeking to identify generic concerns and needs common to all ethnic groups and diverse cultural situations. The Project at the same time sought to identify those needs felt to be unique or more relevant to certain cultural circumstances and situations than to others.

The Project effort was designed by a seven-member Steering Committee and the AACTE Project Staff. The design was calculated operationally to avoid or minimize separateness in the Project's educational approach and product. Simultaneously, it was desired to have reflected the input and points of view from experts on multicultural education within the identified populations and fields.

The members of the Project Steering Committee were selected because of their representativeness and expertise in the areas of multicultural edu-

TABLE 1. COMPOSITION OF STEERING COMMITTEE:

Criteria	Member
Three from Multicultural Commission	1. James Kelly, Jr., Dean, School of Education, University of Pittsburgh, Pittsburgh, Pa.
	2. Elaine Witty, Chairman, Department of Elementary Education, Norfolk State College, Norfolk, Va.
	3. Henrietta Whiteman, Director, Native American Studies Program, University of Montana, Missoula, Mont.
Two jointly named by Teacher Corps and AACTE	1. Atilano A. Valencia, Head, Dept. of Education, New Mexico Highlands University, Las Vegas, N.M.
	2. Mary Hatwood, Classroom Teacher, Alexandria Public Schools, Alexandria, Va.
University of Toledo	1. Richard Saxe, Associate Dean, College of Education, University of Toledo, Toledo, Oh.
AACTE	2. Tomás A. Arciniega, Chairman—Project Steering Committee; Dean, San Diego State University, San Diego, Ca.

cation and competency-based teacher education. Moreover, the composition of the Committee was conceived so that it would have wide and diverse representation from the professional community. (See Table 1.) The membership included three representatives selected from and by the AACTE Multicultural Education Commission, two representatives with special expertise in CBTE selected jointly by Teacher Corps and AACTE (one of these a classroom teacher selected by NEA), one member selected by The University of Toledo (the contracting institution), and one member selected by AACTE.

MULTICULTURAL EDUCATION/COMPETENCY-BASED
TEACHER EDUCATION PROJECT

AACTE Institutional Relationship			Racial Group	Geographic Location	Sex
Size	AACTE Member	Type Inst.			
Large	Yes	Public	Black American	Pennsylvania	Male
Medium	Yes	Public	Black American	Virginia	Female
Large	Yes	Public	Native American	Montana	Female
Medium	Yes	Public	Spanish-speaking American	New Mexico	Male
	NEA	Public	Black American	Virginia	Female
Large	Yes	Public	White American	Ohio	Male
Large	Yes	Public	Spanish-speaking American	California	Male

The substantive content of the document was written by scholars of multicultural education from throughout the academic community. Although it was recognized that all facets of cultural diversity could not be accommodated in this Project effort, the Project design set the initial phase of research to be the identification of competencies through the perceptions of representatives of the three largest minority racial groups, emphasizing that multicultural education is not synonymous with or limited to racial identities and minority status. As a beginning, and as a means to an end, four educators and/or teams from the Black American, Spanish-speaking American, and Native American academic communities were invited to write position papers on the competencies unique (if unique) to teaching identified racial groups in ethnic settings, as well as in general group settings.

Thirteen such papers were written and critiqued by a panel of eight consultants consisting of a teacher educator, psychologist, anthropologist, curriculum specialist, communication specialist, sociologist, political scientist, and psychometrist. A panel of eight writer-editors for each ethnic group and a cross-cultural panel of eight read the position papers and the consultants' critiques.

The Project Writing Conference was convened at the University of Oklahoma's Continuing Education Center, Norman, Oklahoma, June 16-22, 1974, during which the position paper writers interacted with each other, the panel of consultants, and the panels of writer-editors. (See Appendix I for Conference Program.) Together these professionals wrote Parts II, III, IV, and V constituting this publication. For each group, a prime writer and his or her associate were responsible for pulling together the position papers (and concerted views about them), the critiques and reports of the consultants, and the collective views of the interacting individuals and groups about the chapter content. Part II treats teacher competencies from the perspective of the Black American educator. Part III treats teacher competencies from the Spanish-speaking American educator's perspective, (including views of Puerto Rican Americans, Chicano Americans and Cuban Americans). Part IV treats teacher competencies from the perspective of the Native American, recognizing the divergencies of views among the nearly 300 tribal groups. Part V seeks to identify teacher competencies common to all groups as well as those competencies recognized in the general society as evidence of accepted requirements and standards.

The AACTE Project staff was largely responsible for assembling and providing the background information for the document. This information is reflected in Part I—Prologue. The background sections of the book were written by the AACTE Project Staff with significant assistance from associates at AACTE Headquarters.

Karl Massanari, associate director, AACTE and director of the AACTE/ PBTE Project, and Richard James, dean, College of Education, Morgan State College, Maryland, were largely responsible for writing the grant proposal and initiating the multicultural education project. Throughout its operation, Dr. Massanari served as a constant advisor, consultant, and resource person as well as liaison with the AACTE performance-based program. Joost Yff, John Aquino and Moira Mathieson of the Eric Clearinghouse on Teacher Education, and David Imig of the AACTE Special Projects Office gave invaluable assistance in providing bibliographic listings, literature reviews, and abstract information.

The fifty state departments of education were requested to provide the certification requirements of their states. A summary of these requirements was compiled and analyzed by Geneva Watkins, program assistant for the Project.

The authors gratefully acknowledge the help of many other people in making this publication possible: Kay Shoemaker and Shirley Bonneville, AACTE program associates, for their suggestions and assistance relative to the Writing Conference; Joel Burdin, AACTE associate director; Annette MacKinnon, and Hedy St. Denis and associated staff in editing and publication; and Iran Khan for her untiring efforts in typing the manuscripts.

Special thanks are given to Edward C. Pomeroy, AACTE executive director, for administrative facilitation and continuous encouragement throughout the Project operation; the consultants, writer-editors, and prime and associate prime writers who gave unstintingly of their time.   5

The consultants to the Project were:

PANEL OF CONSULTANTS

TEACHER EDUCATORS

George E. Dickson
Dean, School of Education
University of Toledo
Toledo, Ohio

Richard E. Lawrence
Professor of Higher Education
University of New Mexico
Albuquerque, New Mexico

CURRICULUM SPECIALIST

J. Hugh Baird
Professor of Secondary Education
Brigham Young University
Provo, Utah

ANTHROPOLOGIST

Nancy Modiano
Diag. Arriaga No. 8
San Cristobal de las Casas
Chiapas, Mexico

PSYCHOLOGIST

Helen V. Foster
Professor of Education
Division of Educational Studies
State University College of Arts and Science
Geneseo, New York

SOCIOLOGIST

James E. Anderson
Associate Professor of Curriculum and Instruction
College of Education
University of Houston
Houston, Texas

POLITICAL SCIENTIST

Rudolph O. de la Garza
Professor
Department of Political Science
University of Texas at El Paso
El Paso, Texas

This document is a report of the first phase of a continuing effort to assist colleges and universities in the development of multicultural education as a component of teacher education programs. It is hoped that it will assist faculties in interfacing multicultural concepts and sensitivities into the curricula and full scope of learning experiences in the colleges and universities as well as school classrooms and communities.

The need for continued efforts in this area is more than evident. Since 1954, the principles undergirding 20 years of effort toward quality education, which must accommodate cultural diversity, do not appear to be understood even by the leadership of our nation. Regressive trends of 1974 make it more apparent than ever that America still has not found its democratic soul, nor does it see the urgency to fulfill its educational potential. Until it becomes abundantly clear throughout this nation of divergent cultures that the country's progress and survival depend on its people living together with understanding, contributing to the general welfare with dignity and integrity, the country's future is threatened.

It is apparent that the people of America have to learn to live together; a beginning to this end is learning together. A tremendous responsibility rests upon those agencies—such as schools, colleges, and their agents, e.g., teachers—to prepare its people to participate as Americans, with Americans, in the American society.

William A. Hunter
Director, Multicultural/
CBTE Project

October 1974

7

Participants at the Multicultural Writing Conference
Norman, Oklahoma, June 1974

These pictures capture in part the rich diversity of Americans who came to significant agreement on education needed by both minority Americans and the total cultural mix of our society.

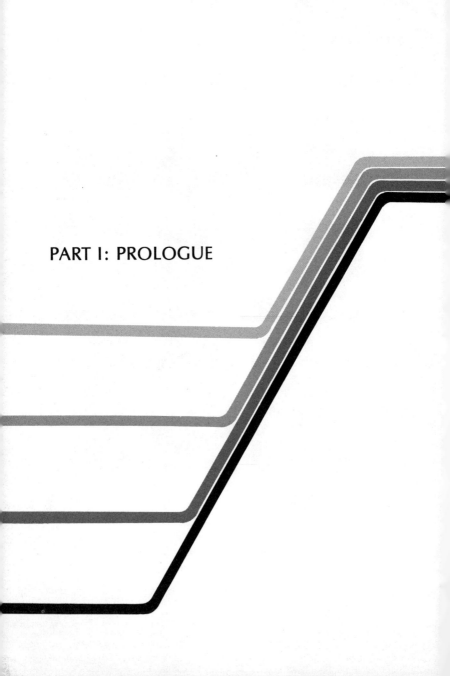

PART I: PROLOGUE

Antecedents to Development of and Emphasis on Multicultural Education

10

ANTECEDENTS TO DEVELOPMENT OF AND EMPHASIS ON MULTICULTURAL EDUCATION

William A. Hunter
Director, Multicultural/CBTE Project
Director, Research Institute for Studies in Education
Iowa State University, Ames

Sociological Antecedents

Education in the United States, to be relevant, must be multicultural. This is not a radical assertion but a corollary of a fundamental socioeducational axiom. To maintain and perpetuate itself a society and nation must set forth education as one of their essential institutions and systems to reflect and administer to the diverse needs of their people. The United States as a nation and as a society consists of many different groups of people with many contributory cultural patterns and products of behavior, all characterized by individual and group diversities within systems of relationships. The highly diversified and complex character of this "nation-society" sets forth its culturally pluralistic nature.

Modern American society is a unique mosaic of cultures, linked and interrelated through a pervading way of life contributed to and shared by all Americans, yet recognizing and accommodating its contributory cultures. These cultural variants may be in many forms, such as language, customs, traditions, beliefs, religions, art, technology, national origin, political persuasion, racial identity, ethnic heritage, sex, age group, socioeconomic level, geographical location, and other characteristics or attributes which define and constitute group aggregates. It is therefore apparent, if education in the United States is to meet the needs of its peoples, that it must have a life blood of multicultural content in order to be sociologically relevant, philosophically germane, psychologically material, and pedagogically apropos.

Historical Antecedents

A special Task Force on Human Rights was established July 1967 by the Representative Assembly of the National Education Association. In defining its functions, the Task Force expressed an awareness that the responsibilities of a human being were not limited to a profession, and that the educational enterprise cannot be isolated from other forces in society. The Task Force's Study included reexamination and study of the Declaration of Independence, the Bill of Rights of the *Constitution of the United States*, the United Nations Declaration of Human Rights, as well as other documents; it visited every region and section of the country and heard testimony during hearings involving witnesses and experts from all walks of life in obvious trouble spots throughout the country.

DISPARITY BETWEEN U.S. PRINCIPLES AND PRACTICES

The Report of this Task Force was published in 1968.[1] It chronicled the disparity between principles and practices of human rights in America.

> America was colonized by people who, in fleeing from repressive governments in lands where their rights were limited or nonexistent, had great reverence for human rights. America was founded upon the recognition that human rights are universal and innate—something a man is born with, not something he can be required to learn. This is the legacy of ideals to the present generation from the fathers of our country. But the present generation of Americans has another legacy from America's past as well—a dismal legacy of discrimination and denial in practice of human rights to certain groups—in violation of the ideals.[2]

America has perceived the character of its society and the roles of its different peoples in different ways. The historical choice open to members of disparate cultures or communities has been to assimilate and disappear into the mainstream of the American Anglo-Saxon character of society or to be isolated and relegated to second-class citizenship—or no citizenship at all, as in the case of the Native Americans.

What are some of the facts which portray this legacy and the need for multicultural education? Is there agitation over this question of multicultural education? Is it really "old hat" as so many say? Is it a problem which has actually been solved and therefore needs no more consideration? Let us examine some facts and further assess America's need for multicultural education.

GENESIS OF AMERICAN CULTURAL DISCRIMINATION

The United States is unalterably a multicultural nation made up mainly of immigrants and migrant peoples. All through the history of humankind, people have moved from over the face of the earth seeking more satisfactory circumstances. Yet not until the 1800's did such movements become of

12

concern; they were judged to cause economic, social, religious, political, and education problems in America.

The Indian constituted the original American population, as the Spanish established influence from Florida through Texas and New Mexico to California, and the French moved up and down the Mississippi and Ohio river valleys before American colonies were settled.

Cultural discrimination emerged during the early development of the United States as a nation. Discrimination took the form of opposing certain nationalities and religions through immigration laws. The English, first settling in 1607 at Jamestown, Virginia, were followed by Germans, Scottish, Scotch-Irish, and Welsh. French Huguenots settled in the Carolina area, Swedish Lutherans in Delaware, and the Dutch in the New York area, Roman Catholics in Maryland, and Greek Orthodox in Florida. The first census of the United States, taken in approximately 1790, showed that more than half the population consisted of African, Scotch-Irish, Welsh, German, Dutch, Swedish, French and other non-English inhabitants![3]

The Rise of Discriminatory Practices. Kopan reports that before 1880 immigration was viewed to present few obstacles to Americanization![4] The fact that Irish Catholics in establishing church schools were viewed as a menace to national security led to the burning of schools and convents and riots in Boston, Philadelphia, and New York. By 1853, open discrimination became organized politically in the form of the Know-Nothing Party.

13

With the change in America's immigration patterns—from immigrants coming mainly from northwest Europe in 1885, to 75 percent coming from southern and eastern Europe by 1905, bringing additionally different cultural entities (religions, customs, education, and political process); even greater discriminatory practices arose. Organizations were formed to restrict so-called "inferior" people in America. An outgrowth of these efforts was the Chinese Exclusion Act of 1882 which applied not only to Chinese but eventually to all immigrants. Such reports as made by the Dillingham Commission,[5] authorized by Congress in 1907, sought to prove the inferiority of new immigrants. The Dillingham Report, in addition to giving credence to the desultory champions of discrimination who had begun to label new immigrants "inferior" because of national origin, laid the foundation for stereotyping.[6]

The report of the Dillingham Commission (which was eventually discredited), and such popular writings as Madison Grant's The Passing of the Great Race,[7] which insisted on laws to restrict immigrants in order to protect Anglo-Saxons in the United States from non-Nordic race inundation, plus subsequent espousements by writers, politicians, and educators of racial superiority or inferiority (on spurious grounds), have created cumulative deep-seated hate, distrust, and animosity which have never been undone.

Although there were obvious multicultural elements in the country such as religious, ethnic, and national origin groups, no real effort was evident that sought to recognize or accommodate the disparities. Instead, after World War I a concept developed which assumed the existence of a complete American culture which, in effect, required assimilation of all to live in it. It became unlawful in many states (until declared unconstitutional by the Supreme Court as in the Oregon Case) to teach a foreign language.[8]

Beginning in 1881, stricter, more discriminative immigration laws were passed. The Chinese Exclusion Act, 1882, sought to end the immigration of Chinese and eventually applied to all immigrants. In 1887, the Dawes Act made it legally possible for individual Indians to move into the white American society if they were willing to leave their reservations and give up their property. In 1890, immigration quotas were set; then in 1917 legislation was passed restricting immigration on the basis of ethnic origin, particularly forbidding further southern European and southwestern Asian immigration.[9]

Starting in 1921, immigration laws were changed to accommodate selective nationalities. The 1924 "National Origins Act" reduced annual immigration quotas in ratio to the numbers of each nationality in the country as of 1890. This act excluded all Asiatics from citizenship. In 1943,the Chinese Exclusion Act was repealed and quotas were set. In 1952 the Immigration and Nationality Act (the McCarran-Walter Act) set forth additional national and ethnic restrictions. These laws remained in effect until 1965 when President Lyndon Johnson signed the Reform Immigration Act.[10]

World War II provided the nation with compiled, interpreted, yet questionable results of physical and mental tests of soldiers and various other groups examined in the war effort. Implications drawn from these data led to additional discriminatory practices which were becoming more pronounced against races, and evident in the areas of housing, education, employment, health care, and justice under the law. Migrations throughout the United States of Puerto Ricans, Mexican Americans, Black Americans, and Native Americans brought on second-generation discrimination and the outright practice of open and legalized segregation. The Italians, Slavs, Greeks, and Jews who were looked down on by the Irish, Germans, and Scandinavians, who were in turn looked down on by the English or others of Anglo-Saxon origin—all looked down on, discriminated against, and segregated the color-visible groups—particularly Blacks (who also had been recently subject to slavery), Chicanos, Native Americans, and Puerto Ricans.

THE MELTING POT CULTURAL CONCEPT

As the ideas of an American culture, an American self-image, and American nativism grew, the *melting pot* idea was seized upon. Israel Zangwill's play, *The Melting Pot*, first performed on Broadway in September 1909, set forth this concept of America as a new country. One of the play's characters, David Quizano, a Russian-Jewish immigrant to New York City, describes the new country as follows:

> America is God's Crucible, the great Melting Pot where all the races of Europe are melting and reforming! Here you stand, good folk, think I, when I see them at Ellis Island, here you stand in your fifty groups with your fifty languages and histories, and your fifty hatreds and rivalries, but you won't be long like that, brothers, for these are the fires of God. A fig for your feuds and vendettas! Germans and Frenchmen, Irishmen and Englishmen, Jews and Russians—into the Crucible with you all! God is making the American . . . The real American has not yet arrived. He is only in the Crucible, I tell you—he will be the fusion of all races, the coming superman.[11]

Various related methods developed as continuing efforts to build a nativistic American culture, such as the labeling of groups as "unAmerican," and the use of English in the public schools to establish a unilingual, unicultural base.

The melting pot ideology failed. Although it was recognized that America was culturally diverse, no national effort was made to understand and accommodate different cultural groups; in consequence, ethnic communities or enclaves were maintained.

15

RISE OF THE CONCEPT OF CULTURAL PLURALISM

Ethnic groups—rebuffed socially, exploited economically, ignored and disenfranchised politically—began to develop within-group institutions, agencies, and power structures for services within community areas. Some of these have been referred to as Little Italy, Chinatown, Jewtown, Greektown, The South Side, The West Side, Harlem, Little Lithuania, Little Warsaw, Cicero, Dark Hollow, Foggy Bottom, and many others. Movement among these communities increased as education, economic development, political coalition, intermarriage, and cooperative mechanisms were needed to cope with external forces attempting domination.

What resulted was the continual development of a different concept of nationality; a concept accommodating and dignifying subnationalities and contributing cultures. This move toward a central tendency which defined a new kind of national ethos and cultural mosaic characterized the rise of the concept "cultural pluralism." History chronicles the sequence of events from 1916 when John Dewey introduced the concept of cultural pluralism in an address before the National Education Association[12] to 1924 when Horace Kallen unsuccessfully sought to show how cultural pluralism made American life richer.[13]

CULTURAL PLURALISM AND MULTICULTURAL EDUCATION

The United States is unique among the nations of the world—having developed a national commitment to education, centered in the states, without a national educational system. Even so, the national approach toward establishing fast and gaining recognition for the concept of cultural pluralism was made through local education systems and the schools as agencies. In addition to the efforts of some school systems and schools to provide for greater understanding and interaction among cultural groups (community resistance notwithstanding), the real thrust came only when the profession, government, and social action mandated certain changes.

Prelude to the Present Era. During the period 1900-1954 an ever-increasing voice of protest arose against racial discrimination, oppression, violence, and segregation. Evidence of the need for development of multicultural education came in many forms—e.g., natural population growth, the growth of international responsibilities, and the emergence of religious tolerance. The significant *natural* increase in the population for 20 years after 1900 signaled the vast growth of the mosaic of contributing cultures, making the interrelationships among them more crucial and multicultural understanding more imperative.

During the period 1900-1945, the United States, having participated in two world wars, increasingly emerged as an international power. This international posture, as well as the newly created interrelationship between the world's citizens, imposed a new dimension on the multicultural imperative—the intercultural view.

Racial Tolerance. It must not be forgotten that the multicultural concept also includes religious integrity. A more tolerant attitude toward religion was developed in several U.S. Supreme Court decisions. In 1919, the right of a private religious school to teach a subject in a foreign language (other than English) was prohibited by law; but in 1923 the U.S. Supreme Court ruled against such a posture.[14] The right to attend a religious school as well as the right for such schools to exist was upheld by the U.S. Supreme Court in 1925.[15]

After World War II a large segment of Americans evidenced concern about and commitment to learn of the welfare and nature of other cultures, nationalities, and races. There was a beginning of efforts to broaden classroom content in the schools to include multicultural contributors, as well as a movement to equalize educational opportunity over all the nation.

The issue of educational opportunities, and the wide differences in the provisions for different youth which have existed in this country for over 200 years, gave rise to social ferment in the civil rights movement, which led to the Supreme Court decision in 1954 in *Brown* v. *Board of Education of Topeka:* "Today, education is perhaps the most important function of state and local governments . . . In these days, it is doubtful that any child may reasonably be expected to succeed in life if he is denied the opportunity of an education. Such an opportunity, where the state has undertaken to provide it, is a right which must be made available to all on equal terms."[16]

16

Growing agitation and frustrations, especially with differences and disparities in economic, social, educational, employment, and housing opportunities based on differences in religion, national origin, sex, and race, led to a period of aroused public indignation, especially among minority groups. What followed was a period giving evidence of recognition of multicultural inequities, and a growing awareness and understanding of the multicultural dimensions of the American society. Significant developments during this period include:

1957 Civil Rights Commission established by Congress to investigate complaints alleging that citizens are being deprived of their right to vote by reason of their race, color, religion, or national origin, or by reason of fraudulent practices, etc.

1961-1962 Lawsuits to eliminate discrimination in public schools instituted in large cities and small communities in North and West, covering gerrymandered school boundaries, transfer policies and practices, discriminatory feeder patterns, etc.[17]

1963 Voting Rights Act (Congressional action)

1964 Civil Rights Act (Congressional action)

1966 James S. Coleman (Johns Hopkins University) survey concerning lack of availability of equal educational opportunities for individuals by reason of race, color, religion, or national origin in public institutions at all levels[18]

1971 School busing for equal quality education

1972 Proposed Constitutional amendment on equal rights for women, passed by Congress, awaiting ratification by a total of 38 states[19]

1972 Court orders allowance bilingual programs (Spanish); *Serna* v. *Portales Municipal Schools*[20]

1972 Instructors' rights—such as *Board of Regents* v. *Perry*[21]—dealt with refusal to rehire college instructors without explanation or hearing

1973 Litigation by Native Americans for adequate compensation for lands of South Dakota Black Hills Native Americans and their gold, silver, and timber taken by abrogation of 1866-68 treaty

1973 Student rights—Court actions sustaining student rights to due process, *Board of Regents* v. *Roth*[22]

1968-1974 The six-year study of educational practices affecting Mexican Americans in the southwest by the U.S. Commission on Civil Rights[23]

1974 Job discrimination in employment practices challenged

The course of events, here briefly outlined, indicate the nature and intensity of concern and commitment to do something about the problems in America stemming from the continuing growth of its pluralistic character.

17

The Schools as a Vehicle for Multicultural Education

The schools have been significantly involved during recent years in efforts to ameliorate disparity in educational opportunity. These efforts have included school integration, compensatory education, special programs for the "disadvantaged," special education classes, opportunity education, adult education programs, and talent search programs.

Education is considered the process and product of continuous interaction of the individual with stimulation and motivation in his or her environment and society. (See Figure 1.) Therefore, schools must of necessity be concerned with the needs of a multicultural society and reflect its diversity throughout their organizational structure. Thus, multicultural education must become a part of the educational programs as well as a part of the philosophy of education threading throughout the educational enterprise.

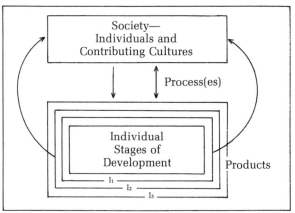

FIGURE 1. The Educational Process-Product System

Efforts of the American Association of Colleges for Teacher Education in Multicultural Education

In 1964, the ground swell of problems attending educational integration and their implications for teacher education called forth reactions from education groups. At the American Association of Colleges for Teacher Education (AACTE), one effort in providing leadership to the education profession was to develop some advanced thinking and considerations for *change in teacher education* in keeping with changing societal needs. In June 1966, under a Title XI Contract with the U.S. Office of Education and Ball State University, Muncie, Indiana, the AACTE NDEA National Institute for Advanced Study in Teaching Disadvantaged Youth was established. In 1969, the product of the Institute was a publication, *Teachers for the Real World*.[24]

Teachers for the Real World, in examining social complexity and teacher education, addressed itself, among other things, to deprivation, racism, and relevancy of teacher education. The *relativity* of the term *disadvantaged* in a pluralistic society laid a firm foundation for fuller understanding of and appreciation for the concept of multicultural education.

In 1965 the displacement, misassignment, nonreemployment, and dismissal of teachers who were favorable toward, involved in, or suspected of involvement in either integration efforts, civil rights, or related activities caused great concern to the profession and in quarters in the federal government. The National Education Association and the U.S. Office of Education instituted an investigation of these developments through colleges, universities, state NEA organizations, and professional agencies. The results of this survey, published by the NEA Commission on Professional Rights and Responsibilities, became the report, *Task Force Survey of Teacher Displacement in Seventeen States.*[25]

Colleges and universities of AACTE, as well as its Board of Directors, expressed equal concern about the developments in the field and felt that some initiatives should be taken, with the view of expressing in a significant way national displeasure about this punitive behavior against teachers in the educational enterprise. Yet, one problem stemmed from the unpreparedness of the members of the profession to understand and cope with some of the problems attending school integration, desegregation, equalization of educational opportunity, and quality education in a pluralistic society.

In February 1970, the Board of Directors of the American Association of Colleges for Teacher Education appointed a Subcommittee for the Establishment of a Commission on Human Rights in Teacher Education. This Subcommittee was to draw up a charge for this Commission and make its recommendations to the Board of Directors. On May 4, 1970, the Subcommittee submitted its report to the Board of Directors recommending the following:

> That the American Association of Colleges for Teacher Education establish a Commission on Multicultural Education, to serve at the pleasure of the Board of Directors, for the purpose of focusing the resources of its members and the Association itself to meet specific issues of teacher education as they apply to racial and ethnic minorities in the United States. It is anticipated that this Commission will be engaged in bringing all educators and all institutions into a unified effort to better serve the preparation of teachers and thereby the education of all American children.
>
> To meet this charge, it is recommended that the aims and thrust of the Commission encompass the following:
>
> Provide information, stimulation, and motivation to member institutions, the Board of Directors, and AACTE committees about multicultural education as a major concern of institutions preparing teachers. . . .
>
> Encourage member institutions to include in their teacher

19

education programs components aimed at the understanding of the multicultural nature of American life and the strengths of this diversity. . . .

Facilitate varied cooperative institutional programs designed to promote intercultural understanding.[26]

The Multicultural Education Commission was formed. On February 5, 1971, the Multicultural Education Commission submitted the following resolution:

WHEREAS the Board of Directors of the American Association of Colleges for Teacher Education has recognized as one of the most critical problems in teacher preparation the lack of understanding and acceptance of cultural and racial differences, and

WHEREAS the Board of Directors has appointed a Commission on Multicultural Education "for the purpose of focusing the resources of its members and the Association itself to meet specific issues of teacher education as they apply to racial and ethnic minorities in the United States," and

WHEREAS the Commission was charged to "encourage member institutions to include in their teacher education programs components aimed at the understanding of the multicultural nature of American life and the strengths of this diversity," and

WHEREAS it is imperative that AACTE assume a major and more effective role now in the area of multicultural education;

THEREFORE, BE IT RESOLVED

THAT AACTE and its member institutions, in its efforts at curriculum and instructional change, establish as one of its top priorities provisions for multicultural education;

THAT AACTE and its member institutions recommend as an aspect of the proper role of higher education in modern society the development of multicultural education;

THAT in matters such as role identification of personnel, evaluation of products of teacher education programs, definition of content of teacher education, the full dimensions of multicultural education be given conscious attention and action; THAT AACTE and its member institutions, in all its efforts including communication, research and development, accreditation, international education, professional development of faculty members, long-range planning and evaluation, influence on decision making and teacher education, promote activities which will respect and develop the multicultural aspects of world society.[27]

NO ONE MODEL AMERICAN—A STATEMENT ON MULTICULTURAL EDUCATION

In an action reflecting its commitment to alleviating social problems through education, the AACTE Commission on Multicultural Education, formed in the aftermath of the Kent State and Jackson State tragedies, is the outgrowth of the Association's long history of involvement in building a more effective and humane society through the betterment of teacher education. One of the first major works of the Commission was the development of a definitive statement on multicultural education. The Multicultural Statement, *No One Model American*,[28] is a significant product of the Commission's work. The Statement, which was adopted officially in November 1972 by the AACTE Board of Directors, was prepared for AACTE, its member institutions, and other centers of higher learning as a guide for addressing the issue of multicultural education.

Commission members caution that the term *multicultural* is not a euphemism for *disadvantaged*. Rather, the Statement encompasses broad ethnic and cultural spheres. A product of Commission interaction with a number of higher education institutions and personnel, the Statement was presented in the interest of improving the quality of society through an increased social awareness on the part of teachers and teacher educators. The official Statement follows:

Text of Multicultural Statement. Multicultural education is education which values cultural pluralism. Multicultural education rejects the view that schools should seek to melt away cultural differences or the view that schools should merely tolerate cultural pluralism. Instead, multicultural education affirms that schools should be oriented toward the cultural enrichment of all children and youth through programs rooted to the preservation and extension of cultural diversity as a fact of life in American society, and it affirms that this cultural diversity is a valuable resource that should be preserved and extended. It affirms that major education institutions should strive to preserve and enhance cultural pluralism.

To endorse cultural pluralism is to endorse the principle that there is no one model American. To endorse cultural pluralism is to understand and appreciate the differences that exist among the nation's citizens. It is to see these differences as a positive force in the continuing development of a society which professes a wholesome respect for the intrinsic worth of every individual. Cultural pluralism is more than a temporary accommodation to placate racial and ethnic minorities. It is a concept that aims toward a heightened sense of being and of wholeness of the entire society based on the unique strengths of each of its parts.

Cultural pluralism rejects both assimilation and separatism as ultimate goals. The positive elements of a culturally pluralistic society will be realized only if there is a healthy interaction among the diverse groups which comprise the nation's citizenry. Such interaction enables all to share in the richness of America's multicultural heritage. Such interaction provides a means for coping with intercultural tensions that are natural and cannot be avoided in a growing, dynamic society. To accept cultural pluralism is to recognize that no group lives in a vacuum—that each group exists as part of an interrelated whole.

If cultural pluralism is so basic a quality of our culture, it must become an integral part of the educational process at every level. Education for cultural pluralism includes four major thrusts: (1) the teaching of values which support cultural diversity and individual uniqueness; (2) the encouragement of the qualitative expansion of existing ethnic cultures and their incorporation into the mainstream of American socioeconomic and political life; (3) the support of explorations in alternative and emerging life styles; and (4) the encouragement of multiculturalism, multilingualism, and multidialectism. While schools must insure that all students are assisted in developing their skills to function effectively in society, such a commitment should not imply or permit the denigration of cultural differences.

Educational institutions play a major role in shaping the attitudes and beliefs of the nation's youth. These institutions bear the heavy task of preparing each generation to assume the rights and responsibilities of adult life. In helping the transition to a society that values cultural pluralism, educational institutions must provide leadership for the development of individual commitment to a social system where individual worth and dignity are fundamental tenets. This provision means that schools and colleges must assure that their total educational process and educational content reflect a commitment to cultural pluralism. In addition, special emphasis programs must be provided where all students are helped to understand that being different connotes neither superiority nor inferiority, programs where students of various social and ethnic backgrounds may learn freely from one another; programs that help different minority students understand who they are, where they are going, and how they can make their contribution to the society in which they live.

Colleges and universities engaged in the preparation of teachers have a central role in the positive development of our culturally pluralistic society. If cultural pluralism is to become an integral part of the educational process, teachers and personnel must be prepared in an environment where the commitment to multicultural education is evident. Evidence of this commitment includes such factors as a faculty and staff of multiethnic and multiracial character, a student body that is representative of the culturally diverse nature of the community being served, and a culturally pluralistic curriculum that accurately represents the diverse multicultural nature of American society.

Multicultural education programs for teachers are more than special courses or special learning experiences grafted onto the standard program. The commitment to cultural pluralism must permeate all areas of the educational experience provided for prospective teachers.

Multicultural education reaches beyond awareness and understanding of cultural differences. More important than the acceptance and support of these differences is the recognition of the right of these different cultures to exist. The goal of cultural pluralism can be achieved *only* if there is full recognition of cultural differences and an effective educational program that makes cultural equality real and meaningful. The attainment of this goal will bring a richness and quality of life that would be a long step toward realizing the democratic ideals so nobly proclaimed by the founding fathers of this nation.[29]

MULTICULTURAL EDUCATION IN THE EDUCATIONAL SYSTEM

The infusion of multicultural education into the educational structure would be through its philosophy of education. How this permeates the entire educational system is demonstrated in Figure 2. Curriculum, learning materials, teachers, the educational climate—all would be infused with multicultural educational accommodation. The cultural factors would be understood, appreciated. and set into the educational experiences of all within the system. A major factor in these considerations is the ethnic groups and cultural factors associated with them.

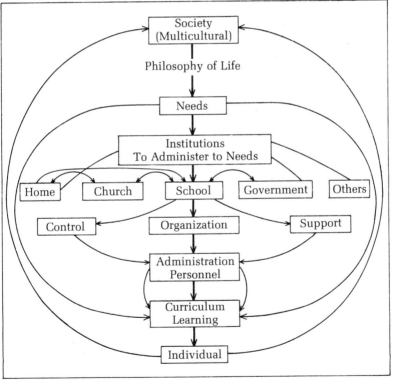

23

FIGURE 2. Primary Elements of School Systems
Showing Multicultural Interfacing

Ethnic Group Education

Although cultural diversity is recognized to be an aggregate of all cultural variants, the AACTE Multicultural Education Project limited the scope of its coverage to three large minority groups. The groups selected were those on which special study already had been focused, and where there existed an institution, agency, or channel through which further study efforts could be made operative. As a beginning, and as a means to a more comprehensive end, the project effort on competencies in multicultural education was focused on educational problems and situations of Black Americans, Spanish-speaking Americans, and Native Americans.

It may be helpful to illustrate the racial breakdown of the school enrollment and the proportions represented by various ethnic groups. The 1972 enrollment in the nation's schools was delineated by Samuel B. Ethridge, director of Teacher Rights, National Education Association, at the 1973 National Bilingual Institute conference.[30] The data Ethridge quoted, from National Education Association (NEA) research resources, indicated that in 1972 the enrollment in the nation's public schools was 44.6 million students. The enrollment in terms of ethnic identity was as follows:[31]

Black Americans	6.7 million
Spanish-speaking Americans	2.3 million
Asian Americans	333,000
Native Americans	322,000
White Americans	35.5 million

BLACK AMERICAN EDUCATION

The current status of education for Black Americans may best be perceived through the cumulative views of studies made during the period 1954 to the present. In 1954 the status of education for Black Americans was set forth by Ashmore, from studies of the status and structure of biracial education in the United States.[32] (The studies from which Ashmore drew his information were supported by the Fund for the Advancement of Education of the Ford Foundation.) Ashmore described and documented the educational effort of the South at that time, pointing up the education provided whites and Blacks, the magnitude of the gaps, and efforts needed to close the gaps.

In 1964 Conant published his observations of schools and Black education from his Carnegie Corporation study. The prestige and influence of Conant had impact in awakening educators and responsible citizens to the intolerable and explosive condition of Black education, particularly in the ghettoes. Conant's views were educationally provocative.[33]

In 1962 Clift, Anderson, and Hullfish, as editors, presented the views of 14 educators and scholars in a comprehensive and candid analysis of education for the Black American from the perspective of facets of Black culture with background for the problems.[34] Among the ten appropriate goals and plans recommended were the following:

1. The public as a whole must become better informed on the many far-reaching facets of desegregation.
2. Communities should use means appropriate for them in dealing with desegregation.
3. Resource people should be available to provide the community with advice regarding problem-solving techniques.
4. The moral and ethical aspects of desegregation must be emphasized sufficiently.
5. Attitudinal changes must be made in order for desegregation and integration to be effective.
6. Teacher-preparing institutions must provide for effective experience which will enable teachers to deal with factors of desegregation and integration.[35]

In 1964 Silberman, in addressing the question of the educational needs of Blacks, sought to put the problems of Black education in perspective with public education for all. In addition to relating the history of education in America and the status of Blacks in this country, Silberman analyzed the circumstances, the chain of events, the writing as well as the statistics about education for Blacks, pointing up the continued urgent need for upgrading education to quality levels.[36]

Some statistical background about education for Black Americans from 1954-1963 was compiled by the Southern Education Reporting Service, through its publication *Southern School News*[37] and its reports such as *Southern Schools: Progress and Problems*.[38] The data from these reports reflect the statistical developments in education for Blacks vs. whites from 1954-1964.

In 1971, the Education Commission of the States supported a project for the National Assessment of Educational Progress.[39] The main purpose of the assessment was to measure change in what children and young adults know and can do. Science, among other subjects, was assessed in 1969-1970 and again in 1972-1973. The nature of these reports reflects the performance of Blacks at different levels of education from different types of communities, giving some characteristics of the performance of Blacks in educational subjects.

The major results of the 1970 study in science regarding the performance of Blacks was as follows:

Blacks performed between 12 percent and 16 percent below the national average at the four age levels: 9, 13, 17 and young adults (26-35). When results were partially adjusted ("balanced") for disproportionate representation of Blacks on the variables of size of community, level of parental education, sex and region, the reduced difference between Black and national performance was between -7 percent and -10 percent at the four age levels.

Blacks performed best on those science exercises largely dependent upon daily experience and common knowledge, and worst on those which involved a detached research attitude toward the objectives and phenomena of science.[40]

Thomas Sowell discusses public schools, students, and Black colleges in his recent comprehensive treatise on the myths and tragedies in Black education.[41]

In a recent analysis regarding the status of Blacks, the Census Bureau reports that during the period 1970-73 the Black population increased 5 percent—from 22.8 million to 23.9 million. In that same period, the nation's white population increased by 2 percent—from 179.5 million to 188.5 million.[42]

The implications of these studies would indicate a greater upward mobility of Blacks by virtue of numbers, improved education, growth, and political power, and other cultural factors associated with the Black presence.

MEXICAN AMERICAN EDUCATION

A six-year study of the Civil Rights Commission was focused on the education of Mexican Americans. The final report of this study, made in February 1974,[43] reflects problems in the education of all Spanish-speaking Americans. The reports for the entire period of the study (1968-1974) documented different aspects of failure of education to meet the needs of this segment of the population. Among these findings, some causes of failure were indicated:

1. Students must attend schools separate from their Anglo counterparts, isolating them by districts and within districts.
2. Teachers and counselors are underrepresented in decision-making positions. In addition, parents of these children are largely excluded from participation in school affairs.
3. Language and culture of the Spanish-speaking American group are being ignored and even suppressed by schools. School curriculum rarely includes programs or courses designed to meet the particular needs of these students.
4. There is unequal school financing. Schools for Chicano children are underfinanced in comparison to schools in the same section financed for Anglo-American children, with Chicano parents bearing a heavier financial burden for schooling.
5. The quality of interaction between the students and teachers degrades and downgrades the Spanish-speaking child.[44]

The sixth-year report examined two other basic questions: What aspects of the schools' educational program and staffing patterns bear on the schools' failure to provide equal educational opportunity to Mexican American children?; and What changes in educational policy and practices at the local, state, and national levels are needed to bring about equal educational opportunity?

The five areas of study in the sixth-year report were examined in terms of its effect on the Mexican American child. Those five areas of study included:

1. Curriculum—the educational program of the school
2. Three widespread school practices—grade retention, ability grouping, and assignment to classes for the educable mentally retarded
3. Teacher education
4. Kind of counseling afforded Mexican American children
5. Civil rights of Mexican American children and their right to equal educational opportunity.[45]

The results of the above areas of study and the recommendations made by the Civil Rights Commission can be found in Appendix II.

EDUCATION OF NATIVE AMERICAN CHILDREN 1973

Native American children attend public, federal, private, and mission schools. In fiscal year 1973 there were 187,613 Native American students, aged 5 to 18 years, inclusive, enrolled in these schools in the United States.

In nine states, the education of Native American children is the responsibility of the state (California, Idaho, Michigan, Minnesota, Nebraska, Oregon, Texas, Washington, and Wisconsin).

In 1973 over 62 percent of all school-aged (5-18) Native American children attended public schools (68.5 percent in public schools, 25.6 percent in federal schools, and 5.9 percent in mission or other schools).[46]

The Multicultural Education/Competency-Based Teacher Education Project

The Multicultural Education/Competency-Based Teacher Education Project was developed jointly by the AACTE Commission on Multicultural Education and the AACTE Performance-Based Teacher Education Committee to explore the potential of competency-based teacher education (CBTE) with respect to the preparation of teachers in and for multicultural school settings.

Two critical situations justified the Project: (a) wide variation existing in the education afforded to young people of various cultural and ethnic groups, and (b) the inadequate preparation of teachers. Although significant efforts in assessing and dealing with the problems of educational content and strategies in a culturally diverse society have already been made by agencies such as the Teacher Corps, the National Center for the Improvement of Educational Systems, and the Career Opportunities Project, the Multicultural/CBTE Project has attempted to synthesize the results of these separate and diverse studies by focusing broadly on the generic concerns and needs of all ethnic and cultural groups.

In America various cultures have been viewed to exist in isolation. Often these isolations have been geographical or intellectual and/or emotional. The education of the children of these groups has rarely included learning experiences which include substantive positive contributions of all groups in the culture as well as provide interaction with members of other cultures and ethnic backgrounds. The education of all children has suffered as a result.

The Project rests on two basic premises: (a) teachers need certain competencies accommodating cultural diversity to function in any situation; once these competencies have been identified, they must be incorporated into preservice and inservice programs; and (b) teachers need certain unique competencies in order to teach in culturally diverse situations. The competencies can be classified into two categories: (a) competencies generalizable to the teaching of all groups, and (b) competencies that can differ among groups.

Competency-based teacher education programs are being implemented in a number of colleges and universities. These programs presuppose the identification and demonstration of prerequisite teacher competencies before trainees can successfully complete the program. While this approach has demonstrated promise for teacher educators, its potential has been only superficially explored with respect to preparing teachers for multicultural settings, according to CBTE advocates.

28

PURPOSE AND RESULTS OF WRITING CONFERENCE

The method of procedure for obtaining the needed information to accomplish the objectives of the project was through a writing conference, the end result of which is this publication. The purposes of the AACTE Multicultural Writing Conference were—

1. to identify teacher competencies needed by all teachers to teach in a culturally diverse society;
2. to identify teacher competencies needed by teachers to teach culturally different youth;
3. to explore the potential of competency-based teacher education as a strategy for preparing teachers to work effectively with children of diverse cultural backgrounds; and
4. to formulate recommendations for the improvement of preservice and inservice preparation programs, whatever their type.

DEFINITIONS AND BASIC ASSUMPTIONS FOR THE WRITING CONFERENCE

For purposes of clarification and consistency in thought, and as a part of the preliminary planning procedure, members of the Multicultural/CBTE

Steering Committee found it necessary to formulate mutual definitions and make basic assumptions prior to the Writing Conference. Those definitions and basic assumptions were the following:

Definitions or Basic Constructs

1. *What is teaching?* Causing learning to occur. . .
2. *What is learning?* Process of affecting changes in the organismic functions resulting in the development or modification of behavior. . .
3. *What is competency?* Mastery of a relevant body, scope, and field of knowledge, high-level skill in applying that knowledge to affect specified learning outcomes, mastery of behavior modifications, strategies for causing desired learning outcomes at an assessed level of performance in orchestrating these factors to affect the outcomes. . .

Basic Assumptions

A. Based on information documented from many sources and statements regarding teacher competencies, it is assumed that there are certain acts, procedures, and characteristics of teaching, the performance and essentiality of which are considered to constitute and define level of teaching competence.

B. Teaching competence is what authorities say and seem to agree on defining it to be—including mastery of a body of knowledge, high-level skill in applying that knowledge to affect learning, mastery of knowledge of behavior modifications with strategies for causing desired learning to occur—and the level of performance in orchestrating these factors in affecting outcomes.

C. Effectiveness of teaching performance can be assumed, evaluated, or measured and can provide an index of level of teaching competence in modules and domains of learning.

D. There are certain teaching competencies related to cultural diversity—evidenced through—
   1. teaching effectiveness with curriculum content made relevant by inculcating diverse cultural considerations in the curriculum and instructional programs in any situation (encompassing competencies that all teachers need);
   2. teaching effectiveness involving the teacher's personal sensitivity through personal cultural identity for working in cultural setting different from one's own;
   3. teaching effectiveness involving the teacher's personal sensitivity through personal cultural and self-identity for working in a cultural setting the same as one's own.

E. There are certain unique competencies needed by teachers who teach culturally different children:
   1. Competencies that might differ from group to group
   2. Competencies that are generalizable to teaching all groups

THIS PUBLICATION

The working papers of the Writing Conference constitute the substantive information of the Project and the core of this book. This publication will hopefully become an important resource in support of the effort to bring improved educational services to all children and youth. This publication will be of continuing benefit to educators working to improve existing programs or start new ones. Other positive results may be forthcoming as a result of the anticipated dialogue and interaction among educators who will be working on shared problems and concerns.

REFERENCES

1 "Certain American Truths." *Report of the Task Force on Human Rights.* Washington, D.C.: National Education Association, 1968, pp. 3-28.

2 Ibid., p. 3.

3 Kopan, Andrew T. "Melting Pot: Myth or Reality." In *Cultural Pluralism,* edited by Edgar G. Epps, Berkeley, Calif.: McCutchan Publishing Corp., 1974.

4 Ibid., p. 41.

5 For the Dillingham Report, see U.S. Senate 61st Congress, 3rd session, Senate Document No. 747, *Abstracts of the Reports of the Immigration Commission, II* (Washington, D.C.: Government Printing Office, 1911).

6 Kopan, in Epps, *Cultural Pluralism,* p. 42.

7 Grant, Madison. *The Passing of the Great Race in America.* New York: Charles Scribner & Sons, 1916.

8 Spurlock, Clark. *Education and the Supreme Court.* Urbana: University of Illinois Press, 1955, pp. 162-8.

9 Kopan, pp. 44-5.

10 Ibid.

11 Zangwill, Israel. *The Melting Pot.* New York: MacMillan & Co., 1909, p. 37. For further discussion, see Nathan Glazer and Daniel Patrick Moynihan, *Beyond the Melting Pot* (Cambridge, Mass.: MIT and Harvard University Press, 1963), p. 289.

12 Dewey, John. "Nationalizing Education." *Addresses and Proceedings of the National Education Association* 54 (1916): 84-5.

13 Kallen, Horace M. *Culture and Democracy in the United States.* New York: Boni and Liveright, 1924.

14 Meyer v. Nebraska 262 US 390 (1923).

15 Pierce v. Society of Sisters 268 US 510 (1925) Oregon.

16 Brown v. Board of Education of Topeka, Shawnee County, Kansas et al. 347 US 483 (1954).

17 U.S. Commission on Civil Rights. *Civil Rights U.S.A.: Public Schools, Cities in the North and West, 1962.* Washington, D.C.: Government Printing Office, 1962, pp. 1-2.

18 Coleman, James S. et al. *The Evaluation of Equality of Educational Opportunity.* Washington, D.C.: Government Printing Office, 1966.

19 Equal Rights Amendment—Women's Equality Act HR 476 Rev. HR 8123 (1972).

20 Serna v. Portales Municipal Schools 351 F. Supp. (D.N.M. 1972). In *Equality of Education,* no. 14 (Center for Law and Education, Cambridge [Mass.]Press, July 1973). p. 49.

21 Board of Regents v. Perry 92 S Ct. 2694 (1972).

22 Board of Regents v. Roth 92 S Ct. 2701 (1973).

23 U.S. Commission on Civil Rights. *Toward Quality Education for Mexican Americans. Report VI: Mexican-American Education Study.* Washington, D.C.: Government Printing Office, February 1974.

24 Smith, B. Othanel et al., eds. *Teachers for the Real World.* Washington, D.C.: American Association of Colleges for Teacher Education, 1969.

25 Commission on Professional Rights and Responsibilities. *Task Force Survey of Teacher Displacement in Seventeen States.* Washington, D.C.: National Education Association, December 1965.

26 AACTE Board of Directors Subcommittee for the Establishment of a Commission on Human Rights in Teacher Education. "Recommendations for the Establishment of a Commission on Multicultural Education." Unpublished report, May 4, 1970.

27 AACTE Commission on Multicultural Education. Commission Minutes, February 5, 1971.

28 AACTE Commission on Multicultural Education. "No One Model American." *Journal of Teacher Education* 24, no. 4 (Winter 1973): 264-5. This statement has been published separately and is available from AACTE.

29 Ibid.

30 Ethridge, Samuel B. "Statistical Projection of Need for Spanish-Speaking Teachers—Fifty States and 18 Leading Cities." Speech delivered at the National Bilingual Institute, Albuquerque, New Mexico, Nov. 30, 1973.

31 Ibid., p. 2.

32 Ashmore, Harry S. *The Negro and the Schools.* Chapel Hill: University of North Carolina Press, 1954, p. v.

33 Conant, James B. *Slums and Suburbs: A Commentary on Schools in Metropolitan Areas.* New York: McGraw-Hill, 1961.

34 Clift, Virgil A., Archibald W. Anderson, and H. Gordon Hullfish, eds. *Negro Education in America: Its Adequacy, Problems and Needs.* Sixteenth Yearbook of the John Dewey Society. New York: Harper and Brothers, 1962.

35 Ibid., pp. 292-300.

36 Silberman, Charles E. "The Negro and the School." *Crisis in Black and White.* New York: Vintage Books (Random House), 1964, pp. 249-307.

37 *Southern School News.* Monthly newspaper published by Southern Education Reporting Service, Nashville, Tennessee, June 1965.

38 McCauley, Patrick and Edward D. Ball, eds. *Southern Schools: Progress and Problems.* Nashville, Tenn.: Southern Education Reporting Service, 1959.

39 *National Assessment of Educational Progress.* Series of Reports on 1969-70 Assessment/National Results by Region, Sex, Color, Size and Type of Community, and Parental Education. A Project of the Education Commission of the States, Denver, 1970-73.

40 *National Assessment of Educational Progress. Report 7: 1969-70 Science.* p. i.

41 Sewell, Thomas. *Black Education: Myths and Tragedies.* New York: David McKay Co., 1972.

42 "Intelligence Report—Blacks Outpace Whites." *Parade, The Sunday Newspaper Magazine.* September 15, 1974, p. 18.

43 U.S. Commission on Civil Rights. *Toward Quality Education for Mexican Americans. Report VI.*

44 Ibid., pp. 1-2.

45 Ibid., pp. 71-82.

46 *Statistics Concerning Indian Education, Fiscal Year 1973.* Washington, D.C.: U.S. Department of the Interior, Bureau of Indian Affairs, Office of Indian Education Programs, 1973. p. 1.

PART II

Prime Writer

Richard James
Chairman, Department of
Education
Morgan State College
Baltimore, Maryland

Associate Prime Writer

Paul B. Mohr, Sr.
Dean, College of Education
Florida A & M University
Tallahassee, Florida

Writer-Editors

Gwendolyn C. Baker
Assistant Professor
Chairperson, Multicultural
Program
School of Education
University of Michigan
Ann Arbor, Michigan

Anne R. Gayles
Chairperson, Department of
Secondary Education and
Foundations
Florida A & M University
Tallahassee, Florida

Asa G. Hilliard
Dean, School of Education
San Francisco State University
San Francisco, California

Charles R. Payne
Director, Multicultural
Department of Secondary,
Adult and Higher Education
Teachers College
Ball State University
Muncie, Indiana

Multicultural
Education
From a Black
Educator's
Perspective

34

INTRODUCTION

Multicultural education is the structuring of educational priorities, commitments, and processes to reflect the reality of cultural pluralism as a fact of life in the United States. Educational priorities must focus on developing and maintaining an awareness of cultural diversity as reflected by individuals, groups, and communities. It requires the commitment of educators to the basic concept of diversity as it is expressed through dimensional aspects of ethnicity and cultural group lifestyles. Multicultural education recognizes that the maintenance of cultural diversity is crucial not only to a particular group's survival, but to the basic tenets that support the democratic ideal.

Multicultural education values differences and fosters the development of an appreciation for these differences. It further recognizes similarities that exist among and between individuals and groups. It is the prime responsibility of education to internalize those attitudes and behaviors that are crucial to the elimination of unequal treatment based on physical appearance, behavior, and lifestyles. The elimination of racism and racist practices in this society is a major responsibility in teacher training institutions and schools.

The Need for Multicultural Education

The need for multiculturalism in education is multidimensional. It concerns itself with relationships between pupil and teacher, parent and teacher, teacher and community, and the host of interpersonal and intrapersonal relationships that are central to the educational process. Maximum utilization of the benefits that accrue from these relationships requires an atmosphere of mutual respect and acceptance. It is not enough to understand cultural differences that may be involved. What is required is the positive endorsement of such differences.

Multicultural education provides such leverage by recognizing the plurality of the ethnic and cultural backgrounds of individuals, accepting such plurality and building upon it, thus enriching the total society. The panel of Black American writer-editors recognizes that monoculturalism or ethnocentrism has been in vogue for such a long time that drawing upon the rich cultural and ethnic diversity of our nation is a difficult but necessary task. Fortunately a dramatic response to the debilitating effects of these two "isms" can be multicultural education.

Multiculturalism must permeate all aspects of teacher training. Therefore, experiences provided for teacher interns, inservice teachers, and teacher trainers must reflect multicultural concepts. The concern here is not only directed at the teacher intern or teacher, but includes those educators responsible for designing, structuring, implementing, and assessing teacher training programs.

Presently, teacher preparation is structured to perpetuate the status quo. The status quo approach has not provided the type of teacher needed for preparing individuals to function as educators in today's society. Therefore, fundamental restructuring of teacher training programs is required if teachers are to be trained and prepared with the necessary skills, attitudes, and behaviors that will allow for children to have the freedom to learn and live a full life in a culturally pluralistic environment. Approaches used in teacher education are not as important as the quality of the product—the product being a teacher who is capable of implementing the objective necessary for satisfying the requirements of multicultural education. This implies that competency-based teacher education (CBTE) is one approach that may be utilized to obtain these goals and objectives. However, consideration must be given to the reality that CBTE can be employed in teacher education and not address itself to multicultural constructs. Competency-based teacher education, *if* planned and programmed for multicultural reality, can be an appropriate vehicle for it. Regardless of the approach utilized, there are some basic considerations that all teacher training programs need to include if multicultural education is to become a reality.

BASIC CONSIDERATIONS FOR TEACHER TRAINING PROGRAMS

1. Establishing a knowledge base
   This component is viewed as a means through which individuals involved in the learning process can explore and learn about culture. Individuals, teacher educators, or prospective teachers are obligated to become knowledgeable about their own culture—the effect it has made upon their individual lifestyles and personalities, as well as what they have contributed toward the development and maintenance of their particular culture. They are then ready to expand this knowledge base by exploring and learning about other cultures. This exploration is an all-encompassing task, and one that must be individually prescribed. An exploration may include historical background, cultural aspects, and any other areas considered essential toward building an individual's knowledge base.

2. Developing a supportive philosophy
   It is assumed that as individuals move from the first stage, they will begin to develop the sensitivity and awareness level that is a requisite for philosophical consideration of multiculturalism. A supporting philosophy is extremely necessary because it determines the attitudes and/or perceptions individuals may have about the concept of diversity. This stage is essential for the implementation of multicultural education.

3. Implementing multicultural learning experiences
   The implementation stage involves the strategies, techniques, methods, and evaluation procedures used in the learning environment. It is at this point that the attitude and behavior of those involved in the process of learning are seen in "product" form. It is here that the ability to design

and plan for academic achievement and social interaction is evident. Nonracist behavior will serve to embrace the learning environment and allow the learner to function productively in an atmosphere of equality and freedom.

Position Papers on the Black Perspective

The aforementioned views are those of several Black writers, consultants, and a panel of Black writer-editors selected by AACTE to present a Black perspective on multicultural education and CBTE. These views are expanded in the following position papers that have been written by Asa G. Hilliard, Allen R. Sullivan, L. Eudora Pettigrew, Cordell Wynn, and Helen Vance Foster and Norman R. Dixon.

Hilliard's paper on restructuring teacher education for multicultural imperatives is an overview. It contains definitions, a rationale, a discussion of general aims, methods, and content, and key recommendations for the implementation of multiculturalism in teacher education. His discussion goes beyond the description of program objectives and includes a treatment of the idea of individualizing instruction for teachers who vary considerably along the principal dimensions of multiculturally experienced sensitivity and skill. In addition, Hilliard describes the special environmental support and system which will permit monocultural teachers to become free enough to deal honestly with the sensitive matter of self-evaluation. Of special interest here is the author's observations regarding some common responses of teachers as they progress through programs. These responses should be quickly recognized by those who have had long experience in teaching for multicultural objectives. Hilliard deals with competency areas without developing the specific competencies in great detail. Papers that follow are more specific in this area. The author then argues for a redefinition of performance or competence in PBTE away from atomism and toward more clustering. 37

Hilliard's general position leads into the position taken by each of the members of the Black writing committee. Multicultural competencies are considered to be generic. However, from a Black perspective, many essential generic competencies are missing from most programs of teacher education, and few programs as now established are able to offer the required teacher education.

Sullivan discusses "Cultural Competence and Confidence: A Quest for Effective Teaching in a Pluralistic Society." As a prelude to his treatment of competency-based teacher education, he reviews six study-group proposals that provide a historical context for the vicissitudes of American education. These proposals range from those of the Committee on the Reorganization of Secondary Education's *Cardinal Principles of Secondary Education* to Frederick Mayer's "broad goals of education."

Sullivan cites these proposals as being more rhetorical than realistic.

He presents a realistic approach in his views on CBTE and specific reference is made to the enhancement of minority youth educational experiences via this approach. Sullivan's discussion of "Racial-Cultural Challenges to Competency-Based Teacher Education" is a response to criticisms in which many readers have expressed an interest. CBTE's limitations in terms of student spontaneity or creativity are also cited. Last, he presents several other issues under the rubric: "Teaching Competencies from a Black Perspective." These issues range from racism, language, and the visibility of minorities, to the affirmation of minorities.

"The urban school . . . as a learning environment has not provided for the acquisition of competencies by ethnic minority pupils in the competitive marketplace," according to Pettigrew. She contends that "it is imperative that teachers recognize the influence they exert" if a learning environment is to be structured to counteract the aforementioned deficiencies. Pettigrew emphasizes that teacher concerns and influences should "foster academic growth and achievement within a multicultural setting." Competency-based teacher education is cited as the kind of learning environment that emphasizes the competence of teachers and the successful social, physical, emotional and intellectual growth of learners— necessary ingredients for a good learning environment. In presenting the larger issue of competencies for all teachers, regardless of culture or ethnicity, Pettigrew states that "faulty learning is the product of a classroom environment rather than a faulty student." Some other issues that Pettigrew presents are: the lack of empirical evidence reflecting a direct relationship between multicultural school settings and minority pupils' achievements; and the accent that multicultural education places on differences rather than differences and similarities. She also highlights assessment procedures in CBTE, indicating that they are designed to "minimize the effects of negative teacher expectations about minority children."

Wynn has conceptualized, in his paper, a comprehensive frame of reference that facilitates a broad understanding of CBTE as a viable strategy for effectively establishing a commitment to multicultural education. Attention is focused on the change role of the teacher and learner in emphasizing the importance of collaboratively identifying specified competencies needed by all teachers to teach effectively in a culturally diverse society. A common thread runs throughout his paper that parallels the competence of the teacher as a facilitator of learning and the quality of the curriculum as an initial focus in designing and implementing multicultural teacher education programs.

Wynn views quality control as a primary element of CBTE as it provides a way of monitoring the skill levels and progress of learners. He sees this educational process as a systematic way for insuring consistent and efficient teaching in a pluralistic society. Much attention is addressed to sharpening the focus of CBTE as a procedure that changes education from an "art" to a "science."

The paper by Foster and Dixon focuses on competencies in the area of assessment that teachers need to develop in order to function in a multicultural education system. The paper briefly reviews the social and cultural biases of standardized tests and develops areas of assessment in which teachers can be educated in order to function adequately in a diagnostic and perceptive program of multicultural education. Within this framework, general and broad competencies are established dealing with mental growth and achievement. The writers discuss how periodic evaluations that include both objective measurement and structured observations are established as part of assessment programs.

Foster and Dixon then suggest teacher responsibilities for developing adequate skills in test construction, the selection of evaluation instruments, and the use of interpretations of evaluative data. This includes communicating such testing information to students and parents as well as educational program planning. It is through such progression that achievement can be charted to serve as rewards for behavior as well as to point out the needs in the educational program for more effective assistance for Black children. In this manner, education can be developed to be more realistic than it has been in assisting the learner from a multicultural background to become a real achiever in both cognitive and affective growth.

CHAPTER I

RESTRUCTURING TEACHER EDUCATION FOR MULTICULTURAL IMPERATIVES

Asa G. Hilliard
Dean, School of Education
San Francisco State University

Ralph Ellison has explored and developed the concept of "invisible man."[1] This concept seems to be commonplace now. Yet, within the United States, minority cultures were simply not seen or taken seriously for many years. It was then possible for many Americans to maintain the myth of the United States as a complete melting pot. A few mainstream Americans talked about cultural differences as a part of America, but this was largely in the abstract.

Combining that abstraction with the way experience was presented in the mass media, it certainly did seem as though the United States was a melting pot. Likewise, to look at the board of directors of a large corporation, the top leadership in politics and government, and the top leadership in the educational establishment was testimonial to a sterile and crippling sameness in American life. Many cultural groups were simply left out.

Since the late 60s, there has been a small crack in the facade of America, the melting pot. Self-conscious activism permeates many areas of American life among minorities. Affirmative action in hiring has resulted in more of a mosaic for America, albeit a limited one. The events of the past few years in America have made it easier and more possible for educators to deal with multiculturalism in our schools.

Many people have had the view that schools were somehow isolated from the normal cultural milieu. In fact, schools more than anything else are reflections of processes that go on in the culture at large. We are the same citizens who participate in other areas of American life. It is unlikely, as George Counts suggested many years ago, that it will be schools that will "dare to build a new social order."[2] Schools cannot operate independently of the culture as a whole, and schools tend not to be the most potent segment of our society anyway. We must do our job better by preparing students who have the skills, attitudes, and understandings to survive and to enhance their lives and to develop concern for the growth of their fellows. I would settle for these modest objectives. I hope that we now are ready to deal realistically with multicultural imperatives in education.

Symptoms of the problems stemming from our failure to deal with our varied pupil population are everywhere apparent. Yet we cannot talk about multicultural education assuming that there is a common understanding when the term is used. Therefore, it is necessary to clarify the basic issues and definitions.

Some Definitions

One impediment to the development of better teacher education is the general fuzziness of terms and constructs which we use. *Multicultural teacher education, performance-based teacher education,* and other commonly used terms have varying meanings and are used in highly idiosyncratic ways by educators. Not only are the terms fuzzy, but there is also no generally accepted taxonomy for this area of inquiry which we loosely call teacher education. Therefore, it is necessary to offer some tentative definitions of terms used here.

Multicultural: The term *multicultural* is used here to define a society—in this case the United States—made up of a number of cultural groups based upon race, ethnicity, religion, language, nationality, income, etc. Multiculturalism here is not a euphemism for the term *minority.*

Multicultural Education: Multicultural education is used here to mean learning about various cultural groups. Ethnic studies programs and cultural appreciation studies are examples.

Multicultural Teacher Education: The term *multicultural teacher education* means the focus in teacher education which is designed to help teachers to function effectively with pupils in a culturally diverse society. The focus here is upon teaching behavior that facilitates or retards pupil growth. This does not refer to teacher education exclusively for working with a single cultural group, either by a member of the single group or by a person external to the group. The fundamental assumption here is that teachers can improve their teaching of school subjects to their own or other cultural groups if the appropriate attitudes, cultural experiences, and self-understanding are present.

Performance-Based Teacher Education: The terms *performance-based teacher education* (PBTE) and *competency-based teacher education* (CBTE) are used interchangeably. Both are used to describe teacher education programs which attempt to specify, to the extent possible and as clearly as possible, teaching behaviors which impede or promote pupil growth. Performance or competence here refers to clusters of teacher behaviors more than to isolated skills. A performance has meaning and must ultimately be demonstrated in clinical situations—in the school environment, not simply in a teacher training seminar or conference. A performance includes but is not limited to face-to-face, teacher-pupil interaction. It also includes all other areas of teaching activity such as conferring with parents and peers, evaluating tests and records, assessing the learning environment, and using community resources. Teaching is more than the sum of individual competencies. Effective teaching performance will always require a selective and creative blending by teachers of skills, attitudes, and understandings which will be reflected in pupil gains.

On the Interface between PBTE and Multicultural Teacher Education

For many Black educators, PBTE along with PBE has aroused suspicions and mistrust. Although the reason for this mistrust is not altogether clear, several possible explanations exist. First, there has been little indication that the leaders in the early days of the movement saw multicultural teaching as a priority concern. They regarded the development of a generic set of competencies as the answer to minority concerns. The problem was that few Blacks could find evidence in any of the PBTE materials that teachers would learn the vital things pertaining to the teachers' adequacy for work with children whose cultures differed from their own. Undoubtedly, PBTE comes in for some suspicion too because of its perceived and sometimes actually happy acceptance of behaviorism as its theoretical base. The atomistic and mechanistic dependency is inimicable to the learning and general cultural style of Black people.

Blacks tend to trust more in holistic approaches, gestalts, approximations, and person-centered modes. For most Blacks, bad teaching or oppressive teaching is most often less a matter of a teacher's deficit in commonly practiced teaching skills than a matter of the reflection of a teacher's fundamental negative feelings about or negative expectations for Black children. Skilled teachers may often fail or be unable or unwilling to apply generic teaching skills equitably to minority children. With PBTE practitioners ignoring these conditions by design, by default, or by expressing inability and perplexity in the area of attitude change, the grounds for a basic lack of faith in PBTE become clear. Perhaps there are other reasons as well. However, PBTE might rapidly gain more acceptance among Black parents and educators if this highly ballyhooed magical movement could be shown to result in Black children's learning to read, compute, and succeed generally in school where there has been only a long line of teaching failures before. Successful teaching performance reflected by pupil growth must precede the accolades! We have had too many fads in education.

Multiculturalism in Education: What is the Real Issue?

America is made up of many cultures. The benefits of citizenship are distributed unevenly among these groups. Symptoms of inequity are easy to spot. For the poor and many ethnic or racial minorities, we educators see: abnormally high drop-out rates, extremely poor attendance at school, very limited participation in the curricular or co-curricular school program, disproportionately higher representation in "educationally handicapped" programs, disproportionately lower representation in "gifted" programs, and strange phenomena such as a decrease in intelligence quotient *with age* for Black children who were at the same level as white children on measures of infant intelligence taken during the first 15 months of life. The list goes on, and it shows that some subgroups in our country are still in real trouble. Why? Many educators and social researchers have sought the answer by attempting to study the culture in trouble to find out why it is "deficient" or "ill." Millions of dollars of federal and private money have been spent to follow leads growing out of the deficit or pathology hypothesis. Explanations based upon deficit and pathology have claimed the mainstream of professional attention. Conversely, little or no professional attention has been paid to the study of means by which subcultures are victimized or the way in which victimization influences behavior. This distinction concerning the origin of the problem is critical, since the adoption of either explanation will lead educators to a quite different set of expectations for the affected students and a different set of professional responses to problems.

Turmoil characterizes the educational scene in many other ways such as (a) the recent law decision in the federal courts requiring instruction for students in their native language;[3] (b) the Detroit Board of Education proposal (February 1974) to require multicultural teacher training for faculties in schools having 25 percent or more minority pupil population; (c) the U.S. Civil Rights Commission study showing that white teachers tend not even to look at Chicano children in classrooms;[4] (d) the Bay Area Association of Black Psychologists and NAACP case of Larry P., which resulted in a moratorium on group psychological testing in California because of clear abuses where Black children were concerned;[5] and (e) the national distribution of a disproportionate number of Black male students in classes for the "retarded" or "emotionally handicapped." These examples are all clear indications of the roots of concern which bring us to consider multicultural teacher education. Damage is being done in educational institutions to minority populations. Herein lies the problem.

The real issue in multicultural education is how to gain a clear sense of cultural dynamics as they affect education and how to develop effective strategies for guaranteeing real equity in educational opportunity for all. For some educators, multicultural education is simply a matter of infusing regular school content with material which deals with different customs, dress, food, or other matters which fall under the label of cultural appreciation. This is a very limited perspective and will contribute little to the solution of the fundamental problem of inequity. The main reason is that it leaves out consideration of individual and institutional racism or other prejudice as part of the foundation for victimization. As painful as it may be to deal with racism and other prejudice, it is impossible to approach problems realistically while ignoring these matters. To do so is to be like the man who was looking for a lost coin two blocks away from where it was lost because the light was better at the new spot. If he were to continue in that way, the problem could never be solved. Similarly, educators must deal directly with the problem where it is.

Our task as professionals is not only to help others but also to deal with ourselves as well. Self-diagnosis and remediation are necessary in order to see ourselves accurately and to function properly as a part of the dynamics of the school. We simply cannot take a detached academic or uninvolved look at the school context. We affect it and are affected by it as well as by other aspects of our culture.

The Essential Multicultural Content for Teacher Education

Given the fact that most teachers will ultimately function in some kind of culturally heterogeneous environment and the fact that there is a problem in gaining equality of opportunity for some groups within our culture, what are the essential multicultural content and understandings for teaching education programs?

ESSENTIAL UNDERSTANDINGS

1. *The Teaching Process Is Always a Cross-Cultural Encounter.*

Teachers are representatives of a particular configuration of subcultures. Age, socioeconomic status, geographical background, education, belief systems, are examples of sources of a teacher's cultural configuration. It is out of this unique cultural configuration that the teacher notices variations among students and frames questions, develops expectations, and plans action. Similarly, each student brings a unique configuration as a basis for perceiving and responding. Therefore, when a teacher and a student meet each other to deal with learning tasks, it is not simply a matter of academic content which must be handled. In fact, the very selection of content to be considered, the way in which that content is to be considered, and the use to which the content is to be put are all influenced by what teacher and student bring to the context. Consequently, it becomes important that teachers experience enough to expect a cultural encounter so that they do not make errors in assessing classroom dynamics. Teachers must feel in their bones that each student in a given class is having a unique rather than standard experience, and that the teachers' own experience is equally unique. To understand this is to see how meaningless a question such as the following can be when discussed in the abstract. "What should a teacher do when a student is disrespectful of the rights of others?" Which teacher? Which student? Which context?

2. *The Personality, Values, and Social Background of the Teacher Are Critical Cultural Inputs.*

The teacher is the primary professional "tool" in a classroom. As seen above, there is no "standard" teacher. Teachers vary in the ways mentioned above and in several other significant, personal ways. Teachers do not have the same self-concepts and motivations. They are not alike in terms of courage, fear, comfort, threat, loneliness, guilt, personal growth, personal deficit, lifestyles, feelings of power, or powerlessness. These and other dimensions of teachers' personal configurations bear heavily upon the interchange which takes place between them and pupils and have positive or negative effects upon pupil growth independent of course organization, school physical facilities, textual materials, etc.

3. *All Teaching Tools Are Culture Bound.*

The easy availability and slick format of most standardized teaching tools such as tests, textbooks, and courses of study tend to mask the fact that the orientation of teaching tools favors the mainstream of American culture. Economically and administratively this makes for a simple straightforward process of education. But this ignores differences and sends negative messages to the poor and to racial and ethnic minorities. These groups readily sense that they are being ignored, that they are not being valued, and that they are in an oppressive environment when the school as a major cultural institution is operated as if their cultures do not exist. Teachers in training must understand how the tools are culture bound and the impact that this has upon students.

4. *The Classroom Is Not a Benign Context but a Potent Matrix.*

Too little attention has been paid to the real world of the classroom. Philip Cusick spent several months as a "participant-observer" in a high school subgroup.[6] What emerges from his report is a picture in clear relief of the school and classroom culture. Even to experienced teachers, he presents new information on "invisible activities" of high school students. Even though many teachers have little awareness of much that goes on among students, the students themselves are often acutely aware of what is happening to them. In every classroom the following things occur directly and indirectly. Teachers and students become involved in judgments, sanctions, rewards, labeling, control of time, control of space, paying attention, blaming, intimidation (using knowledge, power, or status), employing paternalism, valuing, loving, selection of content for study, selection of means of academic presentation, including others in activities, excluding or isolating others, and so on ad infinitum. It is precisely through these activities that conscious or unconscious inequity can intrude into the transactions among teachers and students. There is literally no escape for the student who is victimized by the unequal or nonculture-specific application of these processes. Similarly, this tends to explain the "greased slide" for students who happen to be in the proper rut. A teacher training program must cause these processes to be fully eliminated.

45

5. *Teachers Must Understand How the Student Can Be a Victim.*

It is important that teachers understand and recognize when students respond as victims or oppressive conditions, as opposed to responses to perceived pathology. A school environment which exhibits indifference to a student's culture, one in which the deck is seen as stacked or one in which the rules of the game favor other cultures most of the time is in fact an oppressive environment. Oppressed students are skilled at detecting not only direct oppression but also the very subtle or unconscious acts of oppression as well. There are a few potent options available to those students even though they do not control the environment, make the rules, or set the standards. There are many possible responses which may give the students some psychological relief and may even affect the environment. They may strike out aggressively, sometimes indiscriminately, at real or imagined tormentors.

Assertive behavior may be verbal, physical, or manipulative, such as the contest of wills often occurring between teachers and students in classrooms. While the aggressive behavior is not socially desirable, neither is it necessarily evidence of pathology. It simply is for some students the only way they see open to them to cope. Thomas Hilliard, in a study of Black student activists,[7] found them to be more healthy psychologically than students who made no particular response to their oppressed condition. There is a suggestion here that the student who is ill may well be the one in a second category. This is the one who perceives no problem when there really is a problem or the one who, seeing the problem, simply yields. Often teachers tend to treat the student who strikes back as bizarre and the one who yields as healthy. It is certainly easier to deal with the quiet one. If, however, teachers recognize aggressive behavior as a symptom, they may be able to help a student find ways to develop more effective strategies for survival and enhancement. Further, teachers who understand will not tacitly sanction withdrawal behavior by accepting it as normative and desirable.

6. *Teachers Must Understand That All Minds Are Equally Complex.*

Teachers must see how every complex mind demonstrates its potential with the material and problems which it must confront in its own cultural setting. The universality of mental operations and skill and the specificity or relativity of cultural content is carefully documented in Levi-Strauss' *The Savage Mind.*[8] Depth experiences in relevant professional literature and experience with students from different cultures are essential for developing a real respect for and understanding of the real potential of all students.

7. *Teachers Must Be Helped to Understand That the Poor and Racial or Ethnic Minorities Can and Actually Have Been Able to Learn at the Same Level as Others When the Proper Environmental Support Was Provided.*

A Berkeley, California high school teacher of mathematics was able to demonstrate that Black elementary school children were able to master abstract mathematical processes at a level precisely equal to their white middle-class counterparts, with no apologies for cultural difference. Further, these poor, low-achieving, ghetto, "failing" students mastered many college-level mathematical skills.* If teachers know that these things happen frequently, their level of expectation and strategies will certainly be reflective of that understanding.

8. *Teachers Must Understand That Learning Is Related to a Sense of Power Over Some of the Forces Which Impinge Upon Our Lives.*

Motivation is low when students feel powerless, and vice versa. Charnofsky[9] has presented a full treatment of the role of power and powerlessness in learning across all groups. Freire[10] has treated the same subject from a slightly different perspective. Both authors, however, demonstrate the connection clearly.

9. *Teachers Must Understand How Their Own Expectations Are Determining Factors in Building a Climate for Growth of Students.*

Rosenthal and Jacobson have studied this phenomenon and described it in *Pygmalion in the Classroom*.[11] Rist corroborates this.[12] Even when criticisms of their experimental design or statistical procedures have been taken into account, the principle remains and reaffirms what many writers, teachers, and other students of human behavior have found in their daily lives and work: A part of what we all are is determined by the kind of feedback which we get from others. Victimized students require positive and accurate feedback if they are to grow.

10. *Teachers Must Intimately Understand the Culture of Their Students.*

Clear communication, the possibility of understanding students and being understood by them, requires an intimate knowledge of and involvement in the culture of the students.

Essential Skills for Multicultural Teacher Education

Programs of teacher education must insure that, among other things, the following skills are developed by teachers for teaching students from cultures different from their own.

1. *The Ability to Communicate with Students from Other Cultures*

This skill must be demonstrated by teachers in training, and validated with feedback by students who are being served and by lay persons and professionals from other cultures. Communication has occurred only when all parties to the effort have been engaged. This feedback must be provided for as a part of the training program.

2. *Diagnosing the Knowledge and Abilities of Students from Other Cultures*

Teacher education programs must provide for teachers the opportunity

---

*This math program has now received federal funding nationwide and is known as "Project Seed."

to demonstrate that they are able to glean relevant data regarding students' ability, interests, values, concerns, and perception of the school.

3. *Skill in the Evaluation of Professional Literature Bearing upon Multi-cultural Education Problems*

Teachers, as consumers and interpreters of professional literature, must be able to deal critically with that material in order to find and utilize relevant information and to detect distortion, inaccuracy, and incomplete information. This is especially important in view of some of the exploitative research and program development which has been done and which is sometimes cited in professional literature. Teachers should be helped to detect racism and exploitation in research and not to be awed by pseudo-scholarship which is sometimes used to cover inadequate research. This new-found critical skill should be exercised by teachers to analyze textbooks for racism and sexism and heighten student awareness to their existence.

4. *Self-Diagnosis*

Teachers must be helped to demonstrate skill in self-diagnosis regarding their own behavior in a multicultural context. For example, they must be able to recognize when they begin to foster dependency in students growing out of the teachers' need to be needed. They must recognize when they are projecting their fears and insecurities on the students. They must recognize when they live vicariously through students and support negative student behaviors for that reason. Many such teacher behaviors must be examined, understood and, if need be, changed.

5. *Recognizing Cultural Equivalencies*

Teacher education programs must help teachers go beyond the superficialities of form or style in communication or thinking and detect substantive activities in which pupils are involved. For example, does a teacher recognize reasoning skills when they are exhibited through the vehicle of nonstandard English or slang? Conversely, does the teacher miss shallow reasoning when it occurs if the student speaks beautiful standard English? Differences may be seen easily. Equivalencies are often missed.

6. *Detecting Conscious and Unconscious Negative Signals*

Teachers may explore this through such material as is developed on interpersonal interactions at the Far West Regional Laboratory for Education Research and Development in San Francisco.

Essential Attitudes

Teacher attitudes toward students from other cultures can become more positive as they gain depth experiences with individuals from other cultures. For some teachers it will be necessary to provide a supportive environment while they experiment for the first time. For others, little help may be needed. For still others, it may be that their fears, prejudices, and other inadequacies are too much to overcome. For these few, it is necessary that they be helped to find work where so much does not depend upon cross-cultural understanding and commitment.

Among others, the following teacher attitudes should emerge as teachers work cross-culturally.

1. *Teachers Must Be as Free of Bias as Possible and Must Be Open to Continuing Self-Examination.*

2. *Teachers Must Honor and Value Cultural Alternatives such as Language, Beliefs, Values, and Behaviors.*

Teachers must see these alternatives as valuable in their own right and not simply starting points for "growth" into standard patterns. For example, excellence in all music is good. Teaching jazz in school should not be regarded simply as a way of seducing students to learn "better music" later. Jazz is an equivalent art form, not a subordinate one. Similarly, all art forms in all cultures should be regarded as equivalencies rather than primitive stages of standard American-European forms.

3. *Teachers Must Feel That a Multicultural Orientation Is Beneficial to Them Personally.*

"Benevolent multiculturalism" says that oppressed groups are being given help and have little to offer a helper. Nothing could be further from the truth. As Freire suggests, it is vital to both helper and the person being helped that a "dialog" be established.[13]

Packaging

The trend in PBTE toward the development of packaged or canned materials for teacher education gives some cause for concern. Some content may be packagable. However, the skills, attitudes, and understandings described above for multicultural teaching competence do not lend themselves to packaging. What an individual teacher's attitude or misunderstanding may be or how it will be revealed cannot be determined in advance. Therefore, teacher education must be responsive rather than "preprescriptive." Feelings cannot be evoked on cue. Competencies can be described; however, the work in developing them in teachers must be in an interactive clinical environment.

Structuring the Essential Clinical Context for Multicultural Teacher Education

1. *The Program Must Provide Feedback on Candidate Behavior.*

If teachers are to work successfully with students from cultures different from their own, it is imperative that the training program provide for more than intellectualization about cross-cultural issues. Teacher growth in this area is possible only to the extent that the teacher's own behavior in cross-cultural settings is the subject of examination and experimentation.

2. The Clinical Setting Must Contain a Multicultural Pupil Population.

It should represent all socioeconomic levels between and within as many diverse cultural groups as possible. It should be clear from this that some sites are unsuitable for clinical placements. Teachers whose only clinical experience is in a monocultural environment will be severely limited.

3. The Clinical Context Must Involve a Multicultural Candidate Class.

It is vital that candidate groups have broad cultural perspectives represented within the class. Group discussions involving only those who are from similar backgrounds tend to be seriously circumscribed. Cross-cultural peer feedback is needed in addition to information from supervisors, students, and the teacher candidate in order to get the most from the clinical setting.

4. The Clinical Context Must Contain a Multicultural Professional Staff in Public Schools and Training Institutions.

A true multicultural perspective begins with multiculturalism among those who are responsible for planning, executing, and evaluating programs. The multicultural perspective is required in all phases of program development. Judgments regarding site selection, master teacher selection, student teacher performance with pupils, professional library resources, etc. require a variety of cultural viewpoints.

5. The Clinical Context Must Contain Staff Who Have Demonstrated Their Own Ability in Fostering Growth in Pupils from Cultures Different from Their Own.

Theory and practice are partners. The credibility of the professor or supervisor is directly affected by his or her ability to perform. This is especially true of multicultural teacher education programs. Hope for a new teacher comes from those who have had real and successful cross-cultural experiences in facilitation of learning.

6. The Clinical Context Must Provide Access to Diverse Communities.

Teacher candidates become more able in cross-cultural settings if their clinical experience extends beyond the school and into diverse communities which are served.

7. The Clinical Context Must Provide Each Candidate with Multicultural Contact over Time.

Attitudes and values do not develop instantaneously. It is necessary that teacher education programs provide for early guided cross-cultural contacts beginning in the first years of college and extending throughout the program. It may be that basic subject matter requirements may be specifically designed for teachers so that new content need not be added. Courses in the behavioral sciences and history can be adapted to serve as vehicles for early cross-cultural experiences.

Common Teacher Responses in Multicultural Training Programs: Signs of Teacher Development

Patterns of teacher responses to multicultural teacher education activities which have been observed by this author will follow. Those who are responsible for teacher education programs can compare these to their own experiences with multicultural teacher education. This review should serve to indicate potential "normative" teacher behavior and also to illustrate why certain general objectives mentioned above must be treated systematically in a clinical environment.

1. Initially, many teachers say, "I treat all kids the same." This may represent either an attempt to indicate a willingness to value minorities positively or an attempt to close off discussion on sensitive areas by suggesting that a problem does not exist.

2. Many teachers say, "We really have no need to call attention to differences, since that will only call attention to areas and create problems where none exist." Such teachers tend to have a personal investment in having things come out all right regardless of the real situation. They often genuinely believe what they say and tend to maintain their beliefs in spite of clear evidence to the contrary.

3. By saying, "Your situation is not like mine," the teacher-in-training attempts to disqualify proposed solutions or exemplary practices. Often this is less related to the inadequacy of the proposal than to the teacher's fear that his or her own work will somehow be disqualified.

4. Negative feelings or expectations about minorities will usually be disowned by teachers-in-training at the early stages. This may be either a conscious or unconscious defensive maneuver.

5. Teachers-in-training prefer to deal with multicultural ideas in the abstract rather than to examine their own behavior in a multicultural setting.

6. Exposure of feelings and behavior in multicultural settings can bring on both defensiveness and guilt. When this happens, a teacher is not open to information or suggestions in direct proportion to the degree that these feelings are deeply felt.

7. Humor is preferred as a vehicle for communication during the early stages of a teacher's multicultural training.

8. Teachers-in-training prefer to keep the trainer, facilitator, or consultant talking. By having someone else dispense information or do demonstrations, it is possible to avoid the necessary examination of behavior. Training session leaders are vulnerable to this maneuver because of its seductiveness. Groups will show genuine appreciation for a stellar performance by the leader. Unfortunately, the results for teachers-in-training are meager.

9. Teachers-in-training prefer to focus upon instructional materials, not behaviors. This is another method of avoidance or resistance. It fits our general American disposition toward fascination with gimmicks and reliance upon canned assistance.

10. White teachers who are inexperienced in multicultural settings prefer to focus upon learning information about minorities rather than upon interactions with minorities. There is no clear indication that information about a cultural group leads to more supportive treatment of that group. This is easy and can be done at leisure. However, it is the interactions themselves which provide the grist for learning.

11. White teachers who are inexperienced in multicultural settings often find it difficult to accept minority colleagues as peers. Attempts are often made by the teacher-in-training to establish paternal or protective positions directed toward minority peers. A frequent potential symptom is the easy use of superlative judgments for ordinary things. "She is the most articulate and beautiful person I have seen." This may often be the speaker's means of elevating herself or himself to a position of "one who is qualified to judge or label." It is also possible that this could be either genuinely intended, an expression of nervous surprise, or simply an indication of limited experience.

12. Minority teachers often feel that no training for them is necessary in matters of multicultural concern. Nothing could be further from the truth. Cross-cultural experiences for minority teachers are necessary.

13. Teachers-in-training are reluctant to work individually. A teacher who seriously engages in a process of self-examination will usually require the support of a peer group. This provides a tangible sense of normative behavior, a sounding board for ideas, and a ready source of acceptable criticism.

Basically, the dominant theme among teachers-in-training is the tendency to prefer a detached, uninvolved observer role.

Goals for the Context for Changing Teacher Behavior

Given the general predispositions mentioned above, a context for training must be created which will enable trainers to help teachers focus upon behaviors. In general, the goals for this training context are as follows:

1. *Fracturing stereotypes with direct experience.* This requires trainers to determine what stereotypes there actually are for each teacher. Experiences can then be developed for learning.

2. *Teaching behavior in the teaching context* must be the chief source of data for consideration.

3. *The management of evaluation functions should be in the hands of the teacher-in-training to the extent possible.* This means that the teacher-in-training should generate and control the input of all data by which he or she is to be evaluated. Naturally, minimum criteria for success are estab-

lished in advance. The control of data will reduce the threat to the teacher and will help to keep him or her open to evaluation.

4. *Qualified clinical judgment must be trusted.* This judgment is to be validated by peers in the training context. Quantitative data is necessary but not sufficient for understanding behavior.

5. *The training context must build doubt.* A teacher must develop a predisposition toward caution regarding the validity of professional tools such as standardized texts, instructional materials, experts, etc.

6. *The training context must build confidence.* Teachers must have success experiences. They must see that they can teach children from other cultures successfully. Their freedom to be creative can never come later if they must live with the knowledge that they cannot teach successfully in a multicultural context. They must not leave teacher training programs being afraid to try and wondering if they can make it.

7. *Teachers-in-training must see minority strength to believe it.* No training program can produce teachers who will be able to work successfully with minority children unless they see minority children being taught successfully. Even minority teachers sometimes succumb to the temptation to expect little of minority children. It is small wonder that this is so if we place student teachers in schools where teachers are unequal to the task of teaching. *Seeing is believing!* There are teachers who *can* make the grade. These teachers must be included in the program.

8. *Teachers who try to improve their skills can be critically evaluated. But, they must be shown a way out.* It does no good to browbeat a teacher who lacks multicultural skills. Under these circumstances, little learning occurs. To have one's inadequacies illuminated without offering a way of improving one's skills is to create a hardened and nonflexible teacher. If the teacher can be helped, a safe and supportive learning environment must be created. If the teacher cannot be helped to teach, then that teacher must be helped out of teaching.

Certified teachers will in all likelihood be required to teach students whose cultures are different from their own. Their chances of success can be greatly improved by specific training focusing upon multicultural skills, attitudes, and understandings. Some teachers can teach students from other cultures very successfully. Teachers from racial or ethnic minorities require cross-cultural training just as all other teachers do. The training must include an examination of the candidate's behavior in a real context, confronting individual and institutional racism directly as required. Teacher education staff materials and sites must be multicultural.

There is real hope for success in improving the ability of teachers to work with children from cultures different from the teachers' own. However, this does not happen automatically. Training programs must give highest priority to this problem. We can draw upon the successful cross-cultural teaching experiences of some teachers of all races and socioeconomic backgrounds for guidance. Pretending that a problem does not exist is the surest way to exacerbate our number one problem in the schools. By engaging problems directly, openly, honestly, and without fear, teacher educators have a fighting chance of building an environment conducive to growth for all children and one which will enrich the personal and professional lives of the teachers.

The elements of teacher education described above *must permeate all teacher education*. These concepts and practices cannot be viewed as a formula, as an injection, or as a short-term matter. Major commitment to a massive restructuring of teacher education is an urgent requirement.

REFERENCES

1 Ellison, Ralph. *Invisible Man.* New York: Random House, 1952.
2 Counts, George S. *Dare the Schools Build a New Social Order?* Reprint of 1932 Ed. New York: Arno Press, 1969.
3 Lau v. Nichols 414 U.S. 563 (1974).
4 U.S. Commission on Civil Rights. *Toward Quality Education for Mexican Americans. Report VI: Mexican-American Education Study.* Washington, D.C.: Government Printing Office, February 1974.
5 Larry P. v. Wilson Riles 343 F. Supp. 1306, 1315 (N.D. Cal. 1972).
6 Cusick, Phillip. *Inside High School.* New York: Holt, Rinehart and Winston, 1973.
7 Hilliard, Thomas. "Black Psychology: A Comparison of Personality Characteristics of Black Student Activists and Nonactivists." In *Black Psychology,* edited by Reginald Jones. New York: Harper & Row, 1972.
8 Levi-Strauss, Claude. *The Savage Mind.* Chicago: University of Chicago Press, 1966.
9 Charnofsky, Stanley. *Educating the Powerless.* Belmont, Calif.: Wadsworth Publishers, 1971.
10 Freire, Paulo. *Pedagogy of the Oppressed.* New York: Herder and Herder, 1970.
11 Rosenthal, Robert and Lenore Jacobson. *Pygmalion in the Classroom: Teacher Expectation and Pupil's Intellectual Development.* New York: Holt, Rinehart and Winston, 1968.
12 Rist, R.C. "Social Distance and Social Inequality in a Ghetto Kindergarten Classroom: An Examination of the Cultural Gap Hypothesis." *Urban Education,* 1972, pp. 241-60.
13 Freire, *Pedagogy.*

BIBLIOGRAPHY

Bess, James L. "Integrating Faculty and Student Life Cycles." *Review of Educational Research* 43 (1973): 377-404.

Chessick, R.D. *Why Psychotherapists Fail.* New York: J. Aronson, 1971.

Grier, William and Price Cobbs. *Black Rage.* New York: Basic Books, 1968.

Cohen, R. "The Influence of Conceptual Role Sets on Measures of Learning Ability." *Race and Intelligence.* American Anthropological Association., 1971.

Ekstein, R. and R.L. Motto. *From Learning for Love to Love of Learning: Essays on Psychoanalysis and Education.* New York: Brunner Mazel, 1969.

Fanon, Franz. *Black Skin, White Masks.* New York: Grove Press, 1967.

Fuller, F.F. and B.A. Manning. "Self-Confrontation Reviewed: A Conceptualization for Video Playback in Teacher Education." *Review of Educational Research* 43 (1973): 469-528.

Ginsburg, Herbert. *The Myth of the Deprived Child: Poor Children's Intellect and Education.* New York: Prentice-Hall, 1972.

Hilliard, Asa G. "A Helping Experience in African Education: Implications for Cross-Cultural Work in the U.S." *Journal of Non White Concerns in Personnel & Guidance* 2 (1974): 733-5.

_____. "Anatomy of a Homicide: How Teachers Kill." Paper presented to Pacific Psychotherapy Associates Bay Area Conference for Helping Professionals, San Francisco, April 1973.

_____. "The Psychology of Teaching: An Idea Whose Time Has Come." *California Journal of Teacher Education.* February 1973 (no pages given).

Labov, William. *Sociolinguistic Patterns in the Inner City.* Philadelphia: University of Pennsylvania Press, 1972.

McDermott, R.P. "Selective Attention and the Politics of Everyday Life: A Biosocial Inquiry into the Causes of Reading Failure and the Persistence of Pariah Minorities across Generations." Unpublished manuscript, Palo Alto, Calif.: Stanford University, 1974.

Mercer, Jane. *Labeling the Mentally Retarded.* Berkeley: University of California Press, 1972.

Nordstrom, C., E.Z. Friedenberg, and H.A. Gold. *Society's Children: A Study of Resentment in the Secondary School.* New York: Random House, 1967.

Ryan, William. *Blaming the Victim.* New York: Vintage Press, 1971.

Silberman, Melvin. *The Experience of Schooling.* New York: Holt, Rinehart and Winston, 1971.

Thomas, Alexander and Samuel Sillen. *Racism in Psychiatry.* New York: Brunner Mazel, 1972.

Waller, W. "What Teaching Does to Teachers." In *Identity and Anxiety,* edited by M.R. Stein, A.J. Vidich, and D.N. White. New York: Free Press, 1960, pp. 329-350.

Weems, Luther X. "Racial Differences and the Black Child." Unpublished paper presented to APA Region Head Start Consultants Meeting, Atlanta, Georgia, February 9, 1974.

Willie, Charles V. and Arline S. McCord. *Black Students at White Colleges.* New York: Praeger, 1973.

Willie, C.V., B.M. Kramer and B.S. Brown, eds. *Racism and Mental Health: Essays.* Pittsburgh: University of Pittsburgh Press, 1973.

CHAPTER 2

CULTURAL COMPETENCE AND CONFIDENCE: A QUEST FOR EFFECTIVE TEACHING IN A PLURALISTIC SOCIETY

Allen R. Sullivan
Associate Professor of Urban Education
University of Minnesota, Minneapolis

56

> The training of youth—the revelation of life, its present techniques and future possibilities to growing people—is a matter of intricacy and difficulty to any people. But it is peculiarly difficult to Black Americans who must, in addition, teach of invisible bonds and concealed social barriers of worlds within worlds, and dangerous waste places, of subtle temptation and unnatural restraints. Every artificial difficulty that surrounds Black children today should be additional incentive to make their education and mental development the highest possible.[1]

The challenge as expressed in this quote by W.E.B. DuBois forms the nucleus of this presentation. The challenge is clearly: How can we develop teachers who feel strongly committed to the effective education of all youth in general and culturally distinct youth in particular? It is also the contention of this paper that *commitment* is the first step, but it must be followed by *competence, confidence,* and *content.* That is, it is not enough to like the children; the challenge is to effectively teach them within a *cultural context.* This paper will address itself to the five "C's" highlighted in this paragraph and use Black educational experiences to illustrate these concepts, being mindful of the fact that the goal is to reflect *cultural pluralism.* It is this author's belief that you must isolate each element before you can fully understand and appreciate its total contribution to the fabric of America. To weave a piece of cloth you lay the strands of differing hues out on the loom before you begin the weaving process.

Urban Education: The Imperative in Contemporary American Education

W.E.B. DuBois stated that race and the color line were the fundamental issues facing America in the 20th century.[2] In America's attempt to grapple with issues of race, some fundamental contradictions have been exposed. In the present quest for a new or alternative system of education to fulfill crucial needs, minority racial communities constitute the decisive social force for this change, because it is these particular communities in which the present educational system has most dramatically failed. Thus urban education is an attempt to apply the principles of group dynamics, creative use of power, and sound educational practices in the correct combinations in an attempt to eradicate this phenomenon of failure. Although there may be alternate methods in achieving this goal, it is imperative that the task be undertaken. Some of the critical issues in contemporary American education are as follows:

1. What is the quality of education presently in the United States? More specifically, what types of fundamental changes in the educational delivery system are needed in urban inner-city schools to have significant positive impact on the quality of the educational experiences and academic outcomes of heretofore educationally neglected cultural and racial groupings (i.e. Latin, Spanish and/or Mexican Americans, Afro-Americans, and Native American Indians)?[3]

2. How can schools be meaningfully involved in the task of fundamentally reversing white racism and the concomitant negativistic assumptions, attitudes, and behaviors generated towards educationally neglected cultural and racial groupings within this society?[4]

3. What types of educational training and retraining programs and experiences are needed such that a cadre of educational personnel may be developed to provide leadership in directing the changes implied above?

4. How can schools systematically and continuously include parents and community persons in collaborative decision-making processes that affect the lives of their children?

This listing of issues and questions is not exhaustive, nor is it exclusive of all the concerns which must be addressed. Several recent studies have indicated that the United States is becoming increasingly factionalized racially because of racism and discrimination. This factionalization is most pronounced when one views suburban schools and compares them to urban inner-city schools. Maybe for this reason, schools have been viewed as the places which provide an available and optimum intervention level to bring about fundamental changes in this society.

A Historical Perspective on Urban Schools

EDUCATIONAL ACCOMMODATION PROCESS FOR IMMIGRANTS

The urban crisis is a fairly recent historical phenomenon (within the past 50 years). Throughout this century, city schools have been called upon to accommodate an influx of immigrants. To accomplish this objective the schools were organized:

1. To give workers' children the elementary skills in the three R's which would enable them to function as workers in an industrial society
2. To give these children proper reverence for the four A's: American history, American technology, the American free enterprise system, and American democracy
3. To provide a smoothly functioning sifting mechanism whereby those individuals equipped by family background and personality to finish high school and go on to college could be selected out from among the great majority on their way to the labor market after a few years of elementary school, or, at most, a year or so of high school

It's interesting to note that Chicanos, American Indians, and Blacks have been, until fairly recently, in rural settings. Thus, the educational accommodation process didn't consider these populations because the process was developed for meeting work force needs using immigrants in urban industrial settings, rather than the populations in rural agrarian settings. With the increasing and continuing influx of these minority populations into cities within the past few decades, there was an increased labor supply with a corresponding decrease in demand because of increased industrial mechanization. Thus a limited number of a new kind of worker was needed. This changed the education process by selecting an elite group for specialized training for industrial purposes; this resulted in a custodial or preventive detention role for a significant number of children not in the elite group. Increasingly, minority communities in particular have seriously questioned these newly formulated objectives, and have begun to demand educational relevancy and accountability, in an attempt to have schools more adequately educate their children in a fashion which will affirm and enhance their humanity rather than deny it.

From the mid-1960s on, considerable attention has been paid to the cultural diversity of this nation.[6] Heretofore, many people have seen this diversity as a divisive force within the United States. Thus they adhered to the "melting pot" philosophy to obliterate these differences. Now many of these culturally distinct groups have proclaimed that this nonacceptance of cultural distinctions must end and that society must be re-educated from the melting pot to the "*tossed salad*" philosophy (i.e. elements mixed with others but maintaining their distinctness and making unique contributions to American life, with no element considered worse or better than others).

Most teachers presently teaching in the American educational establishment went through teacher preparation that paid little or no attention to cultural differences. Thus the attitudes, beliefs, and knowledge that teachers have about specific cultural groups need to be critically examined and enhanced in light of new knowledge and literature on cultural pluralism produced within the past decade.[7]

Historical Perspective on the Goals of American Education: Rhetoric vs. Reality

Since the start of this century, there have been several major study groups dedicated to the articulation of the goals of American education. For example, in 1918 a commission on the reorganization of schools listed several goals of public education:

1. Good health
2. Command of fundamental processes
3. Worthy home membership
4. Vocational efficiency
5. Civic efficiency
6. Worthy use of leisure
7. Ethical character[8]

Later, in 1938, the Educational Policies Commission issued a report entitled "The Purposes of Education in American Democracy." The report outlined four major areas of concern:

1. Self-realization: An inquiring mind; a command of fundamental processes, such as speech, reading, writing, arithmetic; sight and hearing; health knowledge and habits; interest in public health; recreation; intellectual and esthetic interests; formation of character.
2. Human relationships: Respect for humanity; friendship; cooperation; courtesy; appreciation of the home; conservation of the home; homemaking; democracy in the home.
3. Economic efficiency: The importance of good workmanship; occupational efficiency; occupational adjustment; occupational appreciation; personal economics; consumer judgment; efficiency in buying; consumer protection.
4. Civic responsibility: The need for social justice; social activity; social understanding; critical judgment; tolerance; social application of science; world citizenship; understanding of principles of conservation as related to the national resources; devotion to democracy.[9]

Eight years later, in 1946, Sidney Hook listed seven aims for American public education in his book *Education for Modern Man:*

1. "Education should aim to develop the powers of critical, independent thought.

2. It should attempt to induce sensitiveness of perception, receptiveness to new ideas, imaginative sympathy with the experiences of others.
3. It should produce an awareness of the main streams of our cultural, literary and scientific traditions.
4. It should make available important bodies of knowledge concerning nature, society, ourselves, our country and its history.
5. It should strive to cultivate an intelligent loyalty to the ideals of the democratic community.
6. At some level, it should equip young men and women with the general skills and techniques and the specialized knowledge which, together with the virtues and aptitudes already mentioned, will make it possible for them to do some productive work, related to their capacities and interests.
7. It should strengthen those inner resources and traits of character which enable the individual, when necessary, to stand alone."[10]

A somewhat similar statement concerning the aims of a liberal education was submitted in 1952 by the faculty of Washington University in St. Louis:

I. Concerning knowledge:
   1. Of man's physical and biological nature and environment.
   2. Of man's social environment and history.
   3. Of man's cultural history and situation.
   4. Of the processes which make for personal and group fulfillment.

II. Concerning abilities:
   1. To use one's own language.
   2. To think critically.
   3. To make value judgments.
   4. To participate effectively in social situations.
   5. To handle a foreign language.

III. Concerning appreciations:
   1. Of beauty.
   2. Of people.
   3. Of differences.
   4. Of wonder, awe and mystery.
   5. Of man's potentialities.

IV. Concerning motivations:
   1. To develop an adequate hierarchy of values.
   2. To adopt an affirmative, constructive orientation toward life.
   3. To achieve independence.

4. To assume social responsibility as a participant in the world community.
5. To include the interests of others within one's own.
6. To seek self-realization on the highest possible level.[11]

The White House Conference on Education, in 1955, substantially agreed with the statement of the Washington University faculty. Composed of lay persons and educators from all parts of the country, the Conference enumerated 14 goals for American public education:

1. The fundamental skills of communication: reading, writing, spelling as well as other elements of effective oral and written expression; the arithmetical and mathematical skills including problem solving; while schools are doing the best job in their history in teaching these skills, continuous improvement is desirable and necessary.
2. Appreciation for our democratic heritage.
3. Civic rights and responsibilities and knowledge of American institutions.
4. Respect and appreciation for human values; and for the belief of others.
5. Ability to think and evaluate constructively and creatively.
6. Effective work habits and self-discipline.
7. Social competency as a contributing member of his family community.
8. Ethical behavior based on a sense of moral and spiritual values.
9. Intellectual curiosity and eagerness for life-long learning.
10. Esthetic appreciation and self-expression in the arts.
11. Physical and mental health.
12. Wise use of time, including constructive leisure pursuits.
13. Understanding of the physical world and man's relation to it as represented through basic knowledge of the sciences.
14. An awareness of our relationships with the world community.[12]

Finally, in 1963, Frederick Mayer summarized and synthesized what he termed the "broad goals of education:"

1. Reflective thinking.
2. Appreciation of culture.
3. Development of creativity.
4. Understanding and application of science.
5. Contact with great ideas.
6. Moral and spiritual values.
7. Fundamental skills.

8. Vocational efficiency.
9. Adjustment to family life.
10. Effective citizenship.
11. Physical and mental health.
12. Change and develop personality.
13. Permanent interests.
14. Achievement of peace.
15. Perpetual renaissance of man.[13]

In reviewing these six goal proposals covering 45 years of American education, it becomes evident that there is general agreement regarding several points.

1. Schools should be concerned both with the process of, and the products of, education; the goals stipulate what knowledge a student should be acquiring while attending school as well as what kind of human being the student should be when he has completed schooling.

2. Affective learning is stressed as much as cognitive learning; values and beliefs are as much a responsibility of the schools as are knowledge and skills.

3. While the goals generally involve the retention of factual material, the process of thinking, the development of skills and abilities, and the development of attitudes, beliefs and values, the focus is on the student as a developing social and civic human being rather than on curriculum and materials.[14]

The goals stipulate what was felt to be basic values claimed by the "American Culture." One has to compare the development of these goals with the development of race relations going on concurrently in America to understand what is missing. In essence, during the time of significant development of educational goals and public education as we know it, a whole host of negative assumptions concerning the major American cultural groups (minorities) were being formulated, i.e. Native Americans.[15] It seems obvious that post-1954 goals should reflect goals related to desegregation—integration—cultural pluralism. Some of the expressed goals reflect concerns related to "human relations" which can be viewed as antecedents to an emphasis on race relations, and then cultural pluralism.

Many would say that the goals were merely stated goals—rhetoric rather than actual educational practices—reality. It is argued that once teachers close their classroom doors they engage in *idiosyncratic teaching rituals* which may have little specific relationship to the goals. This may be a true reflection of the current state of education, but it is not a desirable state. Several educators have pointed to the discrepancies between rhetoric and practice. For example, Johnson[16] states that teacher trainers often don't practice what they preach to teacher trainees; so for example, classes or small group dynamics often consist of 250 students; classes on new or innovative instructional strategies are given as straight lecture courses. Jersild's studies[17] indicate that the incongruence between the rhetoric and the reality often produces guilt for the teacher. This incongruence must be dissipated to allow for positive educational outcomes.

> Discovery of inconsistencies between opinion and practice is not particularly startling in light of a succession of studies showing similar findings in other fields (for example voting behavior). The opinions expressed by an individual are the result of a number of factors, including the beliefs of members of his immediate reference group, his background and training, and his perception of what kinds of answers his interrogator would like to hear. This behavior, however, is a product of various situation determinants of his role, including formal and informal constraints, the presence or absence of pressures to act, and competing demands on his time and energy. Consequently, it would be surprising if we were to find a perfect correlation between opinion and practice.[18]

I will return to this concept of rhetoric vs. reality later in the section on assessing teacher competencies.

Competency-Based Teacher Training: Aligning Rhetoric and Reality

Competency-based teacher education (CBTE) seems to have the potential for influencing education in general as well as specifically enhancing the educational experience of minority youth. Let me hasten to say that I feel multicultural educational experiences aid all children, but the literature is full of all kinds of documentation of the deleterious effect of current educational practices on minority youth, academic self-concept, and achievement. This author feels that there are several advantages to looking at the competency-based teacher education model to rectify these deleterious effects, namely:

1. The CBTE process takes the onus of responsibility for failures in education off the backs of the minority youth[19] and distributes responsibility for more effective education throughout the total educational system. That is to say, effective teaching, or aligning the reality with the rhetoric, becomes a conscious goal and responsibility of teacher trainers, prospective teachers, and public school personnel. This is far superior to student inadequacies[20] for teacher failure—something often done with minority youth.

2. CBTE recognizes the possibility of *teaching disabilities,* i.e. the inability real and/or perceived to deliver effective educational experiences to select groups of students. The important aspect of this process is that it doesn't stop at identifying impediments to effective teaching. It has posi-

tive philosophical underpinnings because it expresses a faith in people's ability to accept feedback and to effectively change their behavior in a desired direction.

   3. CBTE focuses those involved in a process of clear goal setting.

> Leaving the total direction of American public education in the hands of individual teachers is chaotic and self-deceiving. Since "What will we do tomorrow?" is of paramount importance to many teachers, it becomes relatively easy for them to determine goals after classroom activities have been selected rather than developing learning experiences which will lead to the realization of predetermined goals. Actually, this is a "survival" technique employed by directionless student-teachers which is carried over into professional life. However, there is a vast difference between *survival* and *excellence*.[21]

CBTE recognizes that if education is to be excellent, it must proceed from conscious and deliberate intent rather than accept whatever is done as the intent.

   4. CBTE focuses our attention on process and outcome variables while simultaneously specifying criterion levels of performance and creates an environment conducive to continuous reassessment, allotting positive results and recycling certain ideas and personnel in need of reaching specified criteria of performance.

   5. Lastly, this author realizes that the potentials as stated are not exhaustive. The points seem to address themselves to the concern for accountability heard in minority communities as well as the total educational establishment.

Racial-Cultural Challenges to Competency-Based Teacher Education

There are several criticisms of CBTE indicating that unitary teacher training doesn't provide for spontaneity or creativity. Nash and Agne feel that CBTE may be a way to continue practices as usual rather than further fundamental changes in teacher preparation.[22] With the addition of racial and cultural groups into the equation, no longer will CBTE be allowed to perpetuate that status quo. This would have an adverse impact on minority youth by continuing negative practices which deny appropriate educational experiences for these youth. Let me share a few studies which will dramatize this need for change in training procedures for teachers.

> The study was conducted with 66 white female undergraduates and 264 seventh and eight graders attending three junior high schools in a midwestern community. White and Black junior high schoolers were randomly assigned either the "gifted label" or "non-gifted label." Each student teacher was given the information on student status with a teaching task to perform. Systematic

recordings were taken during the assigned teaching task period. The observation and recording focused on six variables:

1. Teacher *attention* to students' statements, subdivided into requested and spontaneous student statements,
2. Teacher *encouragement* of students' statements,
3. Teacher *elaboration* of students' statements,
4. Teacher *ignoring* of students' statements,
5. Teacher *praise* of students' statements,
6. Teacher *criticism* of students' statements.

The results were of special interest, because of comparisons of teacher interaction with Black and white students. Black students were given less attention, ignored more, praised less, and criticized more. More startling, perhaps, was the interaction between race and label, which suggests that it is the gifted Black who is given least attention, is the least praised, and is the most criticized, even when comparing him to his "nongifted" Black counterpart. Postexperimental interviews indicated that the teachers were not suspicious of the experimental assumptions and hypothesis.[23]

A second study points out the discrepancy between the school's view of Chicano and Black children's intellectual functioning and performance in their community, when compared with school performance.[24] Recently there has been a discussion[25] and study of the negative implications and students' perceptions of children labeled as a result of their performance on academic and intellectual measures.[26]

Implications of these studies are very clear. Teachers need specific instruction and competency experiences related to teaching children of various racial and cultural groups, with very specific attention paid to the dynamics of race involved in the teaching-learning act. Competency-based educational practices have addressed these issues obliquely while addressing human relations competencies of teachers.[27,28] What is being suggested is that more specific attention should be paid to the exploration of racial attitudes and behaviors of pre- and in-service teachers. The author also recognizes that the measurement or monitoring of racial attitudes of teachers generated to students is difficult; suggestions for initial exploration of racial attitudes will be given later in this paper. Suffice it to say that CBTE must address the racial-cultural issue head-on, recognizing fully that this is a difficult task for an emerging method of teacher training.[29]

Teaching Competencies from a Black Perspective

Recognizing that capturing a Black perspective is a difficult if not impossible task, I will outline some issues which need to be addressed in a competent manner by all teachers. These issues are derived from personal observations and summaries of the literature. Consistent with my beliefs, I will outline some of the critical aspects of minority and Black experiences which can be addressed along with a select group of references (indicated by raised footnote numbers). However, the most important issue has to be decided by those directly affected—teacher trainees, community residents, and parents, as well as training and instructional staff in educational institutions. Prospective teachers should have knowledge of all the variables listed.

I. Making minorities visible[30]
   A. The Black contribution to American society
   B. The Native Americans on reservations and in cities
   C. Plight and prospects of Mexican Americans
   D. Economics and U.S. minorities
   E. The rage of minorities: historically and currently
   F. Future options for minority groups in U.S. society

II. This is a racist society[31]
   A. Racism defined for whites
   B. The subleties of racist attitudes
   C. The effects of systemic racism
   D. Racism and its impact on education
   E. Ways of coping with the issue of racism
   F. Ways of changing racial attitudes

III. Language and the minorities[32]
   A. The nature of language
   B. Dialects in the United States
   C. Diverse cultures and language
   D. Standard and non-standard English
   E. Sociolinguistics
   F. Linguistics and the teaching of languages in schools

IV. Innovation and minority education[33]
   A. Recent research: profile of the creative person
   B. Creativity tests and their possibilities
   C. The teacher as innovator
   D. Eliciting creativity in the classroom
   E. Creative needs in American business
   F. Creativity as a measure for occupational choice

V. Affirming minorities in education[34]
   A. The negative connotation of compensatory education
   B. Evidence of the self-fulfilling prophecy
   C. Strengths of the survival culture
   D. A positive look at minority values
   E. Self-concept and ethnocentricity

Components of Multicultural Education

The following topics and subheadings are suggested themes for extended discussion and building blocks for developing skills, sensitivities, and knowledge. These concepts should be discussed and elaborated. It is this author's firm belief that a viable teacher education program can no longer function as a closed system. Components or variables that a multicultural teacher training program must include if it is to be attuned to contemporary problems are—

1. partnership of public schools and colleges in program planning,
2. student involvement in planning and conducting their own programs,
3. teacher involvement,
4. community involvement inclusion of the cultural perspective,
5. interdisciplinary academic involvement, and
6. heavy emphasis on direct student experiences.

An organizational structure that not only tolerates differences among its partners but also is capable of building on them is basic to an open system program, predicated on partnership of diverse interested parties.

SOCIAL AND PSYCHOLOGICAL ASSUMPTIONS

Although the above variables are basic to the program, the following fundamental social and psychological assumptions underline this model:

1. Neither children nor prospective teachers are raw products. Both enter the learning area with hidden personal curricula. Therefore, *this program or model must attempt to provide for individual differences as the building blocks of a teacher education program.*

2. Fundamental to the cognitive structure of children is their cultural milieu; fundamental to the teaching styles of teachers are their sensitivities, perceptions, and understandings as they have been molded by their cultures. Therefore, *we must attempt to provide for socio-anthropological understanding of different cultures.*

3. No one has the complete answer to the teacher education program that will most effectively produce the types of teachers who can most productively enhance the learning of children. All persons who have something at stake in education would help articulate a program; hence, a teacher education model that provides for a broad-based, cooperatively developed program is a necessity. Therefore, *we must attempt to provide for cooperative, broad-based planning.*

4. All university faculty and students, school personnel in the program, and community members must be both teachers and learners. Therefore, *we must attempt to provide an opportunity for all members to function in a number of roles.*

5. A self-renewing mechanism must be devised to assure a dynamic program over time; too often, following the initial Hawthorne effect of innovation,* the maintenance of an intact program becomes the major goal. Therefore, *we must attempt to provide for effective feedback through open communication built into the structure.*

6. Active participation of both students and university faculty in the selected public schools and the community is essential. Therefore, *we must attempt to provide for schools and the community as the extended university classroom.*

7. Teaching is a support process through which student and teacher interact as learners. Therefore, *we must attempt to provide for one-to-one and small-group interaction among all participants.*

Assessing Teacher Competencies Related to Culturalism

Recognizing that there are still many unanswered questions related to CBTE, here are some suggested areas for future discussion and research:

There is a need for a new philosophical belief system and consequently

---

*The Hawthorne effect is a change in behavior as a result of the knowledge that one is involved in an experiment.

new vocabulary related to cultural pluralism. This author's phrase, *educational culturalism*, for example, can reflect the concern for including culture in the schooling process.

Earlier, I discussed the discrepancies between the rhetoric and reality of teaching practice. These discrepancies are observable to those who take time to monitor them. This author is suggesting the use of the polygraph to assist teachers in assessing their attitudes to racial groups and beliefs in competencies. While this may seem an outlandish idea, this procedure has been used as a feedback mechanism in prior studies.[40,41] The instrument records continuous changes in respiration, blood pressure, and pulse caused by the emotional state of the subject. Although this approach may seem Orwellian, it is worth exploration if appropriate safeguards of confidentiality and supportive supervision are offered upon request of the teacher after receiving feedback from a skilled polygraph operator. Thus, this could be a measure of one's confidence in their competence.

The challenges to educate minority youth are many but they must be accepted. "There is no such thing as a neutral educational process. Education either functions as an instrument which is used to facilitate the integration of the younger generation into the logic of the present system and bring about conformity to it or it becomes 'the practice of freedom,' the means by which men and women deal critically and creatively with reality and discover how to participate in the transformation of their world."[42] In essence we need teachers who are competent—confident in their ability to deliver quality education experience in a pluralistic cultural milieu. We are asking for teachers with faith in what human beings can become, with a driving ethical imperative which requires them to accept responsibility for helping students achieve everything that is possible, and with the finest technical preparation for carrying out this obligation.[43]

69

REFERENCES

1 DuBois, W.E.B. *The Crisis*. Organ of the NAACP, July 1914.

2 DuBois, W.E.B. "Words of Color." *Foreign Affairs* 3 (April 1925): 423.

3 Stone, James and Donald P. De Nevi. *Teaching Multi-Cultural Populations: Five Heritages*. New York: Van Nostrand Reinhold Co., 1971.

4 Kovel, Joel. *White Racism: A Psychohistory*. New York: (Random House) Vintage Books, 1970.

5 For a more detailed discussion of this process, see "Education: The Great Obsession," by Grace L. Boggs, in *Education to Govern: A Philosophy and Program for Learning Now* (Detroit: All African Peoples Union, 1968), pp. 11-32.

6 Banton, Michael. "1960: A Turning Point in the Study of Race Relations" *Daedalus*. Spring 1974, pp. 31-44.

7 Stent, Madelon et al. *Cultural Pluralism in Education: A Mandate for Change*. New York: Appleton-Century-Crofts, 1973.

8 Committee on Reorganization of Secondary Education. *Cardinal Principles of Secondary Education*. Bulletin No. 35. Washington D.C.: U.S. Office of Education, 1918, pp. 11-15.

9 Mayer, Frederick. *Foundations of Education*. Columbus, Ohio: Charles E. Merrill Books, 1960, p. 9.

10 Callahan, Raymond. *An Introduction to Education in American Society*. N.Y.: Alfred A. Knopf, 1964, pp. 287-8.

11 Ibid., p. 28.

12 Ibid., p. 289.

13 Mayer, *Foundations of Education*, pp. 10-13.

14 Bowman, Gary L. *Humanistic Education: Personal Growth Through Creative Dramatics*. M.A. Thesis. University of Minnesota. June 1972, pp. 10-11.

15 Jacobs, Paul et al. *To Serve the Devil: A Documentary Analysis of America's Racial History and Why It Has Been Kept Hidden*. 2 vols. New York: Vintage Books (Random House), 1971. (These books do an outstanding job of presenting information on the treatment of racial groups within this nation and are a must for teachers seriously concerned about these issues.)

16 Johnson, John L. and A. Seagul. "But Do As I Preach: Form and Function in the Affective Training of Teachers." *Phi Delta Kappan,* Nov. 1968, pp. 166-70.

17 Jersild, Arthur T. *When Teachers Face Themselves*. New York: Columbia University Press, 1955.

18 Goslin, David. *Teachers and Testing*. New York: Russell Sage Foundation, 1967, p. 138.

19 Ryan, William. *Blaming the Victim*. New York: Vintage Books (Random House), 1972.

20 Wilkerson, Doxey. "Blame the Negro Child." *Freedomways*. New York: Freedomways Associates, Fourth quarter, 1968, pp. 340-46.

21 Bowman, *Humanistic Education*, pp. 11-12.

22 Nash, Robert J. and Russel M. Agne. "Competency in Teacher Education: A Prop for the Status Quo?" *Journal of Teacher Education* 22 (Summer 1971): 147-55.

23 Maehr, Martin and Pamela Rubovits. "The Effects of the 'Gifted' and 'Nongifted' on Teachers' Interaction with Black and White Students." Mimeographed. University of Illinois, Urbana-Champaign, 1971.

24 Mercer, Jane R. "Sociocultural Factors in the Educational Evaluation of Black & Chicano Children." Paper presented at The 10th Annual Conference on Civil & Human Rights of Educators & Students. Washington, D.C. February 18-20, 1972.

25 Towne, Richard C. and Joiner Lee. "Some Negative Implications of Special Placement for Children with Learning Disabilities." *Journal of Special Education* 2, no. 1, pp. 217-26.

26 Jones, Reginald. "Labelling Children Culturally Deprived and Culturally Disadvantaged." *Black Psychology*. New York: Harper & Row, 1972, pp. 285-94.

27 Gazda, George M. "A Design for an Inservice Program in Human Relations for Teacher Educators." Athens: University of Georgia, College of Education, 1970.

28 Joyce, Bruce et al. "Sensitivity Training for Teachers: An Experiment." *Journal of Teacher Education* 20 (1969): 75-83.

29 Elam, Stanley, ed. *Performance-Based Teacher Education: What Is The State of the Art?* Washington, D.C.: American Association of Colleges for Teacher Education, December 1971.

30 Jacobs et al., *To Serve the Devil*.

31 Kovel, *White Racism*.

32 Sullivan, Allen R. "Afro-American Communication in America: Some Educational Implications." *Pan African Journal* 5, no. 2 (Spring 1972): 231-37.

33 Sullivan, Allen R. "The Identification of Gifted and Academically Talented Black

Students: A Hidden Exceptionality." *Journal of Special Education* 7, no. 4 (Winter 1973): 373-9.

34 Stent et al., *Cultural Pluralism in Education*.

35 Hamilton, Charles V. "Education in the Black Community: An Examination of the Realities." *Freedomways*. Fourth quarter, 1968, pp. 319-25.

36 Staples, Robert, ed. *The Black Family: Essays and Studies*. Belmont, Calif.: Wadsworth Publishers, 1970.

37 Billingsley, Andrew. *Black Families in White America*. Englewood Cliffs, N.J.: Prentice-Hall, 1968.

38 Jones, *Black Psychology*.

39 Stent et al., *Cultural Pluralism in Education*.

40 Clark, John et al. "Polygraph and Interview Validation of Self-Reported Deviant Behavior." *American Sociological Review* 31, no. 4 (August 1966): 516-24.

41 Jost, Hudson. *The Use of Polygraphic Techniques in Psychophysiological Research and Clinical Psychology*. Chicago: University of Chicago Press, 1953.

42 Freire, Paulo. *Pedagogy of the Oppressed*. New York: Herder and Herder, 1970, p. 14.

43 West, Earl E. "The Ethical Challenge of Teaching." *Journal of Negro Education*. Winter 1968, pp. 1-3.

COMPETENCY-BASED TEACHER EDUCATION: TEACHER TRAINING FOR MULTICULTURAL EDUCATION

L. Eudora Pettigrew
Professor of Educational Psychology
College of Urban Development
Michigan State University, Lansing

Background

Traditional educational philosophy, methodology, and practices have tended to foster differentials in the achievement of ethnic and nonurban minority pupils. Those who are of minority groups and/or low income status have been exposed to learning experiences in the urban classroom which lead to the development of social and cognitive behaviors counterproductive to positive educational achievement. The earliest and most fundamental lesson ethnic minority pupils in American schools learn is that they are second-class citizens, the "inevitable" failures in the social and intellectual domains of American life. They are something less than their white, middle- or upper-income counterparts. They are outsiders, beyond the mainstreams of white, middle-American rights, life, and luxury.

These are the unquestioned and dangerous assumptions held by many educators—themselves products of their social environment and training—assumptions which they take with them into the classroom. It is not difficult to perceive why many ethnic minority pupils learn to become rebellious, or even apathetic, to the educational system. The result, as made clear in the Kerner Report,[1] is that many more Black than white students either drop out of school, are pushed out, or at least psychologically insulate themselves from their adverse environment and from the defeatist expectations of the educational staff. The Kerner Report advises that in the metropolitan North and West, Black students are more than three times as likely as white students to drop out of school by age 16-17. In 1972, the

National Education Association reported that in 238 schools in the southern states, more than 33,000 Black students have been expelled or suspended from predominantly white schools.[2] Even of those minority youngsters who graduate from ghetto schools, many are unprepared to enter the normal job market and have great difficulty obtaining employment. The urban school, then, as a learning environment, has not provided ethnic minority pupils the opportunity to acquire needed competencies in the competitive market-place. If educators are to structure a learning environment which facilitates both the acquisition of academic skills and the development of productive school-related behaviors in ethnic minority pupils, it is imperative that teachers recognize the influence they exert as a stimulus in the classroom.

The teachers' own attitudes and behaviors operate to shape the attitudes and behaviors of their students. This is especially apparent in the early grades where the social influence of peers is not as great as that of the teacher. Research data presented by Becker,[3] MacKennon,[4] Clark,[5] Katz,[6] Gibson,[7] and Rosenthal and Jacobson[8] clearly indicate that children tend to exhibit those classroom behaviors which they believe their teachers expect. In a variety of school settings, it has been found that academic performance by pupils is importantly affected by teacher expectations. This phenomenon has significant implications for ethnic minority children. As recent research by Leacock[9] and by Rist[10] discloses, pupils of low income and/or minority group status are often expected by their teachers to be underachievers or to be intellectually inferior compared to their majority, middle-income classmates. The researchers found that such negatively evaluated pupils, in fact, tend to be given less instruction, less access to educational materials and resources, and less reward-directed, supportive behavior by teachers. Such a learning environment is destined to promote failure in pupils who are the object of negativistic assumptions or expectations. Those pupils who are *expected* to be essentially uneducable tend to be treated as uneducable and consequently may fail to exhibit those competencies which it was assumed they could not learn. This is hardly surprising when no adequate provision has been made to structure a learning environment which explicitly fosters the acquisition of desired skills, nor actively encourages pupil achievements by positively supporting and reinforcing the occurrence of appropriate behaviors. Teachers must have confidence in the ability and academic potential of all their pupils. They must carefully examine the conditions under which learning is to take place, and they must be aware that their own attitudes and behaviors can either help or hinder the pupils' progress in achieving those behavioral competencies which are taken as an index of learning.

Teachers must become more concerned about the differences and similarities between achievements and aspirations of the ethnic minority child and the advantaged majority child. Further, teachers must become more adept in the deliberate design of learning environments that will foster academic growth and achievement within a multicultural educational setting. This setting can be defined in two ways. First, a multicultural educational setting may simply be a school with children and teachers from differing cultural backgrounds. In this type of learning environment, each ethnic group may contribute to and receive from a curriculum designed to give credence to their cultural values and behaviors. Second, a multicultural educational setting may be a school with children and teachers from one ethnic group, but with a curriculum designed to present cultural values and beliefs from all ethnic groups. In designing a multicultural learning environment, it is essential that teachers consider the extent to which such an environment is structured to optimize the opportunity for all pupils to become equally educated. It is inadequate merely to provide equal educational opportunities for urban minority and low-income pupils and expect them to manifest sudden breakthroughs in academic achievement. It cannot be reasonably assumed that all pupils equally possess the specific, prior learned responses necessary to take advantage of such opportunities. Such an assumption fails to consider that environmental experience may influence pupil behavior and progress in school.

To obviate this kind of assumption, teachers need to design a learning environment which is carefully planned to build systematically upon the existing competencies and accomplishments of each pupil. Such an environment is characterized by stability, derived from a program design explicitly structured and sequenced by the teacher to promote the acquisition and maintenance of cognitive skills and behaviors. Many educators call this system a "performance-based system" or a "competency-based system." In addition, such a learning system can be constructed to foster a variety of task-relevant social behaviors such as attending, writing, asking, answering questions, and other participatory responses which are directly related to academic achievement. Classroom behaviors which are incompatible with the learning objectives are, by implication, prevented, reduced, or eliminated in order to optimize educational attainments.

Environmental determinants of school-related behaviors are the focal point of competency-based teaching, for it is the environment which the teacher can control and manipulate in efforts to produce the desirable changes in pupil behaviors that we call learning. The teacher can alter and arrange conditions in the school setting to foster planned educational change. In this sense, teachers are managers of the learning environment. They must be expert in arranging the environment to facilitate multicultural pupil achievement of productive social and academic competencies relevant to educational objectives. The emphasis here is upon effecting planned behavioral change in the form of desired learning. If teachers fail to adequately plan and program the environment for pupils, learning is left to chance and the results may well be counter-productive.

Definition of Competency-Based Education

Competency-based education is defined as a learning environment in which explicit statements of desired competencies and criteria for evaluation are designed and made public to all participants, e.g. learners, teachers, and parents. Competencies are those particular verbal and non-verbal skills, behaviors, and attitudes which facilitate the interaction of social, physical, emotional, and intellectual growth. Evaluative criteria are threefold: (a) cognitive acquisition of concepts, principles, facts, ideas, and postulates; (b) performance skills in utilizing cognitive materials in teacher planning and performance; and (c) product skills—learner growth—used to evaluate teacher performance.

Competency-based methods emphasize planning, programming, and control with respect to environmental conditions in which pupils behave and learn. Focus is upon promoting achievement of educationally relevant behaviors through positive control of the learning environment and its pupil participants. Teacher behaviors, with respect to designing and implementing instructional activities or strategies are empirically evaluated; that is, they are tested in terms of the effects they produce. Those strategies that successfully promote educational attainment are selected for individual pupils on the basis of their demonstrated use and merit, not on the basis of what the teacher thinks is appropriate, useful, or necessary for a given pupil. In this sense, the formulation and selection of operational strategies applied in the learning environment are based upon objective, scientific analyses of the observed effects of actual pupil behaviors, not on a prejudged opinion.

The use of a planned learning environment such as described above permits educators and researchers to adequately evaluate the effects of a multicultural school setting on both majority and minority children. Data which could be acquired from such a situation would concern academic achievements as well as psychological correlates of academic achievement. In addition, data could also be acquired about teacher functioning and its contingent effect upon pupil behavior.

A COMPETENCY-BASED MODEL

In the *competency-based education model,* faulty learning is perceived to be a product of the classroom environment rather than a product of postulated incompetencies and incapacities of a faulty pupil. This construct contrasts with the paradoxical assumption implicit and prevailing in education that the schools cannot educate minority pupils due to the fixed effects of genetic heritage or early family experiences. The competency-based system postulates that learning behavior (change) may be positively accomplished through exposure to efficient and effective learning environments. Barring severe physiological impairment, no pupil can legitimately be deemed to be limited in what and how much he or she can learn. Unfortunately, in our present urban school systems the opposite is assumed.

The competency-based education model, then, does not assume that educational achievement of pupils is determined by some relatively constant level of abilities, aptitudes, and characteristics identified, classified, and labeled by tests or by perceptions of subjective judgment by the teacher. Rather it suggests that the majority of overt behavior is environmentally determined and subject to change as the environment is changed. Behavior is understood to be experientially learned through interactions with the environment. To say that behavior is determined and fixed by forces beyond the school's influence is contrary to the principal thesis delineating the competency-based model of education.

The competency-based trained teacher uses *behavior management techniques* to design an appropriate learning environment and construct relevant learning strategies designed to promote *planned educational achievement*. Usually the program is intended to promote the acquisition and maintenance of behaviors which result in educational achievement. However, learning activities may also be designed to prevent, minimize, or eliminate behaviors incompatible with positive educational achievement. In either instance, the objective is the acquisition of a clearly defined category of observable and measurable behavior.

The assumptions underlying the competency-based model are based upon *empirically validated tenets of social learning*. As described by Clark, Evans, and Hamerlynch,[11] these tenets hold that—

1. individual behavior occurs in the context of a social environment and in interaction with the environment.
2. social behavior is learned in interaction with the environment.
3. behavior is taught and maintained by the social environment.
4. social learning is a process of reciprocal influence. Participants interacting in a social system mutually affect each other's behaviors.
5. the reciprocal influence process may be explicit or implicit, planned or unplanned, but must be considered a factor in social systems.

In accordance with these principles of learning theory, the author suggests that a competency-based model perceives individual pupil behavior as being—

1. exhibited within the context of a social environment called a classroom.
2. amenable to change in the context of interaction with the classroom environment.
3. taught, maintained, reduced, or eliminated as a function of interaction with the classroom environment.
4. reciprocally influenced in form and frequency by those with whom the pupil interacts in the classroom—the teacher and pupils.
5. continually subject to conscious or unconscious influence by others in the classroom.

Thus the competency-based model is centrally concerned with bringing about explicitly defined and carefully planned effects on the learning behavior of pupils in the classroom environment. When minority pupil behaviors are unsystematically changed in the classroom, as in the traditional school setting, they are not involved in a competency-based program of education.

TRADITIONAL MODES OF TEACHING

The latter situation represents one of the most searing indictments against traditional modes of teaching in urban schools in which a significant number of ethnic minority students are frequently labeled "chronic nonachievers," "unteachable," or "emotionally disturbed." In the traditional models of education, behavior is not perceived to be taught and changed in the classroom—particularly not by events manifested in the classroom. Instead, behavior is seen as essentially fixed and determined by factors beyond the realm of the school's or the teacher's influence. But, in fact, as the above-mentioned principles of learning indicate, behavior change occurs as a function of the events which occur within the pupil's social environment. Hence, pupil behaviors are shaped, maintained, and/or eliminated through the unconscious, unplanned, and unsystematic manipulation of environmental events in the classroom. It has been well documented by Bandura,[12] Ramp and Hopkins,[13] and Skinner[14] that the events or consequences which follow behavior affect future probability of recurrence of such behavior. Desirable or reinforcing outcomes generate behavioral increments. Intervening variables, such as the individual's history of reinforcement, the differential efficacy of reinforcers and the temporal relationship between the response and reinforcement, importantly influence the form and extent to which behavior is modified. The implication is clear that teachers may shape pupils' responses which are counterproductive to educational achievement or social control in the classroom, but which may, in fact, be consistent with the teacher's own subjective expectations and assumptions about the pupils and/or their ethnic, racial, or social referent group.

Teachers' behaviors, then, issuing from their own unconscious biases and beliefs, can effectively contribute to the acquisition of dysfunctional, as well as functional, classroom behavior by pupils. It is the teacher who, by verbal and nonverbal communications, prescribes the social, emotional, and academic conditions prevailing in the learning environment in which the pupil behaves. The question arises as to how often the teacher rewards "failure" and ignores (or extinguishes) successes. When a teacher places in a lower track those pupils who cannot work addition problems and fails to reward them for and promote the accomplishments they do demonstrate, is this teacher not programming the pupils for failure? Since academic skills are representative of a complex of chained responses,[15] if discrete desired responses are not systematically and contingently rewarded, the probability that final performance skills will be manifested and that new behaviors will be learned is very low. When pupils learn of teacher negative expectations, though it may not immediately be recognized, this can result in the acquisition of behaviors incompatible with desired learning and in the reduction or elimination of those behaviors which promote positive educational achievement.

Operating within the context of a competency-based model in which desired behaviors are reinforced, teachers have clearly demonstrated that a variety of educationally relevant behaviors are acquired by minority pupils in urban schools. Teachers have shown, for example, that they can efficiently and effectively improve learners' reading, spelling, arithmetic, and verbal skills, and they can increase productive social behaviors which foster educational achievement (Ramp and Hopkins,[13] O'Leary and O'Leary[16]).

Conversely, traditional teaching models see learning behavior as occurring within the context of a poorly defined mechanism called personality, with differential ability relatively determined and unchangeable. In traditional teaching models, the objective of education is essentially reduced to identifying capacity and ability, and to implicitly classifying and labeling such attributes within the context of prevailing socioeconomic norms. Such a process encourages the allocation of pupils to differentiated "learning" programs or tracks with attendant teacher expectancies for success and failure which socially stratify and prepare the pupils for their role in society. The effects of this frame of reference upon the urban minority pupil are well documented (Green;[17] Brookover, Gigliotti, Henderson and Schneider[18]) and need not be further discussed at this point.

Establishing a Competency-Based Learning Environment

The purpose of any planned program in teacher training should be to produce teachers and administrators who manifest skills and behaviors which will result in positive educational achievement for all children. Typically, prior and present-day teacher training focus upon educational theory which does not necessarily result in specific teaching competencies other than verbal. Seldom does teacher training focus upon the basic premise that should underlie all theoretical considerations—that all teaching competencies should be defined within the framework of the definition of learning. Learning has been empirically defined as relatively permanent changes of behavior (Gagne,[15] Hilgard and Marquis,[19]). Learning, then, is inferred rather than observed, and those behaviors that are defined as learning may be called performance behavior.

The statements above explicitly lead to the conclusion that those persons who aspire to be teachers must be able to bring about changes in behavior in their pupils in order to postulate that learning has occurred. In addition, those persons who aspire to be teachers must bring about changes in behavior in a specific direction in order to promote desired educational achievement. If teachers are to be agents of change, then it follows that they must acquire the skills in changing behavior that exist in the bodies of knowledge—both educational and psychological—and they must be able to apply those skills in an educational setting.

Traditional teaching methods have been based upon an assumption that, given an average environment, children will learn when they are "ready." If a child does not learn or does not manifest a mechanism called intelligence, the child, and frequently his/her ethnic group association, are indirectly held to be responsible. It is assumed that the child is incapable of adequate performance, and that the ethnic group has genetic deficiencies which affect the development of intelligence. To counteract this assumption, teaching should establish a learning environment in which there is a predictable relationship between a pupil's classroom performance and the classroom environment. Should a pupil fail to learn what is desired, the classroom environment should be explored and analyzed to determine ways of modifying it to promote the desired learning. In this manner, teaching is based upon the idea that *faulty learning is the product of a classroom environment rather than a faulty student.* This particular approach counteracts or prohibits the association of ethnic group membership with school performance and in addition counteracts the assumption that minority children cannot learn.

Teaching is concerned with observable activities. When a pupil is reading, you are observing "reading behavior" with all of its correlate behaviors, i.e. eye movements, lip movements, etc. When a pupil is talking, we speak of his/her "verbal behavior" (Meachan and Wiesen[20]). The use of observable behavior as the relevant source of information in designing teacher training experiences permits better description of student performance and diminishes the effects of subjectivity in assessment and evaluation. Subjectivity is one of the principal sources of negative assumptions and attitudes about minority students and can be counteracted effectively through the use of less subjective data for teacher decisions.

Meachan and Wiesen[20] have named the methods used in the competency-based model as precision teaching. They suggest that in such teaching the teacher is not merely a conveyor of information as traditionally conceived, but is also a scientist whose area of study is the behavior of pupils in school. Such a framework provides an ideal opportunity for continuous evaluation of presented educational materials and teacher techniques. If a certain type of material does not result in successful learning, it may be modified or even rejected. If a particular pupil does not respond correctly to given material, more appropriate material for that pupil will be tried or other factors will be examined. In this situation, the teacher must be prepared to assume the basic attitude of the scientist and be ready to abandon his or her method if it does not prove effective, for it is the data about pupils which determines the next move, not assumptions about pupils.

Teaching in the proposed model provides an atmosphere in which the individuality of each pupil can be truly realized. The approach requires that the teacher have some knowledge of the particular likes and dislikes of each pupil, his or her present level of performance, and his or her specific preferred activities. The teacher cannot make assumptions about the pupil but must actually conduct scientific observations of pupils in action to obtain accurate data. Above all, this type of teaching emphasizes a pupil's present performance without excessively dwelling upon his or her past. This is not to say that the past has no influence on present behavior, but merely that only certain past events are really meaningful in understanding a student's present behavior. By questioning many of the unfounded ideas about how pupils are supposed to behave, the teacher in this system automatically eliminates ethnic group membership as a correlate of intellectual performance.

COMPETENCIES RELEVANT TO ALL TEACHERS

In order for all teachers to be able to design and conduct a competency-based learning environment, they should be able to manifest the following teaching behaviors:

1. Design behavioral objectives for pupils, i.e. performance, cognitive, and expressive
2. Design diagnostic pretest instruments for pupils
3. Administer diagnostic pretests to pupils
4. Evaluate diagnostic pretests in behavioral terms for pupils
5. Communicate strengths and weaknesses of pupils to parents and pupils
6 Design teaching strategies in behavioral frameworks that will implement achievement of stated objectives based upon diagnosed strengths and weaknesses
7. Conduct teaching strategies in behavioral frameworks that will result in achievement of objectives
8. Select instructional materials that are necessary for the achievement of objectives
9. Provide alternative learning routes for pupils
10. Recycle pupils who do not reach the necessary mastery level for attainment of objectives
11. Design post-test instruments to acquire data about achievement of objectives
12. Evaluate post-test instruments data in conjunction with pretest instruments data to assess effectiveness of instructional materials and strategies
13. Evaluate total learning environment in terms of its effects on pupil learning

In addition to the above competencies, teachers, regardless of the cultural make-up of the school, should also be able to manifest the following teaching behaviors:

1. Categorize behaviors which have led to negative assumptions about minority pupils and their cultures
2. Categorize societal beliefs which have led to negative assumptions about minority pupils and their cultures

3. Examine curriculum materials and specify how much materials have contributed to negative assumptions about minority pupils and their cultures, either by omission of data or inclusion of data which promotes a less than positive view of minority peoples
4. Redesign curriculum materials that will promote a positive set of assumptions about minority students and their cultures

TEACHER COMPETENCIES NEEDED IN A MULTICULTURAL SETTING

In addition, teachers who work specifically in a multicultural school setting must be able to manifest the following competencies:

1. Conduct an inquiry-oriented science and social studies program which is culturally relevant to all pupils
2. Conduct a modern math program which emphasizes structure without losing proficiency in computation, and which can be applicable to all childrens' experiences with numerical variables
3. Develop in pupils the social skills and values necessary for survival in the dominant culture without denying the existence of other values equally appropriate in minority cultures
4. Assess his/her impact on pupils and modify that impact by modifying teaching style
5. Develop and conduct a reading program which will emphasize the multicultural nature of the society as well as develop good reading skills
6. Differentiate between interpersonal relations with other staff members which have a negative effect on the teaching-learning process and those which lead toward positive change
7. Effectively use audio-visual equipment in the instructional program to develop instructional modules which relate to the lifestyles of all pupils
8. Develop and involve community resources as integral parts of the teaching-learning process
9. Interpret the school's program to the community in terms both understandable and acceptable
10. Design curriculum modules which relate to the multicultural population of the school and which provide ways for all pupils to gain positive identification of self-images

Teacher training procedures should concentrate on developing all of the above listed competencies in all future and inservice teachers, not just those who plan to teach or are teaching in multicultural schools.

Problems and Issues

EMPHASIS ON MULTICULTURALISM

Perhaps the most serious obstacle to the achievement of a truly multicultural system of competency-based education is the present professional attention to the multicultural aspect. While little apparent negativism has developed in relation to the concept of multiculturalism, a very real concern is that professional educators of all ethnic groups will spend much of their time attempting to achieve a truly multicultural society, while ignoring the more visible problem of ethnic pupil school achievement. There is no empirical evidence that the development of a multicultural school system has any direct relationship to minority pupils' achievements. In addition, multiculturalism focuses its concepts on behavioral differences exclusively rather than on both similarities and differences between and among all segments of the society. To continue to focus on differences is perhaps to continue subtly to support the inferiority-superiority hypotheses while at the same time postulating an acceptance on a level of parity of differential behavior manifestations from all cultures. There is an inherent conflict in this approach since it tends to reinforce the seldom verbalized, but currently accepted belief that ethnic minority pupils cannot manifest an achievement level equal to that of majority white pupils. At the same time, it proposes that all cultural values and their resultant behaviors are equal. At worst, such a conflict will inevitably promote the continuation of teacher training practices which behaviorally reinforce negative attitudes about ethnic minority children. At best, it will increase the patriarchial condescending view of ethnic minority persons that exists in America today. Presently, it is more feasible for professional educators to concentrate their efforts on the development of competency-based teacher training procedures which can minimize the negatively stereotyped attitudes about ethnic minority children and concurrently promote the development of a multicultural society.

TEACHERS' NEGATIVE EXPECTATIONS

The teachers' stereotypical thinking, whether or not they are sympathetic to the plight of ethnic minorities or low-income pupils, can itself engender a cycle of defeatist or aggressively counteractive behavior by pupil which fulfills negative expectations. In other words, the teachers' behavior vis-a-vis certain pupils, which follows from unfavorable attitudes and expectations of what such people are "really like," fosters those pupil behaviors which fulfill the culturally derived expectations. They tend to react against teachers and the system which tells them that they are inferior, primitive, dull, or unstable. Overt or covert stereotypes, in which ethnic minority youngsters are seen as intellectually inferior, immoral, emotionally unstable, lazy, boisterous, overassertive, lawless, superstitious, happy-go-lucky, untrustworthy, etc., prevail in American society (Allport[21]) and affect the way in which a teacher interacts with pupils perceived in such a light. This in turn influences how pupils will not only react toward the teacher and the learning environment which she or he structures, but also how they will view themselves. This insidious cycle describes the concept of the *self-fulfilling prophecy* in which the expectancy of certain behaviors in others tends to evoke that very behavior (Rosenthal[22]).

Those educators who believe that the problem of education in the urban school lies in the disadvantaged child are likely to harbor beliefs which breed lowered expectations of performance, promote differential and unequal treatment in the form of instructional quality and process, and thereby lower educational results. Such beliefs lead to futile attempts to restructure pupils, often simply to make them behave according to the teachers' notions of proper conduct, rather than structuring the environment to effectively produce desired learning. To the extent that teachers' notions of minority pupil inferiority represent the rationale underlying the quality and process of instruction in urban schools, minority pupils may be expected to exhibit differential and inferior achievement when compared to those who are not subjected to the same kinds of negative evaluation. Stereotypes of socioeconomic status as well as ethnicity have significant implications in the learning situation. In their study investigating the effects of socioeconomic class and teacher bias, Miller, McLaughlin, Hadden, and Chansky found that for college students preparing for careers in education, pupil records containing cues concerning lower-class status resulted in lower estimates of academic achievement, classroom citizenship, and life attainments.[23] This indicates that teachers tend to evaluate negatively the achievements of pupils who are identified as coming from a lower-class background.

Thus, perhaps one of the most crucial issues that influences the education of ethnic minority pupils is a conglomerate of expectancy factors: the expectation (a) that minority pupils in urban settings are part of a lower caste system which is to be distrusted and feared; (b) that ethnic minority pupils are supposed to be different, interpreted to mean deficient, stupid, and inferior; (c) that such pupils can at best have a marginal place in the American population; and (d) that such pupils are difficult to instruct and have little capability to learn required academic concepts. Such expectancies when operative have resulted in a circular effect. Ethnic minority pupils in general manifest a significantly lower achievement level than other pupils, grow up and are employable in marginal positions, if at all, have children who in turn meet the same set of expectancies, and who in essence demonstrate the same achievement level in school and work as their parents. Attempts to counteract this cycle have been for the most part inadequate. The primary mode of counterattack has been conducted through programs called compensatory education. Significant sums of money have been channeled into so-called "innovative, special educational programs for disadvantaged pupils;" yet analysis of the research on these programs indicates little if any significant improvement in the educational outcomes for minority school children. None of the research presents any empirical evidence about the effects of negative teacher expectancies on pupils' performances. Without this kind of evidence, the evaluative conclusions about compensatory and other innovative educational programming are less than valid and provide little real direction for future programming.

What seems to be needed is a conceptual framework of educational

83

practices and procedures that counteracts and minimizes the effects of negative teacher expectancies as they impinge upon urban minority pupils. It is proposed that the concepts of competency-based education have the potential to act as an effective force in the formation of positive teacher expectancies, and reciprocally minimize the impact of negative assumptions about pupils.

The role of teachers' negative attitudes and assumptions about pupils can be largely controlled in competency-based programs through the systematic development and implementation of the competencies defined earlier. A brief consideration of issues and specific operations relating to the design and implementation of these competencies will indicate the means by which a learning environment can be structured to foster positive educational achievement for all pupils, irrespective of their ethnic and/or social class membership.

Assessment Strategies

The initial task in a competency-based education program is to effectively assess the pupils' cognitive and behavioral strengths and weaknesses in academic subject matter. Assessment must be conducted without any preconceived assumptions about expected pupil behavior due to race, ethnicity, age, or sex. Assessment data must function as an empirical base for the design of learning environments which significantly increase the probability that pupils will develop desired competencies in the academic and behavioral domains. In order to function as an empirical base, assessment procedures must succinctly state acceptable performance levels that indicate mastery of a given task or set of tasks. Expected performance levels are made public to pupils prior to the initiation of assessment procedures so that pupils will know exactly what is expected and how and by whom their responses will be assessed. More important, pupils can learn to determine their relative level of performance and begin to assess their own strengths and weaknesses. The latter is a vitally important construct and will be discussed later in this article.

Assessment procedures in a competency-based model of education do not assume that a pupil who has undergone prior instruction is prepared to advance into a higher level of academic performance. Usually this assumption is based upon a required passing grade. But a passing grade does not delineate the performance competencies a pupil can or cannot manifest, nor does it specify in precise terms the prerequisite competencies a pupil must be able to demonstrate before advancement to higher academic levels.

In summary, assessment procedures in a competency-based program are designed to minimize the effects of negative teacher expectations about minority children. They are basically concerned with the observation and measurement of academic strengths and weaknesses, are focused on clear, succinct public performance objectives, and provide a sound data base for the design of future learning environments in the school.

CONSTRUCTING ASSESSMENT INSTRUMENTS

When constructing an assessment instrument in the competency-based model, teachers will not rely upon expectations but instead will design instruments, sometimes called pretests, based on their knowledge of the academic skills needed to perform another academic task.

Briefly, the guidelines for the construction of assessment instruments are characterized by four major phases: (a) planning the assessment instrument, (b) item writing, (c) item analysis, and (d) establishing measures of validity and reliability.

ASSESSMENT OF COGNITIVE AND BEHAVIORAL SKILLS

Special emphasis is given in competency-based programs to behavioral assessment strategies which may be used to measure correlates of many cognitive skills. At the present stage of development in psychological testing and theorizing, it is highly questionable whether any test score can be validly interpreted as an index of immutable or fixed characteristics, capacities, or abilities. Within the context of its fundamental genetic endowment, behavior is a function of interactions with one's environment, and as such it is modifiable. New patterns of response may be predictably instated and current responses may be maintained or eliminated, exclusively as a result of planned or unplanned environmental events. Moreover, new and existing behaviors may be maintained at differential levels of occurrence, duration, or magnitude as a consequence of conditions present in the individual's environment.

The scores derived from appropriately constructed and reliable cognitive assessment instruments can yield only estimates of specific existing cognitive knowledge, interests, or attitudes *as expressed through verbal communication*. Verbal responses represent only one mode of behavior and are meaningful only when a comparison is conducted with an appropriate reference population or with the same population following a period of instruction. As Wicker has clearly shown, the ability to demonstrate writing skills may have little or no relationship to other overt behavioral responses.[24] What pupils actually do or can do in terms of observable performance often cannot be predicted from their written and/or verbal productions. When techniques of assessment focus upon overt behavioral performances which are taken as evidence of learning, the role of interpretation by the teacher is minimized.

Behavioral Assessment. Factors of subjective judgment, biases, expectations, and personal assumptions about minority pupils are largely controlled when educational achievement is evaluated as a part of behavioral assessment. In behavioral assessment, the teacher's personal disposition toward a given pupil with respect to race, ethnicity, or socioeconomic status is irrelevant. The pupil is assessed on the basis of what he/she can or cannot demonstrate in a given curricular domain. Overt behavioral performance is the sole criterion of achievement. Further, behavioral assessment holds that what does not presently exist in the pupil's behavioral repertoire is not as important as what does exist—what the student can actually do. This is the base upon which new behaviors are shaped and structured. The objective is not to isolate, identify, and label judgmental characteristics or attributes of the pupil for negative reports, but to determine the existence of current patterns of performance with the aim of building up new behaviors to demonstrate learning.

Thus the major objective of behavioral assessment is not to evaluate behavior within the implicit context of a judgmental scheme; rather, it is to provide descriptive, reproducible data on quantitative measures of directly observable samples of behavior. This approach attempts to minimize the imposition of negative subjective perceptions, expectancies, assumptions, and biases in judgment by the assessor, in both the collection and analysis of the data; and it curbs the further development of negative teacher expectations.

As suggested by Kanfer and Phillips, behavior assessment is used to provide empirical information that allows the teacher to define objectives for instruction, to identify conditions maintaining undesirable behavior as well as desirable responses, and to permit the selection of the most efficient strategy designed to promote desired learning.[25]

Evaluation of Change. Quantitative evaluation of change in learning responses should be a continuing and integral part of educational programs. Continuous monitoring of progress toward achievement of educational objectives allows the classroom teacher to restructure and adapt instructional activities as needed to optimize conditions for attainment of educational goals, defined in terms of directly observable behaviors. In addition, pupils who are systematically apprised of their strengths and weaknesses relevant to specified performance objectives may contribute to the development of more salient programs, experiences, and procedures facilitating educational achievement. The latter feature could be used to enhance minority pupils' options in learning to gain more control of their own lives.

Design of Behavioral Objectives

A behavioral objective is an essential component in competency-based programs. It is designed to provide explicit information allowing both teacher and learner to be made aware of the educational goals in a learning environment; it specifies what outcome behavior is to be acheived as a result of instruction, how the behavior is to be achieved, and how its achievement is to be demonstrated and evaluated. Behavioral objectives represent a comprehensive statement (or series of statements) serving as the procedural guideline for the teacher as instructor, and the pupil as learner. Behavioral objectives specify (a) substance (content), (b) structure (format or arrangement), and (c) process (methodology) characteristics of an educational program designed to produce learning in the form of planned behavioral change. Behavior-based objectives do not rely upon methods of assessment designed to produce labels and generate inferential speculations about performance skills. Rather, objectives are set and modified on the basis of data derived from direct and systematic application of assessment criteria.

Instructional Strategies for a Competency-Based Classroom

In designing a learning environment, it is essential that the teacher consider the extent to which it is structured to optimize the opportunity for all pupils to become educated. The point to keep in mind is that the classroom is essentially a social situation—with a complex of interacting events, activities, and conditions impinging directly upon all participants in the milieu. To the extent that a social environment is improperly arranged, manipulated, and controlled, the opportunity for achieving predictable and desired outcomes is impaired.

In managing this social system, the teacher must attempt to structure its components in a way that both his or her behaviors and those of the pupils interdependently operate to produce planned behavioral change in the sequential steps intended. This is largely an issue concerned with the design of physical, social, and temporal conditions which facilitate learning, and the manipulation of predetermined consequences to affect pupil behaviors. Basically, this concerns the formulation and implementation of a strategy or programmed procedure in which both teacher-pupil behaviors are to be exhibited in a certain sequence and under specific conditions of occurrence, followed by preselected consequences to regulate performance.

In designing a system in which physical, social, and temporal parameters of milieu are specifically arranged to expedite planned behavior change, it is the environment itself that is altered and programmed. There is no attempt to restructure the pupil in terms of personality or intra-psychic characteristics according to the notions of subjective opinion. The teacher is responsible for identifying and implementing those environmental changes that have been empirically determined to help the individual pupil to learn new skills.

Competency-based methods emphasize planning, programming, predictability, and control with respect to the environmental conditions in which pupils behave and learn. The focus is upon promoting the achievement of educationally relevant responses through positive control of the learning environment. Teacher behavior, with respect to designing and implementing instructional activities, is empirically evaluated; that is, it is tested in terms of the effects they produce. In this sense, the formulation and selection of operational strategies applied in the learning milieu are grounded upon objective, scientific analyses of their observed effects on actual pupil behaviors, not on subjective judgment. If a particular strategy fails to produce desired results, it is replaced by alternative procedures which must prove their effectiveness in each individual case. This represents a novel approach to teaching. It is not uncommon to find pupils exposed to learning programs which totally ignore their experiential background and existing competencies in curricular subjects. A given procedure may be adopted by the teacher simply because it is standard or traditional for certain populations of pupils, irrespective of their individual needs. But in such cases, failure and frustration are also traditions.

Within the competency-based system, the theme is to utilize positive behavioral control to increase successful performance, whether achievements be modest or notable. In its application, the model explicitly fosters the development of positive expectations for successful performance by the pupil. Pupil behaviors are seen to directly reflect the competence of the teacher's performance in terms of designing and implementing an instructional program. Every pupil is perceived to possess some specific, educationally relevant competencies which can be developed and firmly established to facilitate building up related performance skills. In this system, where positive expectations for pupils' growth and achievement prevail, and indeed are provided for in the design of the instructional program itself, pupil achievements provide reinforcement not only for the individual pupil, but also for the teacher who structures and implements the learning program. A model designed to strengthen and recognize existing and future accomplishments will produce outcomes for both teachers and learners that make education an enriching and productive experience. It is the manipulation of environmental variables which underlies learning. It is counterproductive to assume that failure is a product of postulated incompetencies and incapacities of the pupil; rather, the teacher must examine the classroom environment and program he or she structured in order to identify those conditions or elements which interfered with or inhibited the emergence of criterion behavior and rearrange the situation accordingly.

Evaluation

Evaluation in competency-based programs is a continuous process of collecting and interpreting quantitive information. This information is used to make decisions about the learning environment in terms of its resources (inputs), instructional activities (process), and resultant pupil performances (output). Evaluation should provide quantitive information about the level of competencies of pupils when entering a learning system and when leaving the system, and the quality of instructional operation design. As such, evaluation is a tool and a means and process of collecting data which may be used to improve the system.

Pupil performance on various specific criteria is evaluated regularly and frequently as a basis for decisions related to pupils' progress through the program. This serves a diagnostic or guidance function. Performance of pupils and teachers involved in the program can be assessed for the purposes of evaluating the program itself. This serves an evaluation and research function. The teacher must determine which behaviors and activities are effective in facilitating desired pupil outcomes. It cannot be assumed that a program or mode of instructional practices is effective. It must be empirically demonstrated. The program must be open to development or modification on the basis of objectively quantifiable information. The quality of an educational program is evidenced by what it produces in terms of pupil outcomes—assessed with respect to a specified objective and explicit criteria of *both teacher and pupil performance.*

Continuous evaluation provides feedback for empirically grounded decision making regarding the allocation of resources and the modification of instructional processes as may be needed. Competency-based programs depend upon feedback for correction of errors identified in the system and for the improvement of efficiency as it relates to structuring functional learning environments. A system which provides ongoing information about itself regarding the efficiency and effectiveness of its design and operations should provide a means to minimize the role of highly subjective teacher judgment and possible biases about pupils in determining what competencies pupils possess upon entering or leaving the learning system.

The Benefits of a Competency-Based Educational Setting

Benefits accrue to all participants in a competency-based educational setting. Teachers learn to function in a logical sequential manner. They are able to effectively plan instructional activities based upon pupils' strengths and weaknesses. They are able to evaluate their own behavior as teachers with a minimum of threat. They are able to formulate sound educational practices which are observable, measurable, and predictable. They are able to stabilize the learning environment so that a maximum of learning can accrue with a minimum of disciplinary problems. They are able to efficiently measure pupil progress and, if necessary, redesign the learning environment. Finally, they are more able to become accountable to parents and the community.

The most important benefit for children is that they can gradually become more self-directing in their own education and thus begin to gain a sense of control over their future. Self-direction in education is a concept that has received very little philosophical and research attention. Perhaps because of the society's value system of "control and be controlled," educators have given little credence to the concept of self-directed learning for children and especially not for minority children. Yet, if we expect our young persons to be able to develop the competencies necessary to advance the progress of the society, it is pertinent that we begin to develop decision-making skills, as well as other skills, at early ages. The ultimate goal for children in a competency-based education system is that they gain skills in assessing their strengths and weaknesses in establishing long- and short-range behavioral objectives, in seeking out instructional materials to attain those objectives, and in evaluating their progress.

The public nature of the competency-based educational system allows meaningful parent participation. Parents can participate in the development of curriculum in the assessment of pupil strengths and weaknesses, and in the total evaluation procedure. Parents can assess both the program and the teacher's effectiveness and contribute to the redesign of the total educational environment if necessary.

To properly evaluate the efficiency of *assessment* as a component in competency-based programs, teachers, parents, and administrators can utilize measures which allow them to answer three questions:

1. Were appropriate assessment procedures used to yield empirical information on pupil performance?
2. Were assessment data appropriately interpreted, such that the role of subjective judgment was minimized?
3. Does assessment data lead to specific statements of pupils in terms of behavioral strengths and weaknesses?

To properly evaluate the efficiency of *objectives* as a component in competency-based programs, teachers, parents, and administrators can utilize measures which allow them to answer three questions:

1. Were appropriate behavioral objectives formulated, specified, and made public?
2. Were behavioral objectives clearly and precisely stated in terms of explicit classes of measurable and demonstrable behavior?
3. Have behavioral objectives led in step-wise sequence to the terminal goal of instruction?

To properly evaluate the efficiency of *instructional strategies* as a component in competency-based programs, teachers, parents, and administrators can utilize measures which allow them to answer three questions:

1. Has the teacher designed a learning environment which facilitates the production of measurable behaviors indicative of positive educational achievement?
2. Were strategies appropriate (i.e. selection and organization of curriculum content, selection of learning experiences, positive reinforcement procedures) to facilitate learning by individual members of the given pupil population?
3. Were strategies effective and efficient in implementation, and modified as necessary on the basis of empirical data to produce desired outcomes?

To the extent that these questions, in toto, can be answered affirmatively, it is likely that a functional learning environment has been formulated and established to promote positive educational attainments by all pupils exposed to it.

Summary and Recommendations

The competency-based model of education, applicable to the training of prospective teachers, is concerned with behavior change wherein the pupil acquires a specified level of competency in cognitive, social-emotional, and performance domains. Within the competency-based model, learning programs are designed so that pupils and their objectively identified needs are met, in contrast to the restructuring of pupils to fit into a program. Race, ethnicity, sex, income level, and other demographic characteristics of the pupil have bearing in competency-based programs only to the extent that they describe facets of the pupil's social history and prior learning experiences in the culture. Knowledge of these variables is used to the extent that they may contribute to developing relevant learning activities which build upon, and do not negate, pupils' previous learning experiences. Thus, variables of race, ethnicity, income level, social status, and sex reflect the cultural plurality, history, and attendant learning experiences of the pupils. They are not, as many educators and test interpreters believe, indicants of intellectual capacity, aptitude, and ability which may be used to allocate pupils to educational tracks or problems which reduce the likelihood of high achievement and social mobility in American society.

In competency-based programs, measures designed to assess the individual's present level of functioning in a given domain represent objective indices of observable measurable behaviors. Such measures are not designed to provide labels for categories of inferential, subjective constructs which reflect the test constructor's and/or interpreter's own personal experiences, attitudes, value orientation, assumptions, and biases. It is strongly suspected, as Brookover et al. suggest,[15] that these culture-based tests, which label, classify, and are used as an "objective" basis for the placement of pupils in different educational categories and programs, function to stratify and allocate individuals to different social positions in society. That such tests are used to identify, label, and allocate children to different educational programs where their preparation for the positions in the social strata is implicit, represents institutionalized discrimination and bias in its more subtle form.

Such an approach contrasts sharply with the competency-based method by which the teacher determines what skills the pupils need to strengthen and/or expand. The teacher recognizes that pupils' behavior reflects both individual and group characteristics, i.e. some of their behaviors are unique products arising from their own personal learning experiences, while other behaviors are common to their social group, community, geographical region, and the larger culture. Therefore, the unit of analysis by which the pupils' educational needs are assessed is overt behavior. Constructs mired in postulations of personality, values, intelligence quotients, and attitudes, for example, are irrelevant to a competency-based model of education. Objective data describing observable, measurable occurrences of specifically defined behaviors tell the teacher what the pupils actually do in terms of functioning in a given domain. The emphasis is clearly upon present behaviors. What does not presently exist in the pupils' behavioral repertoire is not as important as what does exist. What the pupils can do represents the base upon which subsequent new behaviors can be built, broadened, and synthesized with other relevant responses in a given domain to produce a constellation of chained behaviors which represent performance skills.

Parenthetically, the analogy of the half-full/half-empty water glass is pertinent. A pupil may correctly read and define 50 out of 100 words in his/her lesson book. Is he/she really "dull," "stupid" or "inferior" because he/she "fails" to correctly answer the other 50 items? Or has the student demonstrated success by correctly answering half of the items, which is the foundation for learning the correct response for the other 50 items? The latter situation epitomizes a major issue in education of minority pupils. The teacher who expects less of the minority pupil will see him/her as failing; the more objective, behaviorally based teacher sees the student as learning, with opportunities abounding for structuring situations to foster further learning and achievement.

Pupils who are exposed to a competency-based program know exactly what is expected of them. The instructional activity is designed so that the pupil builds a chain of successive correct responses which culminate in the criterion performance skills. If pupils falter at some point, procedures allow for them to recycle and build upon existing competencies. The criterion by which pupils can identify successful accomplishment of the learning objective is a specified level of observable behavior which the pupils can assess as objectively as the teacher. Because the emphasis is upon exit rather than entrance requirements, pupils of diverse backgrounds and levels of competency may participate in the learning activity as long as they can demonstrate the minimal skills upon which future behaviors are based. The instruction modes in a competency-based model provide a mechanism for specific guidance, feedback, and evaluation which promotes educational acheivement and can foster self-directed learning.

Chief among the important implications of competency-based education in multicultural schools is the limitation and minimization of subjective variables in terms of testing and evaluational judgments which have connotations of good and bad. Explicitly specifying objectives in terms that have observable and measurable physical referents minimizes the intrusion of such intervening variables as subjectivity and bias which have so often functioned to the disadvantage of minority pupils. Similarly, the role of these intervening variables is minimized in designing learning activities, assessment of competencies prior to the learning activity, assessing achievement of learning objectives, and setting criteria for achievement and advancement to new learning programs.

If teacher training institutions are to provide preservice and inservice training which will significantly increase the probability (a) that minority pupils improve their academic achievement levels and (b) that a multicultural philosophic structure will undergird broad educational goals, then they must facilitate the development of educational policy which will foster the following processes in teacher training:

1. Conduct scientific analyses of learning tasks and design teacher functions to maximize the probability of the achievement of those tasks
2. Redesign teacher function within the competency-based teacher education model
3. Instruct teachers in the pros and cons of reinforcement practices
4. Design internships (rather than student teaching) for preservice and inservice teachers which will allow them to test their own competencies in all the areas of the competency-based model
5. Provide instruction for preservice and inservice teachers in the curriculum area of teacher expectancies of minority groups and the ramifications in teacher behavior of such expectancies
6. Instruct preservice and inservice teachers in the evaluation of pupil performance on a pre-post performance continuum

If teacher training institutions could achieve just the above items, many of the negative results of the education of minority children could be obviated and the development of the multicultural concept could probably be realized.

REFERENCES

1 Kerner, O. *Report of the National Advisory Commission on Civil Disorders.* New York: E.P. Dutton, 1968.
2 "Black Students, Teachers Pushed Out of Public Education, NEA Survey Shows." NEA News Press Release, April 24, 1972.
3 Becker, H.S. "Social Class Variation in Teacher-Pupil Relationships." *Journal of Educational Sociology* 25 (1952): 451-465.
4 MacKennon, D.W. "The Nature and Nurture of Creative Talent." *American Psychologist* 17 (1962): 484-95.
5 Clark, K.B. "Educational Stimulation of Racially Disadvantaged Children." In *Education in Depressed Areas,* edited by A.H. Passow. New York: Columbia University Press, 1963.
6 Katz, I. "Review of Evidence Relating to Effects of Desegregation on Intellectual Performance of Negroes." *American Psychologist* 19 (1964): 381-99.
7 Gibson, G. "Aptitude Tests." *Science* 149 (1965): 583.
8 Rosenthal, R. and L. Jacobson. *Pygmalion in the Classroom: Teacher Expectation and Pupil's Intellectual Development.* New York: Holt, Rinehart and Winston, 1968.
9 Leacock, E. *Teaching and Learning in City Schools: A Comparative Study.* New York: Basic Books, 1969.

10 Rist, R.C. "Student Social Class and Teacher Expectations: The Self-Fulfilling Prophecy in Ghetto Education." *Harvard Educational Review* 40, no. 3 (August 1970): 411-51.

11 Clark, F.W., D.R. Evans, and L.A. Hamerlynck, eds. *Implementing Behavioral Programs for Schools and Clinics.* Proceedings of the Third Banff International Conference on Behavior Modification. Champaign, Ill.: Research Press Co., 1972.

12 Bandura, A. *Principles of Behavior Modification.* New York: Holt, Rinehart and Winston, 1969.

13 Ramp, E.A. and B.L. Hopkins, eds. *A New Direction for Education: Behavior Analysis.* Lawrence, Kansas: The University of Kansas, 1971.

14 Skinner, B.F. *Science and Human Behavior.* New York: McMillan, 1953.

15 Gagne, R.M. *The Conditions of Learning.* New York: Holt, Rinehart and Winston, 1964.

16 O'Leary, K.D. and S.G. O'Leary. *Classroom Management,* New York: Pergamon Press, 1972.

17 Green, R.L. "The Urban School Child." In *Racial Crisis in American Education,* edited by R.L. Green. Chicago: Follett Publishing Co., 1969.

18 Brookover, W.B. et al. *Elementary School Social Environment and School Achievement.* East Lansing, Mich.: College of Urban Development, Michigan State University, 1973.

19 Hilgard, E.R. and D.G. Marquis. *Conditioning and Learning.* Rev. ed. G.A. Kimble, ed. New York: Appleton-Century-Crofts, 1961.

20 Meacham, M.L. and A.E. Wiesen. *Changing Classroom Behavior: A Manual for Precision Teaching.* Scranton, New York: International Textbook Co., 1969.

21 Allport, G.W. "The Resolution of Intergroup Tensions." Paper presented at the National Conference of Christians and Jews, New York, 1952.

22 Rosenthal, R. *Experimental Effects in Behavioral Research.* New York: Appleton, 1966.

23 Miller, D.K. et al. "Socioeconomic Class and Teacher Bias." *Psychology Reports* 23 (1968): 806.

24 Wicker, A.W. "Attitudes Versus Actions: The Relationship of Verbal and Overt Behavioral Responses to Attitude Objects." *Journal of Social Issues* 25, no. 4 (1969): 41-78.

25 Kanfer, E. and J. Phillips. *Learning Foundations of Behavior Therapy.* New York: Wiley & Sons, 1970.

CHAPTER 4

TEACHER COMPETENCIES FOR CULTURAL DIVERSITY

Cordell Wynn
Assistant Dean and Professor, College of Education
Alabama State University, Montgomery

Rationale

Planned multicultural education and the incorporation of competency-based education in school systems, colleges, and universities are becoming increasingly recognized as important phenomena in the American educational enterprise. To the extent that multicultural education can be significantly initiated and purposefully influenced, the role of the educational practitioner is central in these phenomena. It is assumed in this paper that there is a positive value to the total educational arena and to the society which it serves in developing and implementing a relevant and viable multicultural educational program for learners based on the concept of competency-based education.

Teacher education is changing in higher educational institutions because there are insistent demands rising, from such groups as Mexican Americans, American Indians, Chicanos, Blacks, and Puerto Ricans, to recognize the importance of cultural differences and modify the curriculum to reflect their concerns. A dialogue is revolving around sound strategies to create a teacher education program which will equip the individual teacher to demonstrate specified competencies which are realistic to our pluralistic society. When this goal is realized, the role of the teacher will change from a bureaucratic functionary to that of a democratic educational practitioner.

Every school in our nation has an imperative mission these days: to help prepare its students for life in a society composed of many diverse cultures, racial and ethnic strands. The extent to which the school equips its young people to work and live within a country graced by an assortment of races, cultures, and lifestyles—each mutually celebrated—is a positive indicator of its overall quality and its relevance to contemporary youth. Therefore, multicultural teaching is the greatest educational challenge of the century. A response to that challenge is a viable multicultural education/competency-based teacher education program, for it is upon the quality of the teacher that all else depends when it comes to facilitative learning.

In developing a multicultural education program, it is necessary to explore the question:, "What does a teacher need to know and be able to do in order to teach effectively in a culturally diverse society?" In seeking answers to this question, the writer talked with teachers, public school administrators, teacher trainers, state department of education personnel, and education researchers. The key idea that emerged, if multicultural education is to become a reality, was competency-based teacher education (CBTE).

It appears obvious that if the aim of teaching is learning, there should be evidence that preservice teachers can bring about appropriate learning in students before they assume responsibility for such learning in the classroom. Therefore, it is believed that this aim can be accomplished by enabling the prospective learner to demonstrate mastery or attainment of specified criteria. These criteria can be stated so that they include areas in the cognitive, affective, and psychomotor domains and encompass all phases of education from preprimary to graduate level.

Competency, of course, is the important concept, the sine que non of CBTE. The learner will have x number of reading skills, will differentiate among several elements of diverse cultures with y percent accuracy, will know z number of economic concepts, and so on. This is different from the usual approach of saying: Given x amount of time, the learner will be taught to the best of his/her and our ability. In this latter approach, time is the major limiting factor; in competency-based teacher education, time is basically a variable element. The development of a teacher education program that generates this kind of evidence is mandatory if we are to provide the best education possible for all American youth.

Assumptions of Competency-Based Teacher Education

1. Competency-based teacher education should have as its base detailed descriptions of the behavioral outcomes expected of the learner. Although already alluded to, this assumption deserves additional comment because, of all the assumptions underlying competency-based teacher education, the emphasis on behavioral outcomes is probably the most controversial.[1]

Behavioral outcomes are variously referred to as behavioral objectives, performance goals, operational objectives, and instructional objectives. But regardless of the nomenclature employed, most would agree that statements of behavioral outcomes should meet three criteria: (a) the behavior itself must be identified, (b) the important conditions under which the behavior is to occur must be defined, and (c) the criterion of acceptable performance must be specified. When these criteria are met, the result looks something like the following:

> The student must be able to reply in grammatically correct French to 95% of the French questions that are presented to him during an examination (2.50).

> The student must be able to spell correctly at least 80% of the words called out to him during an examination (2.50).[2]

The advantages of stating educational outcomes in behavioral terms are becoming recognized. Advantages include giving meaning to broad statements of educational goals, giving direction to the design of instructional strategies, and making obvious the methods used in evaluation. Proponents argue that these are critical elements in the search for a more effective and efficient system of public education. But critics of behavioral objectives point out several potential dangers. One danger revolves around the issue of responsibility. Do teachers write their own objectives? Or do they use objectives which have been preestablished by experts? The critics argue that teachers seldom have time to do the former and that they jeopardize the unique aspirations of their classes by opting for the latter.

2. Competency-based teacher education should provide for differences among learners in terms of their accumulated experience, extent of achievement, and rate and style of learning. In other words, CBTE is based on the principle of individualized instruction and learning.

3. Competency-based teacher education should provide opportunities for the learner to pursue personal goals. The intent of this assumption goes beyond the elements of individualization described above. That is, it means more than providing the learner with opportunities to make choices among alternate learning activities. In essence, the assumption means that the learner is also given opportunities to make choices among various objectives and, in some instances, to develop his or her own.

In a CBTE program, there are certain objectives which are required for everyone. "For example, each learner must be able to do x, y, and z." But there are other objectives, all of which are considered important, but none of which is considered to be as vital as x, y, or z, or more valuable to all learners than another. From this latter group of objectives, then, each learner has the freedom and the responsibility to negotiate a program of studies.[3]

Or, suppose that the learner is interested in a particular area of study for which the school has no objectives. In such a case, the learner is encouraged to become involved, along with the professional staff, in designing learning modules in that area. Certainly, the extent of the learner's involvement will be determined by his or her age and talents.

4. In addition to the assumptions cited above, two others need to be mentioned, if only in passing. One is that CBTE *should be so organized and managed that all persons concerned with or affected by the education of learners share the responsibility for it.* A key concept in competency-

based teacher education then is *involvement:*—the involvement of parents, of community groups and institutions, and, of course, of teachers and learners in the design and implementations of programs. Another key concept is *accountability.* For when one is responsible for the design and implementation of instructional programs, to some extent one must also be accountable for their consequences.

5. The other assumption is that competency-based teacher education should be so *organized and managed that it provides for its own continuous evaluation and revision.* This is a critical area. For there is always danger that the efficiency of any instructional program will become equated with its effectiveness and relevance. In other words, an instructional program may appear to be functioning with no apparent flaws, to be maintaining itself with little difficulty, but upon closer examination, the program may not be achieving its stated objectives, or the objectives themselves may be irrelevant. In CBTE then, questions of efficiency, effectiveness, and relevance are separate questions, and careful attention is given to asking and answering them.

Competencies to Be Demonstrated by All Teachers In a Culturally Diverse Society

There are certain basic competencies that all teachers should be able to demonstrate to teach effectively in a society composed of disparate cultures. These competencies are identified as follows:

COMPETENCY CLUSTER I. UNDERSTANDING HUMAN GROWTH
AND DEVELOPMENT

1. Recognizing that each individual is worthwhile and unique
2. Understanding that each individual reacts as a whole human being
3. Understanding that each individual's behavior is caused and is not arbitrary
4. Recognizing that each individual wants to do something and attain success in doing it
5. Recognizing that each individual has dignity and integrity
6. Recognizing the importance of the individual and his/her individuality
7. Understanding the implications of selected concepts and principles of human growth and development
8. Recognizing the role that environment plays in learning
9. Understanding and analyzing the development of social relationships
10. Evaluating the factors which affect development and measurement of intelligence

COMPETENCY CLUSTER II. PLANNING AND PREPARING FOR
INSTRUCTION

1. Stating desired learning outcomes in behavior terms

2. Organizing classroom for instructional quality and classroom control
3. Specifying indicators of outcome achievement
4. Recognizing the wide range of interests and achievement levels among individual learners
5. Planning instructional activities that relate to desired learning outcomes
6. Recognizing the difference between the value systems of different racial and class subcultures in the classroom
7. Identifying and articulating the use of instructional materials and procedures
8. Understanding learners' environmental backgrounds and language patterns
9. Planning assessment activities that relate to desired learning outcomes
10. Planning instructional materials and procedures appropriate to the individual needs of all learners in a given classroom
11. Planning techniques to foster self-evaluating, self-directiveness, self-diagnosing, self-prescribing, self-motivating to foster independent learning
12. Generating learners' desire to engage in critical and analytical thinking, rational decision making, and linking knowledge to action
13. Stimulating inquiry, creativity, sensitivity, and conceptualization
14. Promoting instructional ideas that will change the learner's role from *reactive* to *participative*
15. Indicating how data on pupil achievement is to be displayed and used in adjusting instruction

COMPETENCY CLUSTER III. PERFORMING INSTRUCTIONAL FUNCTIONS

1. Demonstrating adequate and appropriate skills in oral and written communication
2. Conveying the learning outcomes desired from instruction
3. Generating constructive pupil-teacher interaction
4. Adapting instruction to context, content, individual learning styles or modes, and rate of growth
5. Managing instructional transitions and terminations
6. Managing the effective use of instructional materials, procedures, and activities
7. Facilitating skill in interpersonal communication
8. Managing unexpected activities and events
9. Managing strong feelings and disruptive events
10. Fostering collaborative decision making between learner and teacher
11. Providing for variety in instructional activities and cognitive levels exercised
12. Reassuring, supporting, reinforcing, and analyzing learner responses
13. Utilizing feelings and emotional climates in the instructional process

COMPETENCY CLUSTER IV. PERFORMING ASSESSMENT FUNCTIONS

1. Assessing learning before instruction
2. Assessing learning during instruction
3. Assessing learning after instruction
4. Planning instruction on the basis of learning outcome data
5. Assessing the individual needs of learners
6. Assessing the needs of the community

COMPETENCY CLUSTER V. DISPLAYING PUPIL ACHIEVEMENT

1. Displaying pre- and post-lesson achievement
   a. For knowledge/skill outcomes
   b. For process/attitudinal outcomes
2. Displaying learning gains that can be attributed to instruction
   a. For knowledge/skill outcomes
   b. For process/attitudinal outcomes

COMPETENCY CLUSTER VI. RELATING INTERPERSONALLY

1. Relating sensitively and effectively to learners
2. Relating sensitively and effectively to supervisors
3. Relating sensitively and effectively to colleagues
4. Relating sensitively and effectively to parents

COMPETENCY CLUSTER VII. CARRYING OUT ADDITIONAL
PROFESSIONAL RESPONSIBILITIES

1. Managing noninstructional activities
2. Meeting work schedule demands
3. Maintaining the learning environment
4. Meeting general professional responsibilities

Some of the most promising practices incorporated into achieving these stated competencies are ideas which some teacher educators have supported over the years in different forms and under different labels. Educational leaders and proponents of multicultural/competency-based teacher education will be working to demonstrate that some of these ideas also have their roots in a democratic value system, an appropriate base for the preparation of teachers for schools in American society. This latter fact makes these ideas all the more important in multicultural education programs.

There will be anticipated problems with this approach. The need for further research is urgent, but better preparation of teachers to meet the challenge cannot wait as cultural pluralism continues to be ignored as an important educational ingredient in creating a "No One Model American." The writer sees the *changing role* of the *teacher* and *learner* as the primary problem in implementing multicultural/competency-based teacher education. To deal effectively with this problem, the writer suggests that we have to build a support system for individualizing instruction within the framework presented as follows:

1. To provide a systematic prescribed individualized program for each student in a given class based upon the learner's needs, strengths, weaknesses, interests, and abilities as determined by relevant and appropriate evaluative instruments
2. To provide for a unique instructional mode for each student in a given class which will facilitate an individualized learning plan for *each* learner. Each plan will provide for a specific procedure on an individual basis, as suggested in Table 1.

TABLE 1
INDIVIDUALIZING INSTRUCTION

1. *Diagnosis:*	Assessing the strengths and weaknesses of the learner
2. *Prescription:*	Deciding what course of action to follow
3. *Contract:*	Commitment of learner to perform the prescribed treatment Partners: Student-Teacher
4. *Treatment:*	Actual instructional strategies that are relevant to the learning modes of each learner; the teaching part of teaching
5. *Assessment:*	Did the treatment work?

This process will also have as its key emphasis the change role of the *learner* and *teacher* as suggested in Tables 2 and 3.

The writer sees that one of the major issues with multicultural/competency-based teacher education programs is how to identify specified competencies needed to facilitate substantive pluralistic learning. Another issue is focused on how teaching competency is to be defined. The range of positions taken on the issues can be framed by a series of questions. Is demonstrated mastery of knowledge about teaching to be considered teaching competency? Is skill in performing the behaviors or tasks of teachers the meaning to be given to teaching competency? Or is *teaching competency* a term to be applied only to the demonstrated ability to bring about the outcomes desired of a teacher in certified teaching positions? These varied positions represent markedly different views of what the writer sees multicultural/competency-based teacher education is all about, and set markedly different requirements for program structure and operation.

TABLE 2
THE LEARNER'S ROLE CHANGES

FROM:	TO:
Assignment doing	Planning
	Optional exercising
	Creating
	Viewing and listening
Memorizing	Problem solving
	Hypothesizing
	Analyzing
	Synthesizing
	Concluding
Note taking	Organizing ideas
Reciting	Discussing
	Conceptualizing
	Inquiring
	Listening
	Evaluating
	Debating

TABLE 3
THE TEACHER'S ROLE CHANGES

FROM	TO:
Presenting broad competencies	Special competencies representing cross-cultural and minority teaching/learning situations. Sensitivity to and knowledge of minority students and their culture must be translated into effective teaching skills which enable the student to learn.
Coercing	Motivating
Lecturing	Discussing
Asking questions	Stimulating inquiry
Talking at students	Listening and talking with students
Testing and grading	Fostering self-evaluation
Lesson planning	Writing behavioral objectives
	Establishing competencies
	Diagnosing
	Prescribing

Competencies Needed for Effectively Teaching Identified Culturally Different Youth

The writer endorses the concept that teachers need identified competencies for effectively teaching specified culturally different youth. In this paper, the writer is focusing attention on the needs of Black youths as an ethnic group, inasmuch as the majority of his 22 years of educational experience has been with this segment of the school population.

Since school districts throughout the nations are required by law to eradicate all vestiges of a dual education for Black and white youth, many teachers find themselves teaching students who differ from them racially, culturally, socially, and economically. This is a relatively new experience for these education practitioners, and research points out that many lack adequate skills to deal effectively with the challenge of providing quality instruction for youth from such diverse cultures.

Contrary to the thinking of many education practitioners, the physical reassignment of students and faculty to eliminate racial identifiability of schools which, in turn, increases cultural diversity, is but a first step in the process of achieving quality multicultural education for all youth. An essential and continuing element in this process is the training of prospective teachers and other education practitioners to cope effectively with problems resulting from bringing together these disparate cultures, with their differing values, mores and customs, into close and prolonged contact. Thus, in dealing with these problems, an educational process is needed that provides an element of "quality control," a way of monitoring the skill levels and progress of students. This process is available in the concept of competency-based teacher education.

Competencies to Be Demonstrated by Teachers Who Teach in a Multicultural Education Program

The writer sees the following identified competencies needed for effectively teaching specified culturally different youth:

1. Demonstrating effective techniques and methods to build and enhance the self-concept of learners
2. Conceptualizing the dimensions in which the learner may be expected to grow and learn under diverse home and community environmental conditions
3. Recognizing the importance of overcoming cultural and racial stereotypes
4. Understanding the interdependence needed among the various cultures for the enrichment of learning how to live, grow, and learn in a pluralistic society
5. Understanding the history of minority groups in the United States and, in particular, of the civil rights movement

6. Demonstrating knowledge about the psychology and impact of prejudice
7. Planning viable and relevant means for combating prejudice and negative reactions as reflected in parent and student behavior
8. Understanding that all people are human—with individual feelings, aspirations, and attitudes no matter what cultural orientation they represent
9. Recognizing the importance of being prepared to encounter prejudice and hostility as reflected in parental and community reactions
10. Assuming responsibility for examining own motives—and what disciplines they apply to
11. Supporting self-initiated moves of all people and not condemning or prejudging their motives
12. Assisting all young people to understand and confront feelings of ethnic groups other than their own
13. Staying with and working through difficult confrontations
14. Showing interest in understanding the point of view of all cultural representation
15. Demonstrating directness and openness in expressing feelings
16. Identifying and exploring solutions to problems arising in cultural diversity
17. Recognizing and creating positive ways to cope with racial attitudes of young people as shown in their behavior
18. Creating a climate of mutual trust and constructive interpersonal and intergroup relationships
19. Building intercultural cohesiveness and dispelling myths about the intellectual inferiority or superiority of ethnic groups
20. Demonstrating research skills relating to cultural pluralism
21. Recognizing the importance of stressing the insights of sociology, psychology, cultural anthropology, and other relevant fields in facilitating learning outcomes in a pluralistic setting
22. Demonstrating methods and techniques to offer young people options which allow for alternative styles of learning
23. Recognizing that within the realm of potential of every human being there is a level of awareness and achievement which can make life rewarding, and that most young people want desperately to find that level
24. Assuming the responsibility of helping to devise programs which reach out to students and engage them in a process which is both interesting and fair and will, thus, lead to a level of awareness and achievement which gives them a positive perception of themselves and their relationship to others
25. Developing viable strategies to confront young people with moral, ethical, and spiritual conflicts of their culture and motivate them to devise a system of values which is both personal and internalized
26. Demonstrating that the color of an individual is not nearly as important as his or her competence
27. Developing objectives and activities to enhance the self-confidence

young Black learners use in guarding against the trappings of condescension

28. Planning to include learners in full participation in the decision-making process relative to instructional activities
29. Selecting materials that will not derogate or ignore the identified culturally different group
30. Building and promoting viable channels for meaningful communication among students, colleagues, and parents to lessen language barriers
31. Recognizing the value of various evaluative instruments and their uses with multicultural education

Problems related to the full actualization of the above identified competencies hinge on how teachers condition their own beliefs about the world in which the learners live. A learner's actions seem intelligent to him or her and to those that will teach him or her only if teachers see the world through the learner's eyes. But the learner's views of reality are largely personal, being influenced by individual needs, values, culture, self-concept, physiological structure, beliefs about other people, and opportunity.

An individual behaves in a manner designed to maintain or to enhance self-organization. People are capable of self-initiated behavior which takes them toward self-realization. The most important factors in determining our perceptions are the beliefs we hold about ourselves and other people which are learned in interaction with them. When people perceive themselves as greatly different than others, in terms of adequacy, they are inclined: (a) to be self-rejecting if they regard others as having greater worth, or (b) to reject others if they regard themselves as having greater worth. We are in the best position to perceive ourselves and others accurately when we believe that both we and our peers have worth.

Based on this type of perceptual theory, in preparing teachers to demonstrate competencies needed for effectively teaching identified culturally different youth, the writer believes these implications for education can be derived.[4] In order to teach, one must—

1. understand individual students by trying to view them and their world as they do.
2. discover the differences between the value system of different racial and class subcultures in the community and the implication for the classroom situation.
3. learn the characteristics of an impoverished community and the nature, causes, and effects of cultural deprivation.
4. understand the relationship of student potentials to attained levels of achievement, with emphasis on the effects that educational, social, and economic levels have on this achievement.
5. acquire the professional skill needed in analyzing instructional deficiencies experienced by disadvantaged children.
6. appreciate the controlling personal and environmental factors involved in the teaching-learning process.

7. develop the ways and means of organizing the classroom for instructional quality.
8. acknowledge the problems of school administration unique to the desegregated school situation, including the preparation of school desegregation plans.

Potential Strategy

The writer sees competency-based teacher education as a potential strategy for preparing personnel to work effectively with youth from diverse cultural backgrounds. The initial focus of CBTE is upon the curriculum, the teacher, and the specified skills the learner is to attain. Some schools of thought suggest that educational practitioners should "first look at the child; he will 'tell' them his needs."[5] The writer views this as a basic "cop-out" in designing multicultural education programs. If we have no goals and objectives, we cannot be held accountable; and accountability is an essential element in providing quality learning experiences for all youth in our pluralistic society. What if the learner never shows interest in his or her fellow classmates? And what if the learner decides he or she does not want to interact with peers from other cultures in a meaningful group activity?

106

Logically, it appears understandable that we must first create and design the curriculum and then look at the learner, in relation to that curriculum. To insure that desired behaviors are specified for learners, there is an imperative need to develop behavioral objectives as a first step in constructing a solid multicultural/competency-based teacher education program. Behavioral objectives are referred to by a variety of terms such as *instructional objectives, performance objectives,* and *terminal objectives.* Regardless of the term used, a behavioral objective is a precise statement of the behavior the successful learner will exhibit after completing the learning activity. The writer defines a *good* behavioral objective as one that contains four essential elements. It states (a) who, (b) given what, (c) does what, (d) how well. It does *not* describe the learning activity in which the student will engage. Rather, it describes what the learner will be able to do after instruction, and how well she or he will be able to do it.

To help understand the movement toward competency-based teacher education and its applicability to multicultural education, the writer breaks the growth of education into three phases: (a) Traditional Phase—marked by a great preoccupation with the "inner" characteristics and capacities of the learner (aptitude or ability); (b) Experimental Phase—focus shifted from learner, per se, to the *teaching process;* and (c) Competency-Based Education—an educational process that provides an element of "quality control;" a way of monitoring the skill levels and progress of learners which is vital in a culturally disparate classroom. This process provides a way of systematically *preventing* failure and insures consistent, efficient *teaching.* The writer sees CBTE as a procedure that has changed education from an "art" into a "science."

Assessment in all its stages—pre, formative and summative—is basic to meaningful and relevant multicultural education as well as to competency-based education. This, combined with more equal achievement standards, provides an educational process that is more likely to meet the needs of all youth in our pluralistic society.

It is important to point out that CBTE systems vary depending upon program size, subject matter, etc. However, these systems follow the same general design. Each basic step helps to answer a basic educational question.

The first step is to formulate and sequence objectives. This step answers the basic question, "What will the learner do?"

The second step is that of preassessment. There is need to find out which of the objectives the learner has and has not learned. This helps educational practitioners answer the question, "What does the learner know?"

After preassessment, instructional planning and instruction, per se, occur. The question, "What activities will the learner perform?" is answered here.

Finally, the question, "What has been learned?" must be answered. This is the postassessment phase. Based on the information gained here, basic decisions are made regarding the next steps in the learner's course of learning. These are the basic steps in setting up models in competency-based education.

The position taken in this paper is that the objective of teacher education programs should be to assist prospective teachers in developing the competencies that they require to intervene successfully in the intellectual, emotional, cultural, and physical development of youth from diverse cultural backgrounds. This position has a number of implications both for teacher education programs and for the school curriculum at all educational levels.

Basic Recommendations and Conclusions

If teacher education institutions are to meet the objectives stated above, consideration should be given to the following:

1. Develop teacher training programs that attend to the defined skills, attitudes, and experiences required of individual living and learning in a pluralistic society.
2. Require student teachers to behave as they will expect their students to behave, though at a level of greater sophistication.
3. Replace subordinate content objectives with behavioral objectives.
4. Accommodate the individual differences of potential teachers in the same way the graduate teacher will be expected to accommodate the individual differences of children.

5. Require teachers to demonstrate a minimum level of competence in a range of critical functions in order to obtain professional certification.
6. Move rapidly to employ, in the full range of positions, faculty and administrators from all ethnic groups in our pluralistic society.
7. Implement special training components that provide for competencies needed in crosscultural and minority teaching/learning stiuations. Sensitivity to and knowledge of minority students and their culture must be translated through training into effective teaching skills which facilitate learning in multicultural education programs.
8. Design and implement vehicles to open up effective and honest communication among all those within the school community, thus increasing mutual trust.
9. Unite public school and university personnel in a collaborative effort to prepare teachers. The goal should be to better integrate practice and theory in the training of teachers.
10. Assist school districts in systematic staff development programs to establish learning-teaching effectiveness centers to provide for the renewal and upgrading of professional competencies in the cognitive domain, and to combine personal creativity with the ability to be a resource to the learning process for all youth in a pluralistic society.

Similarly, if teacher education programs are to have any relevance to what actually occurs in the schools, the schools themselves must—

1. provide programs based on a continuum of skills and concepts inherent in specific learning themes rather than in isolated subject matter.
2. adopt a philosophy of continuous progress.
3. provide opportunities within the school for the child to apply rational thinking to real-life problems of living in a culturally diverse society.
4. actively implement new resources and techniques designed to relieve the teacher of non-teaching functions.
5. select instructional resources that will adequately reflect multicultural education.

Multicultural education/competency-based teacher education has many positive elements and few shortcomings when properly designed and effectively implemented. It certainly enables the teacher to continuously increase her or his competencies to cope with areas of reality in such a way that he or she sees new options within the environment. Such a teacher can build educational settings in which innovation rather than imitation is the norm, and in which the learning process for youth in our pluralistic society becomes self-motivating and is fun.

COMPETENCY-BASED TEACHER EDUCATION PROGRAM
GLOSSARY OF TERMS

ACHIEVEMENT LEVEL   How well a person is doing in relation to a specific instructional objective or group of objectives

ANECDOTAL RECORDS	A written record of conversations between students/students, student/parent, teacher/student, teacher/parent
ASSESSMENT DATA	Information that tells how well a pupil is doing or what difficulty the pupil may be having in relation to a specified objective
ASSESSMENT INSTRUMENT	A test or questionnaire designed to provide information to the teacher about any facet of a child's behavior
BOUNDARIES	Boundaries between acceptable and unacceptable behavior—the rules of the classroom
COMPETENCY	A statement of the knowledges, skills, or behaviors expected of the teacher; each statement will be accompanied by at least one *assessment*
CONTINUING ASSESSMENT	The use of evaluation as an ongoing process utilized to continually refine and improve instruction
CORRECTIVE FEEDBACK	Information given a pupil about performance or behavior in relation to an objective or a classroom rule
DIAGNOSTIC INSTRUMENTS	Tests (formal or informal) designed to indicate why a person is having difficulty learning a given skill, knowledge, or concept
FLOW CHART	A method of diagramming a procedure or process, step-by-step
FEEDBACK	Information provided to the learner about how she or he is progressing in relation to a specific objective
GROUPING AND GROUPING STRATEGY	Refers to the way in which a teacher organizes groups of children for instruction; includes entire-class grouping, small-group, pairing, individualization, or combination of these categories
INDEPENDENT LEVEL	The degree to which a pupil can work on an independent basis, without help and without undue frustration
INSTRUCTIONAL LEVEL	That level at which a child understands at least 80 percent of the words or ideas
INSTRUCTIONAL MATERIALS	Books, films, objects and such, used to help a learner achieve a specified instructional objective

INSTRUCTIONAL OBJECTIVE	A teacher's objective for the learner; what the teacher wants the pupil to know or be able to do as a result of instruction
INSTRUCTIONAL PROGRAM	Long-range plans and objectives for children
INTEREST INVENTORY	A check-list or open-ended questionnaire used to determine the range and depth of student interests
LEARNING ACTIVITIES	What the teacher plans for the learner to do in relation to a given instructional objective
LEARNING MODALITY (LEARNING STYLE)	The way or the circumstances in which the pupil seems to learn best; for example, a pupil may respond best in a structured setting as opposed to a more open environment—or may learn best from visuals, as opposed to audio materials
LEARNING MODULE	A curriculum package based on an objective or related group of objectives
NONVERBAL RESPONSES	All the ways we communicate with people other than through the spoken word; writing, facial expressions, gestures, all kinds of body language
PEER RELATIONSHIPS	Social relationship with other children in the class
PEER STATUS	A pupil's standing in relation to all pupils in the classroom in terms of a designated kind of behavior, i.e. social, leadership, athletic, size, weight, etc.

110

REFERENCES

1 Eisele, James E. and J. Michael Palardy. "Competency-Based Education." *The Clearinghouse,* May 1972, p. 545.

2 Ibid., p. 546.

3 Ibid., p. 547.

4 Part of this list is based on the work of Robert E. Bills, *About People and Teaching* (Lexington, Ky.: University of Kentucky, Bureau of School Services, 1973).

5 Lundell, Kerth T. *Competency-Based Teaching.* Kettering, Ohio: Behavioral Products, 1973, p. 3.

BIBLIOGRAPHY

"A Special Issue on Competency/Performance-Based Teacher Education." *Phi Delta Kappan* 55, no. 5 (January 1974).

Anrig, Gregory R. "What's Needed for Quality Integrated Education?" *School Management* 16 (March 1972): 24.

Arnez, Nancy L. "The Effect of Teacher Attitudes Upon the Culturally Different." *School and Society,* March 19, 1966, pp. 16-17.

Baughman, E.E. and W.G. Dohstrom. *Negro and White Children: A Psychological Study in the Rural South.* New York: Academic Press, 1968.

Chesler, Mark A., ed. "How Do You Feel About Whites? and How Do You Feel About Negroes?" *A Collection of Papers by College Students Exploring and Expressing Their Own Racial Attitudes.* Ann Arbor, Michigan: Center for Research on Utilization of Scientific Knowledge, University of Michigan, 1966.

Heller, Steven Ashley. "A Study of Teacher Attitudes Regarding School Desegregation in Selected Tennessee School Systems." Doctoral Dissertation, University of Tennessee, 1971.

"Hunter to Head Multicultural-CBTE Project." *AACTE Bulletin.* Newsletter of the American Association of Colleges for Teacher Education, Washington, D.C., October 1973, pp. 1,4.

Johnson, Charles E. et al. *Georgia Educational Model Specifications for the Preparation of Elementary Teachers, Final Report.* Washington, D.C.: Government Printing Office, 1969.

Lohman, Joseph D. *Cultural Patterns of Differentiated Youth: A Manual For Teachers in Marginal Schools.* Berkeley: University of California Press, 1970.

Lucas, Sammie. *Racial Perceptions of Metropolitan School Desegregation.* Knoxville, Tenn.: University of Tennessee, 1970.

Mager, Robert F. *Preparing Instructional Objectives.* San Francisco, Calif.:Fearon Publishers, 1962.

"Multi-Ethnic—Multi-Culture Classrooms." *Journal of Research and Development in Education.* University of Georgia, Summer 1971, pp. 356-8.

Myers, Douglas and Fran Reid. *Educating Teachers: Critiques and Proposals.* Toronto: The Ontario Institute for Studies in Education, 1974.

Nash, Paul. "Integrating Feeling, Thinking and Acting in Teacher Education." *AACTE Bulletin.* Newsletter of the American Association of Colleges for Teacher Education, Washington, D.C., April 1971, pp. 7-8.

Pettigrew, Thomas F. "Complexity and Change in American Racial Patterns: A Social Psychological View." *The Negro American.* Talcott Parsons and Kenneth B. Clark, eds. Boston: Houghton-Mifflin, 1966.

Rosner, Benjamin. *The Power of Competency-Based Teacher Education: A Report of the Committee on National Program Priorities in Teacher Education.* Boston: Allyn and Bacon, 1972.

Schessler, Karl. *Analyzing Social Data.* Boston: Houghton-Mifflin, 1971.

Silberman, Charles E. *Crisis in the Classroom.* New York: Random House, 1970.

"Symposium on Multicultural Education." *Journal of Teacher Education* 24, no. 4 (Winter 1973).

Wynn, Cordell. "An Investigation of Cross-Over Teachers' Perceptions of Problems Encountered in Five Georgia Desegregated School Systems." Doctoral Dissertation, University of Georgia, 1973.

Wynn, Cordell. "Black and White in Bibb County Classrooms." *Integrated Education* 9, no. 4 (July-August 1971): 10-16.

111

PREPARATION OF TEACHERS FOR OPTIMAL PARTICIPATION IN ASSESSMENT PROGRAMS FOR MULTICULTURAL EDUCATION

Helen Vance Foster*
Professor of Educational Studies
State University College of Arts & Science
Geneseo, New York

and

Norman R. Dixon**
Associate Professor of Higher Education
University of Pittsburgh, Pennsylvania
Director, National Project on Testing

Rationale for Improved Assessment Programs

During the past ten to fifteen years standardized testing has been viewed by many authorities as discriminating against youngsters who were of minority races and/or lower socioeconomic class structure, and the use of standardized tests was reduced. There is abundant research literature to document the fact that current standardized tests of so-called intelligence/ aptitude, achievement, and personality do not assess racial, ethnic, and low socioeconomic groups fairly and accurately. This literature is buttressed by

---

*Helen V. Foster is one of the psychologists who worked on the standardization of the "McCarthy Scales of Children's Abilities," 1972, and the revised edition of the "Wechsler Intelligence Scale for Children." Both were published by the American Psychological Corporation.

**Under the direction of Norman R. Dixon, the National Project on Testing sponsored the first national conference on the testing of minorities in education and employment. This was cited by the American Psychological Association (APA) as "the most far-reaching effort yet to grapple with the problems of bias in the testing of minority groups."

thousands of students who testify to the inequities and injustices saddled upon them by the improper use of biased tests.

Added to the data supplied by scholars relative to poor tests and malevolent testing are testimonies of thousands of students whose life chances were damaged by teachers making improper use of test results. In one case, a tenth grade boy told his teacher he wanted to become a lawyer. His teacher invited the boy's mother and his counselor to meet with him. In the presence of the boy's mother and counselor, the teacher informed the boy that his test scores were too low. "He could never pass college courses to get into law school." Now the student is a senior in Duquesne University in Pittsburgh with a cumulative grade point average of B. Already, he has had counseling toward law school admission. In another case, a boy in a large city in an Eastern state was tested and placed in special education classes. As a senior, he was counseled toward a trade. "You will never make it in college," he was warned. The young man went to a Black college and earned a bachelor's degree. His master's degree was earned at a large, prestigious university in the East. Today, he is a school principal and candidate for a Ph.D. degree in the university where he earned his master's degree.

Another interesting case concerns a Black military officer who decided to go to college. After taking a number of standardized tests, he was then advised by a government counseling agency not to go into dentistry or medicine. He followed his desires rather than the advice of the counselor. After completion of three years toward his B.A. at a midwestern university, where he had been continuously on the Dean's List, he was accepted by the dental school. He finished third in his class and is presently a tenured faculty member in the school of dentistry at that same university. No doubt each reader can recount numerous experiences with individuals whose teachers or counselors made negative forecasts about their future because of low test scores, where the forecasts fortunately were incorrect. Motivation is a very important variable for which as yet we have no measuring instrument.

A counter argument does exist in the fact that there are some realistic goals which can be achieved through the process of testing. If teachers are to be evaluated upon their understanding of tests and measurement, then they also must be exposed to and evaluated upon the major applications of testing, as well as their ability to develop and create programs to meet the needs of individual differences, rather than create endless categories and classifications.

Inappropriate and poorly constructed tests can create obstacles to providing the child with a meaningful and challenging educational program. Youngsters from multicultural backgrounds may be forced into unfavorable positions by being evaluated early in life by tests which are predominantly verbal in content. Such tests rely upon questions phrased in middle-class standard English. Responses are considered correct only when given in the same language. Consider the fact that our two most prominently used individual intelligence tests, the "Stanford-Binet" and the "Wechsler Intelligence Scale for Children," require the use of middle-class standard English. The recently published "McCarthy Scale of Children's Abilities" does allow children to use their own type of language or dialect in some responses. However, this test is only for ages 2½-8½.

This paper focuses briefly on the following topics: (a) poor tests and malevolent testing, (b) competencies needed by teachers for participation in assessment programs for multicultural education, (c) a suggested model for preparing teachers for optional participation in assessment programs for multicultural education, and (d) action pointers for the American Association of Colleges for Teacher Education (AACTE), in the hope that it will demonstrate more than mere lip service to multicultural education, including its assessment. In a paper of this sort, it is impossible to treat these topics fully. The reader should give much thought to means by which to expand the ideas presented and relate them to his or her specific needs. The references cited will be helpful sources in this task.

From the outset, two facts must be made unmistakably clear: First, because this paper recommends preservice and inservice teacher education in how to use standardized tests, this does not imply endorsement of any single standardized test or any group of tests. Second, use of the term *multicultural education* does not imply that American schools, on any level, have accepted and implemented a philosophy which provides educational equity for *all children of all the people.* Perhaps the reason that standardized tests do not reflect the positive values of racial, ethnic, and low socioeconomic groups is that American school objectives are not based upon cultural diversity. It is vital to understand this point in order to absorb the thrust of this paper.

Relationships of Assessment to Teaching and Learning

Assessment of student performance should not be a disconnected, isolated event. Rather, it should be integral with the total sequence of teaching and learning. The general pattern and sequence of interlocking relationships should be as follows:

1. Assessment of student needs
2. Specifications of behavioral objectives to be achieved
3. Specification of academic content to be utilized to achieve the behavioral objectives
4. Specification of instructional media to be utilized to achieve the behavioral objectives
5. Specification of activities for use of academic content and/or activities to achieve the behavioral objectives
6. Identification and use of human resources to achieve the specified behavioral objectives
7. Identification and use of formal and informal assessment techniques for assessing student performance

8. Use of assessment data for refining and improving educational situations and student performance

Each of the eight interlocking, interrelated steps cited above should be suffused with Black, Chicano, Puerto Rican, Native American, Asian, and poor white cultural data. To be sure, there is much to be said about other ethnic groups in America, but the groups identified above are the most woefully neglected and seriously maligned groups in American education. In addition, American schools have deliberately excluded Blacks, Chicanos, Puerto Ricans, Native Americans, Asians, and poor whites from control and operation of the schools. Even today, few school systems invest these groups with power to help effect multicultural education by including them on school boards and employing them as administrators, counselors, teachers, athletic coaches, librarians, school social workers, and psychologists. This is true in large urban areas and in the suburbs as well.

Needless to say, participants from diverse cultures would enrich the education of the majority group—and all school personnel—immensely. Participants from diverse cultures could contribute importantly to the specification of multicultural education objectives and thereby deliver an ultimatum for broader assessment, utilizing multicultural data. Unless the schools apply the multicultural approach to their objectives, academic content, instructional media, activities, and personnel, there is no need for multicultural assessment. The schools as social institutions must also speak directly, loudly, and clearly to test producers, by requiring multicultural tests to assess multicultural school objectives. Unless the schools—including teacher education institutions—are willing to take these steps *now*, papers such as this are futile efforts.

115

Poor Tests and Malevolent Testing

Fair and accurate assessment of students is indeed a difficult but simultaneously a major issue. Many parents, legislators, educators, students, and taxpayers generally perceive assessment results as the hard data confirming (or denying) school effectiveness. With the recent demands for accountability, it has become critical that schools provide students, school boards, and the community with evidence to justify their claims to be institutions which make positive differences in community life. As a result, the schools have resorted to standardized tests as infallible instruments for collecting data on the cognitive abilities and achievement of students. Despite the obvious limitations of such standardized tests, they have been employed without due regard for their limitations—and the need for prudent use of their results. Little or no attention is given to the need for specification and assessment of affective and psychomotor objectives.

Teachers are positioned in the middle of the assessment quagmire. They teach and assess students, kindergarten through grade 12, who end up each year as unbelievably poor performers. At the end of grade 12, thousands of Blacks, Puerto Ricans, Chicanos, Native Americans, Asian Americans, and poor whites spell, read, write, listen, and compute at the elementary and junior high school levels. Many of these students were graduated with a "C" average or higher. If these students are fortunate enough to be admitted to college, they must register in minority programs, remedial classes, and/or noncredit college courses.

In addition, there is the grave problem of thousands of "drop-outs," "push-outs," and "kick-outs" from the schools of America. All too many of these students are labeled "troublemakers," "hard to teach," "constant failures," and "difficult to control." *This alarmingly large number of out-of-school students and the continued ejection of students by the schools constitutes a national calamity!* The large number of Black males, ages 12 through 17, thrown out of school is indeed frightening! The rejection-ejection phenomenon is frequently the result of treatment provided students based upon inaccurate and unfair test data.

RELIANCE ON STANDARDIZED TESTS

In the first place, entirely too much faith is placed in standardized tests. Far too many teachers accord absolute trust and confidence in intelligence, aptitude, achievement, and personality instruments. They seem to believe these devices were forged in heaven by God and His angels rather than their being another imperfect human cultural artifact. there is abundant literature (Barnes,[1] Dobzhansky,[2] Eells,[3] Hurley,[4] Kamin,[5] Richardson, Spears, and Richards,[6] and Williams[7,8,9]) to document the fact that standardized tests inaccurately and unfairly assess cognitive abilities and achievement of racial, ethnic, and low socioeconomic groups.

One of the most bitter critics of standardized tests and the injustices and inequities they inflict on Black communities is Robert L. Williams, professor of psychology, Washington University in St. Louis. For several years now, he has waged vigorous warfare against malevolent testing. In a recently published paper, Williams writes ". . . scientific racism is a part of the racial war, and the practitioners of it use intelligence tests as their hired guns."[10]

The attacks on standardized tests are accelerating. These attacks are indeed wholesome, for they underscore weaknesses in test construction and test use which can lead to fairer and more accurate assessment procedures. A major effort to produce test changes is that of the National Project on Testing, University of Pittsburgh. Its central objective is the improvement of the assessment of racial, ethnic, and low socioeconomic groups. Another emphasis of the project is on helping teachers, counselors, administrators, and parents to use tests with due caution and prudence. A great deal needs yet to be accomplished in order to prevent the use of poorly constructed, inappropriate, and inaccurate tests in multicultural education. For instance, teachers must realize that while there are many "intelligence" tests, "no one seems to have a very clear idea of what it (intelligence) is."[11]

116

Hurley shows the relationship of poverty to mental retardation.[12] The mental retardation syndrome in America includes Blacks, Puerto Ricans, Chicanos, Native Americans, and poor whites. Most of these groups are rural dwellers, urban ghetto dwellers, *el barrio* dwellers, reservation dwellers, and migratory workers. For the most part they are tested, labeled, classified, and then in disproportionate numbers placed in mental retardation classes.

Peter Watson indicates how racial discrimination affects I.Q., referring mainly to improperly assumed (or imposed) misconceptions of self-perception and/or expectations on the part of the child tested.[13] He further illuminates the importance of understanding the perspective of the person involved in the test situation, after which one may ". . . begin to have some idea of the way 'race' and 'ability' get tied up in the mind of the youngster and how this, in turn, can both improve and impair his performance."[14]

MORATORIUMS ON STANDARDIZED TESTING

Because they saw the inaccuracy and unfairness of standardized tests, the Association of Black Psychologists, at their 1969 meeting, called for a moratorium on testing. The statement follows:

> The Association of Black Psychologists calls for a moratorium on the repeated abuse and misuse of so-called conventional psychological tests, e.g., Stanford-Binet (Form L-M), the Wechsler, Scholastic Aptitude Test, Stanford Achievement, Iowa Basic Skills, Graduate Record Examination (GRE), the Miller Analogies Test, and many others. For more than two decades, we have known that these conventional tests are unfair and improperly classify Black children. In spite of the abundance of facts, nothing has been done to correct this abuse. Thus, the Association of Black Psychologists, dedicated to preventing further exploitation of Black people, calls for an immediate moratorium on all testing of Black people until more equitable tests are available.[15]

117

In 1972 the National Education Association Representative Assembly passed a resolution establishing an NEA Task Force on Testing and called for a moratorium on group standardized testing. The resolution reads as follows:

> The National Education Association strongly encourages the elimination of group standardized intelligence, aptitude, and achievement tests to assess student potential or achievement until the completion of a critical appraisal, review, and revision of current testing programs.[16]

Even though those and a few other groups have called for moratoriums on standardized testing, strong steps were never taken to put teeth into their declarations. Worse yet, other professional organizations (such as the Association for Supervision and Curriculum Development, National Council for Social Studies, National Association of Elementary School Principals,

National Association of Secondary School Principals, Association for Child-hood Education International, and others) have not prepared policy statements on the preparation and assessment of multicultural education. Such statements should have been prepared and cooperatively linked with such declarations as those of the Association of Black Psychologists and the National Education Association. The value of such a cooperative venture is obvious. The impact upon test procedures of a call to construct multicultural assessment procedures would be quite telling if powerful test users required test producers to do so. Some test producers might, in fact, welcome such a demand. At least two major test producers have stated openly that they produce the kind of tests which test users demand. To demand fair and accurate tests utilizing cultural content would place the responsibility for change on test producers.

Teacher Competencies Necessary for Optimal Teacher Participation in Assessment Programs for Multicultural Education

LITERATURE ON TESTING

Since 1906, it has been recognized that teachers need special preparation to meet their responsibilities in standardized testing. Twenty-five years later, Ernest W. Tiegs wrote the book *Tests and Measurements for Teachers* because of his teaching experiences.[17] Emphasis was placed on the use of tests rather than on the description of them, and on the activities and problems of educational work and how testing techniques will contribute to their solution rather than on a study of tests that some day may prove useful in the classroom.[18] In parts of Tieg's book, the following subjects are specifically addressed: fundamentals of measurement which are basic to all testing procedures, the chief uses of tests with reference to the educational experiences to which they are related, and the complimentary relationship between teacher-made tests and standardized tests. Also treated are the characteristics of standardized tests and the construction, administration, and interpretation of teacher-made tests. Tieg also disusses criteria for test selection, an often overlooked concern requiring due consideration.

Twenty-eight years after Tieg's book, in 1959, Garrett published *Testing for Teachers*.[19] The book was written for "prospective teachers who want to know how mental tests can be of help in their school. It can also serve as a guide for teachers in service."[20] Nearly the entire book deals with descriptions, limitations, and usefulness of standardized tests. The last three chapters are devoted to the preparation and use of teacher-made tests and how tests can be used in guidance and counseling. There is also a statistical supplement, a list of test publishers, and a glossary.

In 1966, Smith and Adams wrote the second edition of their book *Educational Measurement for the Classroom Teacher*.[21] Part I deals with basic statistical procedures, and Part II is devoted to the construction, use, and evaluation of teacher-made tests. It also deals with assigning marks and reporting student progress. Part III discusses the use of standardized tests. The three books cited above span 43 years of standardized testing. They represent the major concerns about teacher-made tests and standardized tests. In the main, all of these books treat general aspects of the same topic. Smith and Adams include condensed copies of the taxonomies of the cognitive and affective domains. In none of these books is there treatment of race, ethnicity, and social class as related to testing. In all of them, however, are implied some basic competencies which teachers in multicultural educational programs can use productively.

ASSESSMENT COMPETENCIES

Today's teachers need competencies in the following areas:

1. Participation in development of a school testing program
2. Participation in test selection
3. Participation in test administration
4. Participation in test interpretation
5. Participation in using test results for meeting individual and group needs
6. Participation in information-sharing with parents and community groups
7. Participation in assessing learning situations
8. Participation in the development and/or use of procedures for identifying and nourishing talent among Blacks, Chicanos, Puerto Ricans, Native Americans, Asians, and poor whites

In addition to the teacher competencies in areas given above, teachers must demonstrate their abilities to display cognitive behaviors uncontaminated by prejudice and racism. Generalized knowledge, intellectual skills, and abilities are insufficient. Affective behaviors must play a large part in assessing multicultural objectives. Such behaviors should sensitize teachers to ethnic and legal rights of students. More than that, teachers must be predisposed to protect these rights. When testing is used at stated points to provide feedback to students, teachers, administrators, and parents regarding whether progress is being attained in desired multicultural objectives, results can be used diagnostically to improve learning situations and promote student growth.

Model: Teacher Preparation in the Area of Assessment

OBJECTIVES OF TESTING PROGRAM

1. A testing program should not be limited to measuring either I.Q., achievement/performance in the basic skills, or the mastery of subject matter alone, because then only superior acquisition of these tasks will be rewarded. If administrators and teachers are aware that the curriculum should include values and mores that teach academic honesty and self-worth, they will reward evidence of these qualities also.

2. An assessment program should be for specific educational needs, not for the mere collection of data that may or may not be relevant in the future.

3. Standardized tests are used more for comparison with norms (national or large regional), and infrequently for measurement of short-term and/or immediate goals.

4. Informal teacher-made tests are used for immediate assessment data and the establishment of further short-term educational goals that are pathways to overall educational objectives.

TEACHER ROLE IN SETTING TESTING GOALS

Teachers should have a participant role in establishing educational and assessment goals. In order to achieve this, certain understandings are required:

1. Teachers should develop some basic understandings of what intelligence tests are designed to accomplish as well as what they cannot accomplish. These understandings would include knowledge of "culture free" tests and awareness of test biases, thus promoting awareness of how such factors might affect multicultural education.

2. Teachers should develop some basic understandings of achievement testing, with no small thought directed toward teacher-made tests. The statistical data provided by the profiles must be properly interpreted in order to assist teachers in developing a prescriptive type of educational program, both for the class and for individuals. (In achievement testing, proper interpretation is facilitated by an adequate retrieval system which includes individual item analysis in support of teacher-directed planning.)

3. The development of the school testing program should be the result of interaction between teachers, building and district administrators, parents, and students, with each group having an active and ongoing function in the process.

SELECTION OF TESTS

Decisions regarding which tests are most appropriate should be made with the needs of the school in mind. This concern encompasses both the educational goals as well as thorough understanding of the racial, cultural, ethnic, and socioeconomic makeup of the test population.

PARTICIPATION IN TEST ADMINISTRATION

1. Once teachers have been involved as major functionaries in the previous developmental stages, they will then become more willing and effective administrators (and interpreters) of tests.

2. By establishing a more familiar base regarding test administration

(and interpretation), teachers are then more committed to providing a wholesome environment and favorable climate for the testing situation.

3. Test anxiety and test-taking motivation have become significant items affecting student attitude and perceptions. The evidence indicates that usually the middle-class white student develops a "test-wise" approach to standardized testing. If, as has been indicated, the norms are drawn from this grouping, then a caveat need be issued regarding the validity of such tests when applied to children of multicultural backgrounds. Such a problem requires more than merely readjusting the anxiety and motivation levels for ethnic youngsters.

4. The factor of humanism, which has been touted throughout the educational arena, must be applied to standardized test programs as well.

TEST INTERPRETATION

The factor of test interpretation, that is, what the data reveals and what ought to be done with the information, should receive a similar amount of joint attention from teachers, administrators, parents, and students.

1. Attention should be focused on what data is desired from the test.

2. Understandings must be developed concerning test interpretations, in light of the inability to utilize them with perfect fairness when applied to youngsters of culturally diverse backgrounds.

3. It is necessary to predetermine how much credence will be given to the test data as a valid instrument by which teacher and/or educational accountability may be measured, or whether such an approach would receive any consideration at all. This matter becomes a dilemma for many groups faced with the accountability aspect of standardized testing.

4. All parties involved must be prepared to deal with both the strengths and weaknesses which are extrapolated from the data, each being of equal importance, at least in terms of interpretive scrutiny.

5. Consideration of the rights of students, parents, teachers, administrators, and school boards must be maintained pertaining to test utilization, educational implications (whether for innovation or modification), and the overall impact on the immediate school community.

6. The individual's rights of privacy regarding test results and reporting are obvious but often need mention, if for no other reason than to maintain those rights.

7. Evaluation of students is an integral phase of the ongoing assessment program. It is essential, therefore, that the evaluation system, integrated into such a multicultural education program as has been discussed, be one in which assessment criteria have been decided in advance by those involved in educational planning, which includes the community spectrum. This would insure consensus on both appropriateness and applicability of evaluation as it relates to the multicultural education program.

Recommendations

The authors charge AACTE to take an active role in helping school personnel, college faculties, and students at the undergraduate and graduate levels to become prepared for participating optimally in assessment programs for multicultured education. This would require the selection of various communities where there is a representation of two or more racial, ethnic, cultural, and low socioeconomic school children and public school personnel as well as a university setting within a realistic distance with a similar makeup of student body and personnel. Then AACTE can establish centers for a period of at least three years where a model such as the one described in this paper can be established on a functional basis.

AACTE should further establish a cadre of consultants who could function in the preparation of teachers for optional participation in assessment programs for multicultural education. AACTE could assist in the funding of such consultants and workshops and/or institutes.

REFERENCES

1 Barnes, Edward J. *Testing and Minority Children: Imperatives for Change.* National Leadership Institute for Teacher Education/Early Childhood, The University of Connecticut, Storrs, Technical Paper, 1972.

2 Dobzhansky, Theodosius. "Differences Are Not Deficits." *Psychology Today* 7 (December 1973): 197-98, 100-1.

3 Eells, Kenneth. "Some Implications for Schools—the Chicago Studies of Cultural Bias in Intelligence Tests," *Harvard Educational Review* 23 (1953): 284-297.

4 Hurley, Rodger. *Poverty and Mental Retardation: A Causal Relationship.* Jason Epstein, ed. New York: Vintage Books (Random House), 1969.

5 Kamin, Leon. "The Misuse of IQ Testing." *Change* 5 (October 1973):40-3.

6 Richardson, Ken, David Spears, and Martin Richards, eds. *Race and Intelligence, The Fallacies Behind the Race-I.Q. Controversy.* Baltimore: Penguin Books, 1972.

7 Williams, Robert L. "Black Pride, Academic Relevance, and Individual Achievement." *The Counseling Psychologist* 2 (1970): 18-22.

8 _____. "Misuse of Tests: Self-Concept." In *Violations of Human and Civil Rights: Tests and Use of Tests.* Report of the Tenth National Conference on Civil and Human Rights in Education. Washington, D.C.: National Education Association, 1972.

9 _____. "The Silent Mugging of the Black Community." *Psychology Today* 7 (May 1974): 32, 34, 37-8, 41, 101.

10 Ibid., p. 32.

11 Ebel, Robert L. *Essentials of Educational Measurement.* Englewood Cliffs, N.J.: Prentice-Hall, 1972, p. 498.

12 Hurley, *Poverty and Mental Retardation.*

13 Watson, P. "How Race Affects I.Q." *New Society* 16 (1970): 103-4.

14 Richardson, Spears, and Richards, *Race and Intelligence,* p. 67.

15 Williams, "Black Pride," p. 20.

16 "Interim Report of the NEA Task Force on Testing." *Task Force and Other Reports.* Washington, D.C.: National Education Association, July 3-6, 1973.

17 Tiegs, Ernest W. *Tests and Measurements for Teachers.* Cambridge, Mass.: The Riverside Press, 1931.

18 Ibid., Preface, p. xii.

19 Garrett, Henry E. *Testing for Teachers.* New York: American Book Co., 1959.

20 Ibid., p. v.

21 Smith, Fred M. and Sam Adams. *Educational Measurement for the Classroom Teacher.* Second Edition. New York: Harper & Row, 1966.

BIBLIOGRAPHY

Albin. Rochelle. "Quickly! Give The Corps a Middle-Class Answer." *Urban Review* 6 (1973): 32-4.

Anastasi, Anne. *Psychological Testing.* Third Edition. New York: The Macmillan Company, 1968.

Assessment in a Pluralistic Society. Proceedings of the 1972 Invitational Conference on Testing Problems. Educational Testing Service, Princeton, N.J., 1972.

Barnes, E.J. "The Black Community as the Source of Positive Self-Concept for Black Children. A Theoretical Perspective." In *Black Psychology,* edited by R.L. Jones. New York: Harper & Row, 1972.

Beatty, Wolcott, ed. *Improving Educational Assessment and an Inventory of Measures of Affective Behavior.* Washington, D.C.: Association for Supervision and Curriculum Development, National Education Association, 1969.

Beezer, Robert H. "Improve Teachers' Knowledge of Assessment and Evaluation Procedures." Unpublished paper. Washington, D.C.: National Institute of Health (No date given).

Bracht, Glenn H. et al. *Perspectives in Educational and Psychological Measurement.* Englewood Cliffs, N.J.: Prentice-Hall, 1972.

Brim, Orville G. Jr. et al. *American Beliefs about Intelligence.* New York: Russell Sage Foundation, 1969.

Duncan, Otis D. et al. *Socioeconomic Background and Achievement.* New York: Seminar Press, 1972.

Epps, Edgar G. "Motivation and Achievement of Negro Americans." *Journal of Social Issues* 25 (Summer 1969).

Eysenck, Hans J. *The I.Q. Argument: Race, Intelligence and Education.* New York: The Library Press, 1971.

Ginsburg, Herbert. *The Myth of the Deprived Child: Poor Children's Intellect and Education.* Englewood Cliffs, N.J.: Prentice-Hall, 1972.

Goslin, David A. *Teachers and Testing.* New York: Russell Sage Foundation, 1967.

Gottlieb, David and Anne L. Heinsohn. *America's Other Youth: Growing Up Poor.* Englewood Cliffs, N.J.: Prentice-Hall, 1971.

Green, Robert L., ed. *Racial Crisis in American Education.* Chicago: Follett Educational Corp., 1969.

Gunnings, T.S. "Response to Critics of Robert L. Williams." *The Counseling Psychologist* 2 (1971): 73-77.

Hamilton, Judy. "The IQ Boosters." *Florida Accent.* Tampa, Florida, December 30, 1973, pp. 11-14.

Hawes, Gene R. *Educational Testing for the Millions.* New York: McGraw-Hill, 1964.

Holmen, Milton G. and Richard F. Docter. *Educational and Psychological Testing: A Study of the Industry and Its Practices.* New York: Russell Sage Foundation, 1972.

Kaplan, Bert L. "Must Tests Be a Trial?" *Teacher* 91 (January 1974): 20,22.

Koerner, Thomas F. ed. "Will Accountability Work? Initiating Change Programs Computer Capabilities" *Bulletin of the National Association of Secondary School Principals* 58, no. 380 (March 1974).

Labov, William. "The Logic of Non-Standard English." In *Language and Poverty: Perspectives on a Theme,* edited by F. Williams, pp. 153-89. Chicago: Markham Publishing Co., 1970.

Mager, Robert F. *Developing Attitudes Toward Learning.* Palo Alto, Calif.: Fearon Publishers, 1968.

Mayeske, George W. *On the Explanation of Racial-Ethnic Differences in Achievement Test Scores.* Washington, D.C.: U.S. Office of Education (No date given).

Mercer, Jane R. "Socio-Cultural Factors in Labeling Mental Retardates." *Peabody Journal of Education* 48 (1971): 188-203.

Purkey, William W. *Self-Concept and School Achievement.* Englewood Cliffs, N.J.: Prentice-Hall, 1970.

Rosenberg, L.A. "Identifying the Gifted Child in the Culturally Deprived Population: The Need for Culture-Fair Instruments." *American Journal of Orthopsychiatry* 37 (1967): 342-3.

Rosenthal, Robert and Lenore Jacobson. *Pygmalion in the Classroom: Teacher Expectation and Pupil's Intellectual Development.* New York: Holt, Rinehart and Winston, 1968.

Samuda, Ronald J. "Racial Discrimination through Mental Testing: A Social Critic's Point of View." *IRCD Bulletin.* New York: Horace Mann-Lincoln Institute, Teachers College, Columbia University, May 1973.

Schorr, Alvin L. *Poor Kids: A Report on Children in Poverty.* New York: Basic Books, 1966.

Schwebel, Milton. *Who Can Be Educated?* New York: Grove Press, 1968.

Senna, Carl, ed. *The Fallacy of I.Q.* New York: The Third Press, 1973.

Sharp, Evelyn. *The I.Q. Cult.* New York: Coward, McCann and Geoghegan, 1972.

Smith, Charles P., ed. *Achievement-Related Motives in Children.* New York: Russell Sage Foundation, 1969.

Torrance, E.P. *Education and the Creative Potential.* Minneapolis: University of Minnesota Press, 1963.

Vernon, M.D. *Human Motivation.* Cambridge: Cambridge University Press, 1971.

Washington Research Project, Southern Center for Studies in Public Policy. *Title I of ESEA: Is It Helping Poor Children?* Washington, D.C.: The Project, 1969.

Wynne, Marvin D. et al. *The Black Self.* Englewood Cliffs, N.J.: Prentice-Hall, 1974.

CONCLUDING STATEMENT

By the Panel of
Black Writer-Editors

From the five position papers presented, it is clear that multicultural education should be a part of all teacher preparation curricula. It should also be clear that no specific rationales for multicultural education have been given for Blacks only. It is the opinion of all of us that multicultural education is a need of all Americans. The papers did, however, point out some competencies and strategies needed by teachers in dealing with Black children, not because they were Black but because of the racism and oppression that all Blacks have encountered in America. They emphasize the point of cultural diversity as well.

Rationales for Multicultural Teacher Preparation

The rationales for the preparation of teachers in multicultural education as presented by the position paper writers follow:

1. Multicultural education has a positive value to the total educational arena and to the society (Wynn).

2. There are insistent demands on the part of minorities that teachers and schools become sensitive to cultural differences (Wynn).

3. Every school has an imperative mission to assist all students for life in a society composed of many diverse cultural, racial, and ethnic strands (Wynn).

4. If educators are to structure a learning environment which facilitates both the acquisition of academic skills and the development of productive school-related behaviors in ethnic minority pupils, it is imperative that teachers recognize the influence they exert as a stimulus in the classroom (Pettigrew).

5. The teachers' own attitudes and behaviors operate to shape the attitudes and behaviors of the children whom they instruct. This is especially apparent in the early grades where the social influence of peers is not as great as that of the teacher (Pettigrew).

6. Teachers must become more concerned about the differences and similarities between achievements and aspirations of the ethnic minority child and the advantaged majority child (Pettigrew).

7. Teachers must become more adept in the deliberate design of a learning environment that will foster academic growth and achievement within a multicultural educational setting (Pettigrew).

8. If teachers fail to adequately plan and program the environment for multicultural pupils, learning is left to chance and the results may well be counter-productive to educational achievement (Pettigrew).

9. Many people seem to have the view that schools are somehow isolated from the normal cultural milieu, when, in fact, schools more than anything else are reflections of processes that go on in the culture at large (Hilliard).

10. It is not enough to like the children, the challenge is to teach them effectively within a cultural context (Sullivan).

Multicultural education differs from ethnic studies because its methods or teaching strategies can be employed in all disciplines rather than being limited to the social studies. There is, however, a large intersection between ethnic studies and multicultural education. A mathematics class with diverse students, regardless of racial or ethnic composition, should present objectives or mathematical concepts in such a way that the diversity of students' backgrounds are included in the presentation of concepts. This means that a teacher will have to use several examples using more than one idea to explain the same concept. A chemistry teacher would use illustrative examples that occurred in the students' environment, rather than examples that occurred thousands of miles away. This does not mean that a teacher would not use an example because it is abstract, but rather abstractions would be taught with logic in terms of the concepts and understandings which the student possesses.

Multicultural education is an attempt to take those elements and experiences of the students' culture that will enable them to grasp that knowledge which might otherwise be foreign to them as learners in a particular setting. Preparing teachers multiculturally concerns itself with breaking down barriers that hinder teachers from exhibiting positive attitudes and expectations that minority students need in order to achieve. If you believe in the worth and dignity of humanity, then you have to believe in the value of the preparation of teachers for multicultural classrooms. It must be emphasized that multicultural education goes far beyond just loving the students. Teaching the virtues of Blackness is not enough; Black students must experience successful achievement and at the same time retain their identity. They must be able to look out into society or go into a classroom and find successful models and see a continuous flow of successful Black individuals within their environment. This implies a strong connection between what students are told in class and what they know to be true in the real society. Multicultural education should not only assist Black individuals in knowing that they are Black and that Blacks have made numerous contributions to the development of our country. It should also assist them in knowing that many other groups have contributed as well.

The CBTE Approach

The competency-based approach, as suggested by the writers, is one potential vehicle for designing and implementing multicultural teacher education programs, provided that previously suggested precautions are adhered to. Where the CBTE approach is used, the writers suggest the following characteristics:

1. There must be systematic attention given to multiculturalism in the conception and design of the program.
2. All segments of the community being served must participate in planning, implementation, and evaluation of the program.
3. The multicultural perspective must be reflected in the identification of competencies and the specification of objectives.
4. The field-based components of teacher education programs must utilize diverse cultural settings.
5. The ultimate criterion of success in multicultural education is the teacher's demonstrated competence in working with all students.

The position papers provided valuable input for a thorough examination of the relationship between multicultural education and competency-based teacher education as it affects the preparation of teachers. The conclusions that can be drawn from that examination clearly indicate that the panel of Black American writer-editors holds views that vary substantially from the basic assumptions of some multicultural education/competency-based teacher education proponents. One evident difference is that this group of educators has little confidence in the notion that CBTE will be utilized to bring about more effective multicultural education. Reasons for this lack of enthusiasm have been discussed earlier. Further, the Black writer-editors reject the idea that there are certain unique competencies needed by teachers of Black American and other minority children.

Ours is a diverse society. Teacher education programs should provide all teachers an opportunity to develop competencies for functioning in a diverse society. Such programs should include those competencies needed to teach *all* children. To further clarify its position, the panel of Black Americans developed the following statements of principles.

Statements of Principles

1. There is no substantial difference between the competencies needed to teach Black Americans and those needed to teach everyone. To say that there are unique competencies needed by teachers of Black Americans is to say that such competencies can be isolated from the main body of knowledge, skills, and understandings that all teachers need. This position is antithetical to the concept of multicultural education.
2. Any course, workshop, or learning experience provided for prospective teachers must reflect the multicultural perspective. Courses, workshops, or learning experiences that do not reflect this perspective are not credible components of programs for the preparation of teachers. This principle should prevail even where students are likely to teach in

situations that are described as "monocultural." In fact, such situations require additional emphasis on multicultural education as an essential element in the preparation of teachers.

3. CBTE does not indicate a change in the locus of decision-making power in American education. Thus, it does not appear to hold significant promise for affecting the critical problems related to racism and oppression in the schools.

4. The realization of the goals of multicultural education requires a thorough restructuring of American education in general and teacher education in particular. Just as multicultural education cannot be grafted on to traditional educational methods and techniques, it cannot be grafted on to the CBTE movement. A serious commitment to multicultural education must start with real changes in the way in which educators and educational institutions operate.

5. CBTE is an educational process. As such, it does not guarantee adequate consideration of the educational interests and needs of Black Americans or any other minority group. CBTE in itself will not produce teachers who are less racist or less bigoted than they were before experiencing such a program.

6. If CBTE is to impact the preparation of teachers of Black American and other minority-group children, it must cease to be the exclusive territory of the educational "country club set." Representatives of the broad spectrum of America's diverse society must be brought into the movement in positions of leadership and responsibility.

7. The identification of competencies, the diagnosis of learning difficulties, the designing of effective assessment procedures and other critical elements in the CBTE process cannot be accomplished without adequate consideration for multicultural factors. To do so invalidates the entire process as a viable means of providing learning experiences for prospective teachers.

8. The notion that the CBTE process is particularly beneficial to Black Americans and other minority groups represents a perpetuation of the patronizing and condescending attitudes that characterize minority education. Such a notion implies that minority-group children are different with respect to their ability to attain the desired competencies and are, as implied before, inferior to their fellow students.

9. The absence of a need for a white perspective on multicultural education reflects an implicit bias. Multicultural education is not the responsibility of the minorities. It will not become an important priority in education until society as a whole is concerned and involved.

PART III

Prime Writer

Atilano A. Valencia
Chairman, Department of
Education
New Mexico Highlands
University
Las Vegas, New Mexico

Associate Prime Writer

Tomás A. Arciniega
Dean, School of Education
San Diego State University
San Diego, California

Writer-Editors

Rudy Cordova
Vice President for Institutional
Development
University of New Mexico
Albuquerque, New Mexico

Thomas Lopez, Jr.
Associate Professor, Department
of Educational Theory and Social
Foundations
University of Toledo
Toledo, Ohio

Ida Santos Stewart
Assistant Professor in
Curriculum and Instruction
Chairman, Early Childhood
Education Program
University of Houston
Houston, Texas

Spanish-Speaking American Perspective of Multicultural Education and Competency-Based Teacher Education

INTRODUCTION

One of the most pressing concerns found in teacher preparation institutions and agencies is related to the question of preparing teachers who can function with optimal effectiveness in multicultural school environments. Because of the failure of the Anglo-American middle-class curricula to advance the academic and socio-psychological well-being of minority-group Americans, a movement for generating immediate changes in the existing American school system has been initiated. This movement carries identifiable terms, such as *bilingual-bicultural education* and *cultural pluralism*. Bilingual-bicultural education and cultural pluralism as used herein are component features within multicultural education. Since multicultural education affirms the principle of *No One Model American,* it can be envisioned as a dynamic reform movement in American education.[1] This theme clearly reflects the fact that American minority groups, with particular reference to Spanish-speaking Americans, Blacks, and American Indians, will no longer accept the imposition of a school curriculum based on one language and one set of cultural patterns. Spanish-speaking ethnic groups within this country are insisting that their cultural attributes and historical references be recognized and incorporated as integral features of the school. In rejecting the concept of a monolithic American culture in favor of biculturalism, they are furthering the educational principle of an expanding curriculum —of an educational model where students are provided with opportunities to gain experiences related to their immediate perceptual world, while more and more of the greater world is opened. Such curricula would accept the students' cultural being, provide more experiences related to their cultural heritage, and prepare them to function effectively in the larger American society.

The papers that follow address and analyze some of the concerns expressed in this introduction. They take strong positions in exploring the relationship between multicultural education and competency-based teacher education, including:

1. Endorsement of the *No One Model American* concept
2. Recognition of diversity within the Spanish-speaking population, and a rejection of stereotypes and of any educational model based on static cultural concepts
3. Acknowledgement that competency-based teacher education has important potential for promoting multicultural education
4. Condemnation and rejection of the compensatory education model which presumes cultural deficiencies in meeting the needs of the culturally different
5. Strong commitment to equal educational opportunity based on the principle of equal benefits

6. Emphatic endorsement of the principle that teachers should be advocates and practitioners of bilingualism and biculturalism
7. Strong support for collaboration and parity among communities, universities, and schools in planning, programming, and assessing competency-based teacher education/multicultural education programs
8. Contention that multicultural education is imperative for the future of American education

Hopefully, these papers will contribute toward the solution of the most urgent and critical problem in American society, that of realizing our national commitment to equal educational opportunity for all children.

REFERENCE

1 AACTE Commission on Multicultural Education. "No One Model American." *Journal of Teacher Education* 24, no. 4 (Winter 1973): 264-5. This statement has been published separately and is available from AACTE.

CHAPTER 1

TOWARD A RESEARCH MODEL OF MULTICULTURAL COMPETENCY-BASED TEACHER EDUCATION

Luis M. Laosa

Assistant Professor, College of Education
University of California at Los Angeles
Los Angeles, California

Two movements of seemingly great potential are becoming increasingly visible in American education today. These are (a) a trend toward cultural pluralism and multicultural bilingual education and (b) a trend toward competency-based approaches to teacher education. Although neither of these two movements is completely new in education—historical antecedents may be traced for both—recent developments and growing pressures from an increasingly wide variety of sources suggest that both concepts will play major roles in the future of American education. The present paper attempts to integrate these two concepts—multicultural education and competency-based teacher education—and to develop a viable research model of multicultural/competency-based teacher education.

Cultural Pluralism and Multicultural Education

What is cultural pluralism? And what is meant by multicultural education? American society is composed of a wide variety of cultural and ideological communities, each with its own characteristic lifestyle, value system, and all the other components that make up what we call "culture." In societies like that of the United States, societies which themselves comprise multiple cultural groups, each of these subgroups may be said to constitute a "subculture."*

---

*The term subculture as used in this paper should not be interpreted in a derogatory sense.

Whereas a melting pot view of American society called for the amalgamation of all subcultures into a new and superior culture, it has become increasingly apparent that such a model has not provided a healthy outcome for certain groups. It now seems clear that an amalgamation model, when directed by a dominant group, leads to the melting away of subcultures as well as to the preponderance of the dominant group over the others. In the U.S., the melting pot model has favored the white Anglo-Saxon Protestant (WASP) group and has resulted in the neglect—and even in some cases the oppression—of certain "culturally different" groups.

What is the alternative to a culturally homogeneous, Anglo-conformist society? The American Association of Colleges for Teacher Education (AACTE) recently adopted and made available *No One Model American,* a policy statement which reflects the increasing tendency toward a positive recognition of cultural and linguistic differences, and to viewing cultural variability as a societal asset.[1] In this light, cultural pluralism rejects both assimilation and separatism as ultimate goals, and affirms the understanding and appreciation of differences that exist among the nation's citizens. As a corollary to the above . . .

> multicultural education is education which values cultural pluralism . . . . Multicultural education affirms that schools should be oriented toward the cultural enrichment of all children and youth through programs rooted in the preservation and extension of cultural alternatives . . . . Education for cultural pluralism includes four major thrusts: (1) the teaching of values which support cultural diversity and individual uniqueness; (2) the encouragement of the qualitative expansion of existing ethnic cultures and their incorporation into the mainstream of American socioeconomic and political life; (3) the support of explorations in alternative and emerging lifestyles; and (4) the encouragement of multiculturalism, multilingualism, and multidialectism.[2]

Competency-Based Teacher Education

What is competency-based teacher education (CBTE)? Whereas traditional programs generally have as criteria for successful termination the completion of a specified number of courses and practicum activities, competency-based teacher education follows a different principle. In CBTE, criteria of what should make a successful teacher are generally stated in terms of specified measurable acts, and successful completion rests upon evidence that the prospective teacher can perform these criterion acts. As such, CBTE generally has a more individualized focus than traditional teacher education programs, since the emphasis in CBTE is upon exit rather than entrance requirements.

In terms of competency-based criteria, what is a professional teacher in the context of multicultural education? To give a perfectly logical definition, a professional teacher in the context of multicultural/competency-based teacher education is one who is able to provide evidence that she or he can perform the acts which have been specified in advance as constituting successful multicultural testing. Though technically sound, such a definition raises a host of serious questions.

Is multicultural education a socially desirable goal? What are the implications of multicultural education from a wide societal perspective? Is multicultural education feasible with present resources? Is there a sufficiently strong and long-range societal commitment to cultural pluralism which would make multicultural education feasible? Is multicultural education a potentially positive activity toward the cultural, social, economic, and political liberation of heretofore oppressed minorities? Would CBTE in multicultural education, if institutionalized, stifle or rigidify cultural evolution? Are the philosophical underpinnings of CBTE antithetical to the sociocultural values of certain minority groups? What kinds of outcomes should we strive to develop in children? How will these be assessed? Once the desired pupil outcomes are determined, how do we know which teacher competencies will facilitate particular pupil outcomes?

In developing a CBTE model for multicultural education one must consider the above questions. Certain of these issues may be dealt with rationally,* that is, following an analysis based solely on reason and experience. Still others, however, necessitate an empirical approach.

A CBTE model that purports to be adequate, then, must have a sound rational basis. Based on a coherent theory or systematic framework, it must provide a mechanism for ongoing empirical validation of underlying assumptions, extend provisions for answering specific questions that arise during the process of program development and implementation, and offer a plan for testing related hypotheses as well as furthering the scientific body of knowledge in this emerging field.

DERIVING CONCLUSIONS RATIONALLY

Following the earlier discussion on cultural pluralism, we proceed from the assumption that multicultural education is a socially desirable goal, since it is projected to facilitate the societal goal of cultural pluralism.

The question of availability of resources must be approached from at least two levels: (a) human resources, and (b) financial resources. From the perspective of a teacher education model which places emphasis on entrance requirements, the issue of availability of human resources has been indeed a real one. By defining entrance requirements according to specific criteria, potential trainees with certain characteristics have been denied the opportunity to receive training. Partly as a result of such lack of opportunity, the teaching profession is characterized by low levels of employment of personnel from certain ethnic groups.[3] In 1972, the enrollment of U.S.

---

*A rational approach may be contrasted with an empirical one, which relies on experimentation and systematic observation.

public schools was 44.6 million students. Of these, 2.3 million were Spanish-speaking. While there was one non-minority teacher for every 20 non-minority students, and one teacher for every 22.5 American students, there was only one Spanish-speaking teacher for every 107 Spanish-speaking students in the U.S.[4] Of course, it is difficult to separate out the factors which account for the lack of adequate representation of various minority groups in teacher education. One suspects that the truly important factors are wider societal ones, and that the more specific ones, such as potential bias in entrance requirements, are reflections of the society in which they occur.

It could be assumed that some of the problems that minority children have with traditional education institutions stem from the fact that they are taught by individuals from a different ethnic group, usually the dominant Anglo-American middle-class cultural group. A teacher from the same cultural-linguistic background as the pupil, it could be argued, will have a better understanding of that child's motivational and learning styles and other unique culturally related characteristics, and thus be in a better position to maximize the student's learning potential. If this were the case, one could conclude that an increase in the number of teachers from Spanish-speaking backgrounds would solve the educational problems of children from this minority group. Following such a conclusion, one would specify a priori, as a multicultural teacher competency, membership in the pupil's cultural-linguistic group.

Recent empirical evidence suggests that mere membership in a particular cultural-linguistic group does not insure superior teaching ability and success with pupils from the same cultural-linguistic group. While a recent investigation (U.S. Commission on Civil Rights, 1973)[5] revealed that teachers in southwestern U.S. schools were failing to involve Mexican-American children as active participants in the classroom to the same extent as Anglo children, a closer scrutiny of the findings further revealed that Mexican American teachers praised and encouraged Anglo pupils to a strikingly *greater* degree than their Anglo colleagues did, and conversely, these same Mexican American teachers praised and encouraged Mexican American pupils *less* than the Anglo teachers did.

Thus, it seems clear that similar teacher-pupil ethnic group membership is no assurance of multicultural teaching competence. That this is indeed the case could have been determined only through empirical evidence; an erroneous conclusion could have easily been maintained had one relied exclusively on rational analysis.

VALUE OF CULTURAL DIVERSITY

To what extent is multicultural education a potentially positive activity toward the liberation of heretofore oppressed minorities? To the extent that multicultural education is based on the premise of accepting and encouraging cultural-linguistic variability, it should serve as an instrument of liberation for oppressed minorities. The concept of cultural variability in education, however, must go considerably deeper than most current attempts in this regard, which focus merely on the more superficial aspects of culture. It is important to realize that in addition to the more salient manifestations of the different subcultures, such as styles of dress, customs, language, moral codes, skin pigmentation, etc., there are more fundamental and perhaps less visible characteristics, i.e., deep cognitive, perceptual, and personality structures which justify the differing surface manifestations. Although different subcultures certainly have common elements, or "universals," they also differ greatly in many respects; and often such differences are quite deep, although the determinants of their manifestations may be so subtle that most people do not become aware of them.[6] It is probably the case that learner characteristics associated with cultural-linguistic group membership interact in some as yet undetermined manner with the cultural-linguistic group characteristics of the teacher. Before we begin to state teacher competencies for multicultural education (or monocultural education, for that matter), we must both delineate the individual learner characteristics that are culturally (or otherwise) determined, and investigate the nature of the interactions between specific teacher behaviors and pupil characteristics, and then determine which set of teacher behaviors applied to a child with specified characteristics will produce desired pupil outcomes. 139

ROLE OF CBTE

If institutionalized, would CBTE stifle or rigidify cultural evolution? This should be a major concern in developing any CBTE model. As Schalock and Hale (1968) have pointed out, given the elements of continuous societal change, teacher education programs must be planned with an eye toward this change.[7] Any planning or model-building in CBTE should account not only for elements that are likely to be needed in the future, but also provide enough flexibility to accommodate the unexpected. An adequate multicultural/competency-based teacher education model, then, must be based upon a conceptualization of culture that is not static, but rather continuously evolving.

Is CBTE antithetical to the values of certain cultural-linguistic groups? This may be the case, and the issue merits investigation. Given a certain set of sociocultural premises, some individuals may not find the potential emphasis of CBTE on individual study rather than group instruction compatible with their relational style. In this sense, certain aspects of CBTE could be conceived as dehumanizing. It is probable that incompatibilities which surface between a CBTE program and the cultural values of given individuals are more a function of program management than inherent culturally based inconsistencies with the CBTE philosophy. As such, it is important that programs be managed with a sensitivity to these issues.

What kinds of pupil outcomes should we strive to develop in children? That is, indeed, a crucial question in the issue of self-determination. It must be approached from several perspectives. In the context of a free society, the kinds of learner outcomes to be striven for should be determined by each child's parents. Parental choices will be colored, of course, by values, aspirations, socioeconomic status, etc. From a perspective that the individual is subordinate to the larger society, learner outcomes will be dictated by pressing societal needs. So, given these perceived needs, learner outcome projections will be directed toward meeting them. A good example of this occurred in this country in the decade following the launching of Sputnik, when American society saw the need to place stronger emphasis in the teaching of math and science as necessary for survival in the technological race.

In the U.S., learner outcomes have probably been implicitly determined by a combination of the above, plus the influence of tradition and the limits of educational technology. It is obvious, however, that certain cultural groups in this country are having a greater influence in determining which learner outcomes will be strived for than other groups. Thus far, the dominant Anglo group has continued to impose its preferred pupil outcomes on individuals from less powerful groups. Such practices may be labeled enforced assimilation, or attempts at cultural genocide. It is proposed that as a prerequisite for cultural pluralism and multicultural education, each cultural group must have equal power to influence the process of determining pupil outcomes. Until this occurs, multicultural education remains in the realm of tokenism and fantasy.

The Need for an Empirical Model

Several global competency statements are usually identified on a rational basis as those necessary for multicultural education. These typically include such items as (a) the ability to provide a school environment which reflects local cultural heritage and is subject to the desires of the local community; (b) the ability to involve adults from the community in school-related projects, this having the effect of making the school "their" school; (c) when the local community is interested, the offering of history and culture content courses that are relevant to the local culture, along with European and American history; and (d) the use of supplementary materials in the classroom, or provision of library resources which include items that are oriented to the local culture and language, in order to provide cross-cultural experiences and an atmosphere relevant to the child's heritage.

These certainly are seen as desirable competencies for multicultural education and should be required. In this paper, however, the author takes the position that those kinds of competencies, while certainly necessary, address only the more superficial aspects of the incompatibilities that are seen to exist between traditional school characteristics and the characteristics of individual children from minority groups.[8] Not only do such approaches at stating multicultural competencies fail to deal adequately with the underlying problem schools have in meeting the needs of minority children, but also they deal with only one aspect of "culture." As pointed out earlier, there are deeper aspects of culture of which the more visible manifestations—what is traditionally called "culture"—are only reflections. Therefore, an adequate competency-based teacher education model must address these competencies—given the culturally (or otherwise) determined cognitive, perceptual, personality, and linguistic characteristics of a child, it must determine what kinds of behaviors on the part of the teacher maximally facilitate the desired learner outcomes.

Before one begins to state teacher competencies for multicultural education that have any degree of validity,* several questions must be answered:

1. Are there configural patterns of pupil characteristics which are culturally determined?
2. Do such hypothesized inter-learner differences interact differentially with patterns of teacher behaviors in producing pupil outcomes?
3. Can we identify and predict which teacher behaviors, when applied to an identified set of characteristics in the pupil, will provide a certain pupil outcome?

It is a major thesis of this paper that unless we are able to predict and empirically demonstrate *which* sets of teacher behaviors, when applied to particular identified configurations of pupil characteristics—personality, cognitive, linguistic, environmental, etc.—produce certain pupil outcomes, competency-based teacher education will remain only an interesting armchair idea.

141

Previous research shows that children from various cultural-linguistic groups differ with respect to such important educational variables as preferred learning styles, relational and other personality configurations, perceptual-cognitive patterns, family structure, attitude toward the educational process, sex-role development, and linguistic development.[10,11,12,13,14,15] These intersubject differences that are associated with cultural background are hypothesized to interact with teacher behaviors, curricula, and other important education variables. Thus, it is essential to identify the effects of such interactions in determining specific pupil outcomes.

COMPETENCIES AS HYPOTHESES

In light of the previous discussion, we may once again ask: What are the important competencies for multicultural education? At best, teacher competencies may be (a) postulated a priori as hypotheses to be empirically corroborated or discarded; or (b) set dogmatically according to conventional wisdom. Certainly the model proposed here deems the former alternative, (a), as the only appropriate course of action.

The CBTE model proposed here, then, would begin by postulating a set of teacher competencies not as *the* competencies needed, but rather as hypotheses—the relative usefulness of which is to be tested empirically in

---

*The term *validity* is employed here in its psychometric sense.[9]

specified contexts. As a CBTE program proceeds along the lines of the present model, data are obtained in an ongoing manner at each stage of program implementation. These data, collected and analyzed in an ongoing manner, are then used to modify the original set of specified competencies, specifying in further detail the competencies for producing specified pupil outcomes given specific situations, as well as both learner and teacher characteristics.

How is one to proceed in choosing a set of competencies as hypotheses? One may begin with higher-order abstract categories that may be postulated—because they appear likely to be related to desired outcomes—on the basis of (a) previous research findings; (b) conventional wisdom; (c) practices which have already shown positive results on the basis of subjective evaluations; (d) existing theories of learning, education, or human development; and (e) expressed community needs.

Several levels of criteria can be employed to test teacher competency hypotheses and generate feedback for modifying and refining the original set of assumptions. Turner has identified six such levels of criteria.[16] The highest level of criteria, level 1, consists of two parts. First, it calls for the observation of actual behaviors which the teacher exhibits in a real classroom situation. Second, it includes an analysis of the level of outcomes achieved by the teacher with the pupils she/he teaches. This two-part appraisal of teacher performance is to be conducted over a relatively long period of time—at least two years. By including observational data on teachers as well as pupil performance data, the relationships between the observed behavior of teachers and pupil performances can be analyzed. By taking into account entry behaviors in the analysis of outcomes, one may separate out effects due to differential gain.

Turner's criterion level 2 is identical to level 1 except that a shorter performance period is involved—one year or less. In criterion level 3, pupil performance data are not employed; judgments about teacher competence are based solely on observable behaviors of the teachers. The validity of this criterion level is, of course, totally dependent on whether empirical relationships between pupil performance and teacher actions have already been established. Criterion level 4 differs from level 3 in that both the context and range of teaching behaviors are restricted. Microteaching situations involving a few students, or even peers acting as students, would fall in this category. In criterion level 5, the teacher need not perform before a live pupil audience since simulated pupils may be employed. In criterion level 6, the teacher need not even engage in producing a performance, but rather only show that she/he understands some behavior, concept, or principle related to teaching. The same comment made on the relative validity of criterion level 3 is applicable to levels 4, 5, and 6.

In the context of the CBTE model presented here, and of Turner's criterion levels, only levels 1 and 2 are deemed adequate, until sufficient data becomes available to allow reliable predictions of pupil outcomes from particular teacher behaviors. It is obvious that proceeding to develop and implement a CBTE program without empirical data on the *relationships* between specified teacher behaviors and pupil outcomes would represent an exercise in futility. Once data become available on the relationships between certain teacher acts and pupil outcomes, one may adopt Turner's levels 3, 4, or 5 for those behaviors.

As proposed in the present model, however, to begin development of an adequate CBTE program one must go beyond Turner's criterion level 1. It is postulated that intervening variables may influence the relationship between a specified teacher behavior and a pupil outcome. Thus, teacher X may produce the same behaviors as teacher Y, with different pupil outcomes resulting; depending on such types of mediating variables as teacher personality, pupil characteristics, situational variables, etc. Concern here is, of course, with the generalizability of teacher behavior-pupil outcome relationships. Therefore, one must investigate not only observed teacher behavior and resulting pupil outcomes, but also how a multitude of other variables—teacher, pupil, context—affect such relationships.

Summary

Two movements of seemingly great potential are becoming increasingly   143
visible in American education today: (a) a trend toward cultural pluralism and multicultural bilingual education and (b) a trend toward competency-based approaches to teacher education.

After discussing the dangers inherent in developing multicultural (or monocultural, for that matter) competency-based teacher education (CBTE) models which are based on a rational rather than empirical basis, a research model of multicultural/competency-based teacher education is proposed. According to the model proposed herein, an adequate CBTE model program should possess a sound rational basis. Based on a coherent theory or systematic framework, it must provide a mechanism for ongoing empirical validation of underlying assumptions, extend provisions for answering specific questions that arise during the process of program development and implementation, and offer a plan for testing related hypotheses as well as furthering the scientific body of knowledge in this emerging field.

Any planning or model building in CBTE must be based on a concept of culture that is not static, but rather continuously evolving, thus providing the flexibility needed to accommodate the unexpected. As a prerequisite for cultural pluralism and multicultural education, each cultural group must have equal power in determining what pupil outcomes are desirable.

An adequate multicultural CBTE model must address not only the more superficial aspects of culture to which multicultural education programs are usually limited, but also the deeper aspects of culture—cognitive, perceptual, and personality structures; learning, relational, and motivational styles—of which the more visible manifestations are only reflections.

According to the model proposed here, a CBTE program postulates a set of teacher competencies as hypotheses to be tested empirically in specified contexts, using desired pupil outcomes as criteria. Data collected and analyzed in an ongoing manner are used to modify the original set of specified competencies, articulating in further detail the competencies necessary for producing desired pupil outcomes, given specific situations and both learner and teacher characteristics. This is accomplished by going beyond Turner's (1972) criterion level 1, at least until teacher competencies are sufficiently validated to adopt lower levels of criteria for assessment purposes. Observations of teacher behaviors in real classroom situations and analysis of the statistical prediction of level of pupil outcome achieved are conducted over a relatively long period. Intervening variables are postulated to influence the relationship between specified teacher behaviors and pupil outcomes. These mediating variables, such as personality of the teacher, pupil characteristics, situational variables, etc., and the manner in which they affect the relationship between observed teacher behaviors and pupil outcomes, must also be investigated.

REFERENCES

144

1 American Association of Colleges for Teacher Education, Commission on Multicultural Education. "No One Model American." *Journal of Teacher Education* 24, no. 4 (Winter 1973): 264-5. The statement has been printed separately and is available from AACTE.

2 Ibid.

3 Laosa, L.M. "Child Care and the Culturally Different Child in the United States." *Child Care Quarterly* 3, no. 4, in press.

4 Ethridge, S.B. "Statistical Projection of Need for Spanish-speaking Teachers." Paper presented at National Education Task Force de la Raza Conference, Albuquerque, New Mexico, November, 1973, p. 23. A summary of this paper appears in *A Relook at Tucson '66 and Beyond*. Report of a National Bilingual Bicultural Institute. Proceedings of the National Education Task Force de la Raza Conference. Washington, D.C.: National Education Association, 1974.

5 U.S. Commission on Civil Rights. *Teachers and Students. Report V: Mexican American Education Study. Differences in Teacher Interaction With Mexican American and Anglo Students.* Washington, D.C.: U.S. Government Printing Office, 1973.

6 Laosa, L.M. "Child Care and the Culturally Different," and Laosa, L.M., L. Lara-Tapia, and J.D. Swartz. "Pathognomic Verbalizations, Anxiety, and Hostility in Normal Mexican and United States Anglo-American Children's Fantasies: A Longitudinal Study." *Journal of Consulting and Clinical Psychology* 42 (1974): 73-8.

7 Schalock, H.D., and J.R. Hale, eds. *A Competency-Based, Field Centered, Systems Approach to Elementary Teacher Education.* Final Report for Project No. 89022. Washington, D.C.: Bureau of Research, U.S. Office of Education, 1968 (no page given).

8 Cardenas, B., and J.A. Cardenas. "Chicano—Bright-eyed, Bilingual, Brown, and Beautiful." *Today's Education* 62, no. 2 (February 1973): 49-51.

9 Nunnally, J.C. *Psychometric Theory.* New York: McGraw-Hill, 1967 (no page given).

10 Kagan, S. and W.C. Madsen. "Experimental Analyses of Cooperation and Competition of Anglo-American and Mexican Children." *Developmental Psychology* 6 (1972) pp. 49-59.

11 Castañeda, A., M. Ramirez, and L. Herold. "Culturally Democratic Learning Environments: A Cognitive Styles Approach. A Manual for Teachers." Mimeograph. Riverside, Calif.: Systems and Evaluation in Education, 1972.

12 Lesser, G.S., G. Fifer, and C. Clark. *Mental Abilities of Children from Different Social Class and Cultural Groups.* Monographs of the Society for Research in Child Development 30, no. 4. Chicago: University of Chicago Press, Society for Research in Child Development, 1965.

13 Stodolsky, S.S., and G. Lesser. "Learning Patterns in the Disadvantaged." *Harvard Educational Review* 37 (1967): 546-93.

14 Laosa, L.M., J.D. Swartz, and R. Diaz-Guerrero. "Perceptual-cognitive and Personality Development of Mexican and Anglo-American Children as Measured by Human Figure Drawings." *Developmental Psychology* 10 (1974): 131-9.

15 Laosa, Lara-Tapia, and Swartz, "Pathognomic Verbalizations, Anxiety, and Hostility."

16 Turner, R.L. "Levels of Criteria." In *The Power of Competency-Based Teacher Education,* edited by B. Rosner. Boston: Allyn and Bacon, 1972, pp. 3-8.

145

CHAPTER 2

CHICANO CULTURAL DIVERSITY: IMPLICATIONS FOR CBTE

Ernest Garcia
Professor, School of Education
California State College
San Bernardino, California

146   To be or not to be competent is certainly not the question. Even people who have doubts about competency-based teacher education programs would probably agree that the process of education should result in changes in the student which, if they are to be assessed, must be observable. The professor of engineering who is involved with the education of engineers certainly demands that students be able to perform certain tasks or solve given problems. This ability is not only seen as a necessary exit skill from the course, but also as a *basis* for the competence that the engineer will demonstrate when putting her/his knowledge to use.

Likewise, the professor of English insists on performance in order to assess the skill with which a student can analyze a literary work or produce an essay. Those who would employ the product of such a class would look for some evidence of competence in order to select the person who would best fit their needs.

Consider the professor of social service who must inculcate in her/his students the skills and attitudes necessary for their performance as social workers. The focus would certainly be on the question of what the graduates would be able to do. Will they be reasonably successful? Can success be related to specific competencies developed and demonstrated during their training period? Success during the training period should certainly be measured by what the student can do rather than by the number of formal courses she/he took.

Do Chicanos Have Special Learning Needs?

The focus of this paper is on the competencies that teachers should demonstrate in preparation for working with Chicano children. However, before attention can be given to that focus, it is imperative that reasons be established for assuming the Chicano learner has special needs. These special needs must be seen as arising from cultural influences that are different from those which permeate the typical school, including the influence of those who teach in it. The person who will be successful in teaching Chicano learners must have all the skills developed through a good competency-based teacher education program and *more*. The *more* is related to those skills which are heavily influenced by the cultural differences that Chicano children bring to school and which affect the ways in which they perceive their environment.

It is interesting to find that at the turn of the century, the noted structuralist Titchener stressed the need for ethnic psychology.[1] He included language, myth, custom, and art as the important components of culture which set groups apart from each other. Although his brand of structuralism lost influence with the advent of functionalism and behaviorism, his awareness that cultural differences were of importance to the psychologist as well as other social scientists was significant. He stated:

> The collective mind has no existence apart from the separate
> members of the community. But when many individual minds
> come into contact, new complex processes take shape; the ele-
> mentary processes are put together as they would not have been
> had mankind lived solitary lives. The problem of ethnic psychol-
> ogy, then, is to trace the development of these new mental com-
> plexes, and explain them by reference to the conditions of social
> living.[2]

147

If children bring with them different ways of perceiving and responding which are influenced by cultural differences, then teachers must behave in ways which accommodate and enhance this different learning style. Ramirez applied Witkin's concept of field dependence-independence to a study of cognitive styles of Mexican American children to determine some of the strategies for teachers to use in response to cultural differences.[3] Wagner also studied cognitive styles, using Witkin's model as well as others.[4]

In this paper, the concept of the *culture filter* or screen is introduced in an effort to simplify the discussion of learning styles. If teachers need to consider *who* the learner is from a cultural perspective, then the concept of cultural differences must be investigated. The discussion of cultural pluralism which follows serves to point out the danger of having a convenient slogan to categorize the Chicano as a monolithic entity possessing uniform, discernible cultural traits. Pluralism is viewed in a broader sense to include vast differences which exist within the Mexican American group.

Finally, the importance of competency-based teacher education programs in the education of all children and specifically Chicanos is stressed. Recommendations regarding desirable competencies to be developed conclude the paper.

Learning through a Culture Filter

In numerous conferences and inservice meetings, teachers have asked whether the Chicano children they teach learn in ways which are different from those of other children. The question elicits interesting responses which range from the implausible "all children are alike" to the equally untenable conclusion that Chicanos learn in some peculiar way. If the question were put to researchers on human learning, what would be the response? The person whose bias rests with operant conditioning would probably insist that Chicanos learn through reinforcement, and that behavior modification techniques can be just as effective with Chicanos as with other children. A humanistic psychologist would respond that Chicanos, like other people, have a basic drive toward health and actualization, and that by providing an environment where individuals will perceive themselves in a positive way and have the opportunity to develop their own uniqueness, the needs of Chicano students will be met.[5] Instructional theory, emanating from humanistic psychology, would therefore accommodate the learning styles of Chicanos.

Likewise, those interested in cognitive construct approaches to instruction would say that Chicano students, like others, should be considered as people who actively select and interpret certain signals from their environment and, in fact, become processors of information in keeping with their own individualized differences.

If theories and paradigms for explaining the learning process make no distinction in the way Chicanos learn, then does it follow that the education of teachers who will teach Chicanos requires no differentiation? It is a fact that most teachers presently teaching Chicanos did not have an education program which was different from the regular program of all teaching candidates. It is also a fact that the education of Chicanos, when measured with traditional tools and procedures, has been less effective than that of their Anglo counterparts. Data on achievement levels, dropouts, and other indicators show that Chicano students have not fared well.[6] It might even be accurate to conclude that the teacher versed in learning theory, whether of a particular orientation or eclectic, has failed to be productive in the education of Chicanos.

If Chicanos indeed learn through operant conditioning just like anybody else, it would be helpful to view the process through a *culture filter*. If the teacher who uses behavior modification knows things about the Chicano learners that are different from her/his own experience or the experience of other identifiable groups, then this information can be put to effective use in the implementation of the technique. For example, if the teacher is aware of culturally unique nonverbal signals, she/he can recognize potential reinforcers that are culturally appropriate, and realize that there might be conditions such as overly competitive situations where the student would rather withdraw than be engaged in a culturally uncomfortable situation.

148

Similarly, the teacher with a humanistic bent would profit greatly from understanding the uniqueness of Chicano children through familiarity with aspects of their cultural differences. The use of this knowledge to arrange an environment where children would perceive themselves in a positive way would indeed enhance learning. If children's cultural differences are regarded and treated as worthy within the school, then the children see part of themselves, part of their existence, in a positive way.

Cultural Pluralism

Cultural pluralism is a term used as an alternative to *melting pot*. The need to acknowledge and respect cultural diversity is a familiar theme in the literature on the education of ethnic minorities. This emphasis has served a purpose by focusing on the reality that there is nothing un-American in being different. In fact, diversity is very American. Like many good things, however, the focus on cultural pluralism contains the danger that it can be reduced to a popular slogan which is convenient in rhetoric but which lacks the clarity to make it operational. Perhaps the biggest danger to this positive concept is the urge to categorize and classify, to sort and pigeonhole. Writers allude to the *Chicano culture* as if it were a set of values   149 and customs possessed by all who are categorized as Chicanos or Mexican Americans. Romano protests the use of such convenient labeling, stating:

> The Indianistic views, the Confrontationist Philosophy, and Cultural Nationalism with its Meztizaje-based Humanistic Universalism, Behavioral Relativism and Existentialism, when related to types of people who have immigrated from Mexico, those born in the United States, as well as people of Mexican descent who were residents in conquered western lands, all give some glimmer of the complexity of this population, especially when one views it internally from the perspective of multiple philosophies regarding the existence and nature of Mexican-American man. For, in truth, just as *el puro Mexicano* does not exist, neither does the *pure Mexican-American* despite the massive efforts by social scientists to fabricate such a mythical being under the monolithic label of *traditional culture* rather than the more realistic concept of multiple histories and philosphies.[7]

That cultural differences exist among groups is not a debatable question. What does leave ample room for argument is the suggestion that everyone named García, Hernández, Gómez, or Solís somehow possesses uniform cultural differences which must be considered by the teacher in providing better instruction. One author spent much time emphasizing the reality of diversity among people identified as Mexican American, and then proceeded to generalize about their learning styles. This fallacy serves to create the new stereotype which is found in the completion of the statement, "Mexican American children are . . . ."

ETHNIC CHARACTERISTICS STUDIED

Teachers faced with the grim reality that the education of Chicanos has been inadequate at best are quick to accept children as "elements of sociological categories rather than as individual learners; socializing them, in effect, in terms of those categories (ethnically and culturally) rather than educating them."[8] One document designed to help teachers understand Mexican American children and their families is entitled *Characteristic Traits of Hispanic Persons*.[9] It breaks down such concepts as *passion, individualism,* and *humanism* and makes such statements as, "There is a marked tendency among Spanish-speaking peoples to move forward with their back to the future; this is caused by being oriented to a present-past relationship in which the future does not figure in their thinking."[10] The author goes on to explain that this condition is also very much part of the Indian culture and probably resulted from the inbreeding between Spaniards and Indians. He continues, "This is why you will find, when traveling in Latin America, that distances along the highway are given from the point of departure and not to the point ahead."[11] Other statements geared to help the teacher understand and educate Mexican American students are, "Hispanic people are well known for their courtesy, but not for their observance of the law,"[12] and "Individualism causes the Spanish persons to be particularly deficient on those qualities which are based on collective standards."[13] With generalizations like these, it is easy to understand how educational deficiencies can be attributed to the *culture.*

A recent entry in the competition for language arts textbook adoption in California epitomizes the new stereotype of the Chicano. Although the author incorrectly chooses to call the people described in the text "Mexican," the reference is to barrio cultural patterns in the United States.[14] This act of preferring to use "Mexican" to refer to Mexican Americans is the type of fantasizing which Cortes describes as the process of picking up a "frozen village culture" from a remote area of Mexico and transplanting it to Southern California—and declaring that it is alive and well![15] The generalizations in *Tradition in the Barrio* are static, frozen concepts which fit Carter's description of the *noble savage* approach.[16] They don't deal with the dynamic nature of culture, but rather give a distorted view for teachers to use in, once again, completing the statement, "Mexican American children are . . . ."

The new stereotype is, of course, a rebuttal to the old stereotype which attached negative attributes to Mexican Americans. Universal positive attributes have been substituted for universal negative ones. In writing about the compensatory education model, Carter states, "In order to determine the causative differences or deficiencies, studies have been conducted on Mexican American homes, children, and lifestyles. The conclusions of these studies, while often confusing and contradictory, provide an overly generalized or stereotyped description of Mexican-American culture and personality characteristics."[17] On the one hand, some people are busy trying to classify, sort, and label Chicano culture in order to overcome some of the inherent *deprivation* that hinders school progress. On the other hand, Chicanos themselves are eager to give the Anglo a generalized, static description of Chicano culture, romantic in nature and unrealistic at best. Neither effort serves to improve the education of Chicanos. The first apologizes for differences and seeks to overcome them in order to enhance school progress. The second provides for a new stereotype which does not accommodate the vast differences that exist *within* the group. Romano offers four broad categories which serve to emphasize cultural diversity within the group.[18] These differences emerge from the different ways in which people of Mexican descent have had to adjust to life in the U.S. Those who have embraced styles of life aspiring to Anglo-Saxon conformity have attempted to move away from their cultural origins to embrace the ways of the dominant society.

STABILIZED DIFFERENCES

The cultural differences of children from these families will include little more than a Spanish surname if, indeed, it hasn't been changed. Contrast this group with people described as having *stabilized differences*, who have immigrated from Mexico in the last 50 years, and are found in pockets, *colonias, barrios,* where they maintain the basic ways and traditions which are based on the "multiple histories and philosophies from which they came."[19] The subgroups of this category differ throughout the Southwest but the Spanish language, existing in a variety of dialects, is a common feature, along with traditional food. This is the setting that probably spawns the urge to classify all Mexican Americans as being from a "folk culture." In reality they represent different areas of Mexico, and to identify them as a single entity is to deny that differences exist among the inhabitants of Mexico. The simplicity of describing all as members of that "frozen village culture" transplanted north of the border is a convenience we can ill afford in understanding cultural pluralism. It would be wrong to view children of this group as growing up in a static environment because they grow up interacting with the old ways which are Mexican, and with many facets of the dominant Anglo society. The teacher who stereotypes this group might find that the Chicano music preferred by the young is not all traditional, but rather the country western sounds of Johnny Rodriguez or the exciting rock beat of El Chicano and Santana.

Mexican Americans who can be described as in a state of *realigned pluralism* are those who have taken up the ways of the dominant society but have found it necessary to establish activities and institutions that are ethnically oriented and parallel to those of the dominant society. The phenomenon of the third generation return is common within this category. A recent article illustrates the outcome of efforts to set up parallel activities and institutions.[20] The article calls Albuquerque a Chicano Nashville, and goes on to tell how Chicano musicians and artists have formed corporations to control their own destinies and promote their music.

RECOGNITION OF CULTURAL DIFFERENCES

The final group described by Romano is called "bicultural," and is composed of individuals who can function equally well in both cultures. There is hope that effective ethnic studies and bilingual cross-cultural programs in the schools will produce more people who can be called bicultural.

These categories, though admittedly broad, serve to illustrate the differences and dynamics of people called Mexican Americans or Chicanos, who are too often seen as a monolithic group with a uniform set of values and customs. Romano's observation that all of the categories can often be observed in a single Mexican American family further emphasizes its dynamic nature.[21]

Cultural pluralism, then, is not a concept that applies only to the differences between teacher and child when one is Anglo and the other Mexican American. The concept also applies to the culturally pluralistic aspects of Mexican American life. What are the specific cultural differences that the teacher should look for and understand in order to act in ways that accommodate the culturally different? Some differences such as language are obvious but are not always treated in ways that show sensitivity. Monolingual Spanish children who find themselves in an English-language environment need to have a very real cultural difference accommodated. The sensitive teacher arranges a learning environment where children feel good about the way the language they bring to school is accepted, and the ways in which the new language is made part of their instruction. There are many graduates of language differences. The example of the Spanish monolingual indicates a very definite cultural difference but there are many other language differences which are not as readily identified. The child who speaks more English than Spanish certainly has very specific needs which the teacher must recognize, and which require as much attention and sensitivity as those of the monolingual. Beyond the obvious difference of language, people are often hardpressed to be specific concerning other cultural differences. In a recent meeting between interested Chicano parents and teachers who were seeking ways to implement a more effective program for their students, the parents pointed out that the teachers should be aware of and understand the Chicano culture. Aside from the obvious difference of language, the group had difficulty identifying salient cultural differences. Unfortunately the next step in such situations is to begin to cite examples that run the danger of creating stereotypes that provide patent answers for working with Chicano students:

> The Chicanito doesn't pay attention to female teachers because he is taught to be *muy macho.*
> The Chicano child, as a sign of respect, will always bow his or her head while being reprimanded.

While both of these statements might be accurate in certain situations with certain children, the teacher must be able to recognize when such influences are really affecting the behavior of the child and proceed to act in ways which accommodate the differences. Cultural differences should therefore be construed as those characteristics which cause a student to act or react in ways different from the responses commonly anticipated by the institution. If the five elements of culture as listed by Aragón—language, diet, costuming, social patterns, and ethics—are considered, the teacher can have a framework through which to assess differences that exist in the child's home and community environment.[22]

If children come from a barrio where stabilized differences are evident, then the chances that Spanish monolinguals will be coming to kindergarten is more probable. Diet differences might also be more pronounced, so that while discussing the nutritional qualities of a good breakfast at school, the teacher needs to be aware that the ingredients suggested by the National Dairy Council in its colorful posters might be neither relevant nor desirable for a Chicano child. A teacher complained recently that he hadn't been able to find calorie counters that included traditional Mexican foods for his junior high class to evaluate the caloric content of their diets. To the extent that diets would be different, the school should accept and build upon those differences.

Costuming can become an important expression of cultural differences which can occur in subtle and often unrecognized ways. The teacher who looks for *sombreros, sarapes,* and *huaraches* might miss a pattern of dress or body adornment which has become an expression of identity in the barrio, and which, *if understood and accepted by the school,* will enhance learning conditions for the student.

Social patterns such as the extended family, machismo, carnalismo (brotherhood, ethnic kinship), and patriarchy must be understood and seen as appearing in different ways and in different degrees depending on the setting. A common complaint of parents is that the traditional social amenities stressed in some homes are not reinforced by the school. Of particular confusion to a child who comes from an environment where the *Usted* form is used in addressing adults, and the terms *Don* and *Doña* are ways of showing respect, is the situation where the young teacher greets her/his children by saying, "Hi kids, I'm your teacher and I want you to call me Chris."

Expressions of cultural ethics are complex in the dynamic culture of the Mexican American. Aragón mentions nepotism as a concept that is rejected by the American but seen as a positive thing by the Chicano because "you trust the person you love."[23] *La mordida* ("bite," or bribe) is something that few Chicanos would attempt with American officials but which many use with cultural gusto when traveling in Mexico.

Cultural differences that need the attention and sensitivity of the teacher come with each individual. Sometimes there will be several students with the same needs. The important point is for the teacher to promote individuality through recognition and acceptance of cultural differences. The teacher should be aware of those instances when the student is acting or reacting in unanticipated ways. It is at this time that intervention can prove helpful, because the student's chances of success are improved and the feeling that someone cares is fostered.

Interviews with Chicano parents reveal that they are very interested in the performance of their children in school, and that they trust teachers to exhibit certain behaviors that will get children to learn. The following letter was sent home by a teacher.

Dear Mrs. Sanchez:

Ramon can't talk too well in English. He is having a great deal of trouble with his addition combinations, and his reading is very much below grade level. I hope you can come and see me.

Ms. Hewitt

A scribbled note came back:

Dear Ms. Hewitt:

I know what you say about Ramon is true. That's why I send him to school.

Mrs. Sanchez

Parents are basically competency-performance oriented. They want their children to be able to do things well.

Relevance of CBTE

Competency-based teacher education gives us cause to be optimistic that the education of all teachers will improve. The shift in emphasis from requiring students merely to complete a series of courses to requiring instead the acquisition of specific exit skills is indeed a positive move. Although other disciplines require performance on tests and other instruments to measure student progress, the concept of a competency-based course or program is still foreign to many, and sounds mechanistic and rigid when, in reality, it allows for flexibility and innovation. Perhaps the greatest beneficiaries of CBTE will be culturally different childen, because teachers educated on the basis of specific competencies will most likely be specific in identifying the exit skills they expect from their students. Hopefully, they will be less likely to consider the cultural differences that children bring to school as liabilities in the learning process.

THE PROGRAM

It was stated earlier that teachers of the culturally different must have all the competencies developed through a good teacher education program and more. The greatest portion of this paper has been devoted to the definition of more as the knowledge and appreciation of cultural differences that children might bring to school and the sensitivity, good judgment, and skill to use that knowledge for children's benefit. Competencies for being an effective teacher of Chicanos should not be thought of as being a completely different set of behaviors designed only for teaching this particular group. Rather, they must be behaviors that are flexible enough to allow for and promote cultural diversity in the teaching-learning act. The teacher needs to make use of the culture filter to begin to see the situation as students see it, and to modify conditions to enhance learning.

To prepare candidates to be effective teachers in a culturally diverse society, the program should include requirements such as these:

1. Require competencies in teacher-pupil interaction as well as in fostering conditions that promote pupil-pupil interaction; require the prospective teacher to focus on cultural differences that might inhibit participation

2. Require competency in arranging a learning environment designed to accomplish specific instructional objectives; have the prospective teacher demonstrate how the needs of learners will be met, and indicate flexibility of the arrangement to accommodate individual differences

3. Require competency in developing instructional units which focus on a culturally diverse society but which do not result in an "ethnic lunch" curriculum; require teacher candidates to demonstrate how current curriculum materials can be augmented to include themes of cultural diversity, particularly social studies and language arts materials; require student teaching in a multicultural setting where candidates can evaluate themselves as well as be evaluated by others

4. Require competency in conversational Spanish that prepares teacher candidates to understand the spoken Spanish of the area and to be understood while speaking it

5. Require competency in recognizing nonverbal signals that are different from the teachers'

6. Require that students understand and can demonstrate that instruction in a culturally diverse setting and *about* a culturally diverse society should not be determined by "peddlers of ethnic packages," or by those who promote the "let's make piñatas and eat tacos" syndrome

7. Require specific knowledge of the Indian-Spanish-Mexican-Chicano heritage of the Southwest, and demonstrate an ability to include alternative perspectives where other points of view or historical facts have been omitted

ILLUSTRATIVE PERFORMANCE OBJECTIVES FOR CBTE CANDIDATES

1. Demonstrate an ability to assess one's own cultural orientation and biases by describing feelings toward concepts such as: cooperation, competition, family, loyalty, respect, etc.; compare and contrast feelings with those of members of family or friends who appear to think the same way

2. Identify settings which tend to restrict full participation because one's cultural orientation runs counter to the viewpoints and behaviors required for full enjoyment

3. Investigate cultural characteristics that are attributed to Chicanos; select two or three examples that a child could conceivably bring to school, then identify an instructional setting where conflict might arise; describe

155

how to accommodate the child's differences and still attain the instructional objective

4. Assume a group of Chicano students in class; describe how to find out as much as possible about their home and community environment—without invading their privacy; explain what knowledge is necessary before asking questions

5. Describe a situation where a Chicano child is having difficulty; identify possible factors contributing to that child's lack of success; list factors that the child might be injecting into the situation; describe adjustments that could be made to increase chances of success

Summary Statement

From the viewpoint of human learning, Chicanos learn like anyone else. However, cultural differences can hinder learning when the conditions do not accommodate those differences. The teacher should therefore be able to understand and utilize aspects of cultural diversity which will increase chances of success for the learner. The teacher should perceive cultural pluralism in ways that don't stereotype groups as having uniform characteristics. Differences within the group called Chicano or Mexican American are broad and varied.

156

Competency-based teacher education is important to Chicanos because of its focus on *performance*. The lack of school success for Chicanos has traditionally been attributed to cultural differences. Teachers trained in specific competencies will be better able to accommodate cultural differences and enhance pupil chances for success.

REFERENCES

1 Titchener, E.B. *A Primer of Psychology.* London: Macmillan & Co., 1909, p. 292.

2 Ibid., p. 293.

3 Ramirez, Manuel, III. "Bilingual Education as a Vehicle for Educational Change." In *Mexican Americans and Educational Change,* edited by Alfredo Castañeda et al. Proceedings of the May 21-22, 1971 Symposium on "Project Follow Through." Sponsored by the Mexican American Studies Program, University of California, Riverside. Washington, D.C.: U.S. Office of Education, 1971, p. 400.

4 Wagner, Steven R. "Cognitive Styles: Locus of Control and Field Articulation." Ph.D. dissertation, Department of Education, Claremont Graduate School, 1973, Chapters 3 and 5.

5 Snelbecker, Glenn E. *Learning Theory, Instructional Theory, and Psychoeducational Design.* New York: McGraw-Hill, 1974, pp. 482-3.

6 U.S. Commission on Civil Rights. *Toward Quality Education for Mexican Americans. Report VI: Mexican-American Education Study.* Washington, D.C.: U.S. Government Printing Office, February 1974.

7 Romano, Octavio. "The Historical and Intellectual Presence of Mexican Americans." *El Grito* 2, no. 2 (Winter 1969): 41.

8 López, Thomas R., Jr. "Cultural Pluralism: Political Hoax? Educational Need?" *Journal of Teacher Education* 24, no. 4 (Winter 1973): 277.

9 Covey, Don. "Characteristic Traits of Hispanic Persons." Unpublished manuscript available from the author, 1968.

10 Ibid., p. 3.

11 Ibid.

12 Ibid., p. 2.

13 Ibid.

14 Flores, Elvira. *Tradition in the Barrio*. Edited by Julian Nava. Walnut Creek, Calif.: Aardvaark Media, 1974.

15 Cortes, Carlos. "Cultural Pluralism in the Curriculum." Speech delivered at Colton Unified School District Workshop on Cultural Diversity, Colton, California, April 27, 1974.

16 Carter, Thomas. "The Persistence of a Perspective." In *Mexican Americans and Educational Change*, edited by Castañeda et al, pp. 270-2.

17 Ibid., p. 276.

18 Romano, "Historical and Intellectual Presence," pp. 42-3.

19 Ibid., p. 41.

20 Pippert, Wesley G. "Albuquerque: Chicano Nashville." In *San Bernardino* (Calif.) *Sun Telegram*, May 17, 1974.

21 Romano, "Historical and Intellectual Presence," p. 45.

22 Aragón, Juan A. "The Challenge to Biculturalism: Culturally Deficient Educators Teaching Culturally Different Children." In *Mexican Americans and Educational Change*, edited by Castañeda et al, p. 262.

23 Ibid., p. 264.

COMPETENCY-BASED EDUCATION AND THE CULTURALLY DIFFERENT: A RAY OF HOPE, OR MORE OF THE SAME?

M. Reyes Mazón
Director, Institute for Cultural Pluralism, and
Professor, School of Education
San Diego State University
San Diego, California

Tomás A. Arciniega
Dean, School of Education
San Diego State University
San Diego, California

158

Competency-based education (CBE) holds great promise for achieving the ideal of equal educational opportunity in the American school, while giving minority students a positive view of their cultural and historical heritage. An obvious and sad fact is that culturally and linguistically different groups in American society have suffered disproportionately from cycles of poverty and limited opportunities. In order to break such cycles, education systems need to become responsive in a comprehensive manner to the concept and ideal of cultural pluralism. Schools must be organized to promote such an idea. This will mean that school and school-related programs in the areas of teacher education and professional training, curriculum development, and educational administration must necessarily become multicultural. The competency-based movement, with its emphasis on performance and collaboration among community, students, teachers, administrators, and college professors, provides an excellent strategy by which schools can begin to reflect and promote subcultural differences inherent in American society, rather than continue so vigorously to attempt their elimination, to the detriment of minority students.

Competency-based teacher education (CBTE) has been described by advocates as "the most significant lever for educational reform since Sputnik," and as "one of the most influential and important developments in this progressive effort to advance the process of schooling." Its critics, on the other hand, call CBTE "a multi-faceted concept in search of practitioners," "old wine in new bottles," and "a good idea if you could figure out what it is."[1]

The authors are convinced that the movement toward competency-based teacher education (CBTE) is a positive force for change. It is a culmination of a series of change efforts in education which resulted from legitimate public demands for accountability, cost effectiveness, and relevance. The educational technology boom of the 1960s also gave impetus to the CBTE movement. The U.S. Office of Education's support of model elementary programs, the Trainers of Teacher Trainers (TTT) programs, and Teacher Corps have led to more systematic program planning in teacher education, all of which have given rise to more field-oriented professional preparation programs. Minicourses, microteaching, computer-assisted instruction programs, and many other individualized instructional approaches have demonstrated that instruction which permits students to proceed at their own pace is feasible and can be effective. Throughout, the emphasis has been on (a) instruction tailored to specific student needs in relation to identifiable behavioral outcomes, (b) student evaluation as well as program evaluation based on explicitly stated objectives, and (c) a systematic overall plan to achieve program ends.[2]

An important feature of CBTE which grew out of the U.S. Office of Education (USOE) effort is the notion of parity. The Teacher Corps emphasizes program development and implementation in collaboration with community representatives, students, classroom teachers, school administrators, and college professors. Of all the developments, this is the aspect of CBTE that truly goes to the heart of organizational problems, and it is this key element that offers the greatest promise for improving schools and teacher training programs.

Past reform efforts in education have not responded to critical underlying questions and assumptions such as: What are schools for? What is the real world of the school? What is truly occurring in and around schools that has meaning for children? What should be occurring? Are we preparing children for tomorrow, yesterday, or do we know? Do we act as though we even care? If so, we then have a host of additional questions: Which children are we educating for what? Do schools really assume, in form and practice, that all children are equally worthy?

We think the answer to this last question is negative.

Reform efforts have focused largely on curriculum rather than the effects which schools have on children. Educational reform attempts too readily ignore the powerful fact that schools shape and shape well, socialize and socialize well, and ultimately fit and fit our young well for the prevailing order of things. Robert Engler called it "culture-breaking the young and developing loyalty to the social order."[3]

CBTE and Multicultural Education

CBTE offers a process by which educators, university scholars, community people, and students can collaborate and become involved in determining the education process. This is one important ray of hope on an otherwise dismal horizon because educators and scholars have failed miserably to respond to the needs and demands of the culturally and linguistically different. There is no need here to dwell extensively on the well-known litany of wrongs perpetrated on minority students by the typical white middle-class oriented school. Experience with the reforms of the past—whether recent or not so recent, whether Sputnik-inspired or whatever, have demonstrated that conventional wisdom simply does not work well in teaching culturally and linguistically different children. As a matter of fact, it hasn't worked well for most children. Teaching and learning, to be successful, must be interesting to students. Student motivational styles can only be accurately deciphered if schools are made to care enough so that they find out who their students are in terms of their social, cultural, and historical backgrounds.

Given the multiplicity of ethnic groups in this country, increasing national commitment to equalization of opportunity, and the assertion of ethnic pride in groups, education systems cannot continue to ignore the impact and significance of cultural differences in American society. They can't afford the luxury. They must acknowledge and accept in form and practice what children learn in the home and community, as well as in school. Learning goes on rapidly and well with young people. It is only when the incongruities between school and the learning style of its clients are at great variance that negative judgments about the place of the client in the school are made. That is called making value judgments. America's schools have actively chosen not to value cultural, linguistic, and racial differences. This is the crux of current major reform movements in our schools.

This country can no longer afford to continue the isolationism which created the monolingual, monocultural society of white middle-class America. The schools must be restructured to meet the educational needs of the total society. Programs must be developed which will enable children to communicate in at least two languages and function in two cultures by the time they reach their fourth year of formal schooling. Programs are needed that will enable all students to become positive contributors to a culturally dynamic society consistent with cultural origins, and which recognize the worth of other cultural groups. It is only in promoting and practicing this ideal that the rights and needs of minorities—of the culturally and linguistically different—can be effectively responded to.

Current Status of Equal Opportunity

In spite of a recent flurry of reforms and innovations, and large amounts of federal dollars spent on education, the schools remain remarkably unchanged. Books such as *Teachers For the Real World*[4] and *Crisis in the Classroom*[5] have had little, if any, effect on the nation's schools. Silberman writes:

> the 1950's and 60's saw one of the largest and most sustained educational reform movements in American history, an effort that many observers . . . thought would transform the schools. Nothing of the sort has happened; the reform movement has produced innumerable changes and yet the schools themselves are largely unchanged.[6]

We are undergoing a period of extraordinary sociocultural development that demands a change in both the structure and function of schooling.[7] The demand for attainment of equal education opportunity in this country will become the most serious domestic issue in the ensuing decade.

The monolingual, monocultural society reflected in the curricula of the American school began to crumble when ethnic America began to demand its share of the dream of equality. The Black movement accentuated by the 1956 nonviolent bus boycott led by Martin Luther King, Jr. in Montgomery, Alabama spurred the "Movimiento Chicano." The march of the National Farm Workers' Association led by Cesar Chavez in 1966, and the continuing American Indian Movement (AIM) protest against government control, have demonstrated that the culturally different peoples of this country will no longer tolerate inequality.

EQUAL ACCESS VS. EQUAL BENEFITS

A recent review of research and development efforts aimed at the culturally different in this country (by Arciniega, 1973) shows two different points of view concerning what constitutes equality: (a) the "equal access to schooling view," and (b) the "equal benefits view."[8] The equal access to schooling view, which preceded the equal benefits view, contends that equal education opportunity is provided when all segments of the population have an equal opportunity to compete for the benefits of the education system. Green summarizes this view by saying that:

> there be provided for every person within the society some school with approximately comparable curricula, facilities, staff, and management. If there are children for whom no school at all exists, then those children do not have equal educational opportunity. Moreover, if the schools available for some are significantly deficient, then the children who attend those schools do not have equal educational opportunity.[9]

To put it another way, equal education opportunities are provided when there is equal access to the school for all, and when all schools are roughly equal in staffing, instructional material, and physical facilities.

As Coleman noted, this notion of free education assumes the non-existence of inequalities in opportunity because of low economic status and ignores the problem of the poor staying in school beyond the age of employment. Second, it is assumed that through simple exposure to the common curriculum, equal opportunity will be provided. The school is placed in the passive role of being responsible simply for making available the opportunity to learn. The task of benefiting from the opportunity is left to the child.[10]

The equal benefits view, on the other hand, focuses on the benefits derived from schooling. Equality exists only if there is an equal opportunity to benefit from schooling, and not merely equal access to schooling itself. This is not to say that the *range* of achievement should be at the same level for all, but rather that it should be at *about* the same level for the various groups being served. Achievement of this goal may necessitate unequal allocation of resources and substantial increases in accessibility to the opportunities of the school. This position has been affirmed in recent Supreme Court decisions—e.g., *Lau* v. *Nichols* and *San Antonio School District* v. *Rodriguez*.[11]

Given the notion that equal education opportunity is only provided when equal benefits can be derived, there are two divergent approaches concerning how minority groups can best achieve equal benefits from the school system. One is by attempting to overcome the negative effects of their "deprived" home and cultural environments; the other is by focusing on the school itself. The former is reflected in compensatory education and other efforts designed to compensate for supposedly inadequate learning environments in the home and communities of culturally and linguistically different children, efforts which propose to acculturate children into middle-class values and standards of behavior. An alternative and more viable approach would be for teachers to acknowledge the worth and contributions of home and cultural communities in the emotions of children. The intent is to promote cultural and linguistic differences in children as positive values for American education.

Compensatory education is what has prevailed in this country's effort to provide equal education opportunities and equal benefits to children from culturally different groups. Equal benefits for the Chicano, the Black, and the Indian child will not occur in a system that attempts to make them over into the image desired by the white middle-class society.

If America is to fulfill its dream of equality, it must begin with schools that promote and reflect a culturally pluralistic society. The schools and universities of this country must restructure themselves to provide students with basic knowledge, basic skills, and political awareness to enable them to derive equal benefits—to function effectively and contribute to American society as functioning members of their own cultural and linguistic communities.

CBE as a Vehicle for Equal Opportunity

The competency-based education movement offers educators a way to bring about equal education opportunities for the culturally and linguistically different, if the collaboration principle that CBE advocates is adhered to. CBE, as noted by Blosser, involves the identification of competencies which are stated in terms of behavioral objectives the student must master.[12] Competencies are constellations of related behavioral objectives. Time and method vary and are tailored to meet individual student needs.

An advantage of CBE is that evaluation of achievement is in terms of observable behaviors. Behavioral objectives state explicitly—

1. what behavior is to be performed by whom,
2. when the behavior is to be performed,
3. the conditions under which the behavior is to be performed,
4. the proficiency level which is acceptable, and
5. the time permitted to bring about the behavior.

Knowledge of all these factors provides security and assurance of fairness to the learner. The learner knows exactly what is expected. The statement of conditions under which the behavior is to occur assures fairness and validity of assessment. Additionally, the conditions of the objective assure that the teacher will have the necessary materials and instruction plans prior to the time when the behavior is expected to occur.

Another relevant feature of competency-based education for the culturally and linguistically different learner is the manner of evaluation. Evaluation in CBE is based on whether or not behavioral objectives which comprise specified competencies can be adequately performed. Since any one competency is a constellation of behavioral objectives, it is clear that the purpose of evaluation becomes not a decision about whether a learner is competent or incompetent, but rather a diagnosis and prescription of which behavioral objectives need additional treatment before mastery is achieved. Since evaluation in competency-based education is differentially diagnostic, the term incompetent is not relevant in competency-based education.

CBE ASSUMPTIONS, IMPLICATIONS, AND WHITHER?

Where are we? Where do we go from here? In reviewing the variety of CBTE programs, it is safe to conclude that, measured in terms of the issues we have raised, little has actually been done. For example, the impact of CBE on the issue of equalizing opportunities for Chicanos, Blacks, and Native Americans has, at best, been minimal. Some even argue that it has been counter-productive, because the tangible results of CBTE programs have been in methodological and professional-technical areas, rather than in the concerns related to school organizational pathologies. The principal reasons that the CBTE movement has so far failed to live up to its early promise are related to: (a) the continuation of old value assumptions, (b) the unwillingness to effect required major changes in school organization, and (c) the flat refusal of universities and school districts to substantially collaborate with and meaningfully involve the community (parents, students, teachers, and teacher organization groups) in the business of education. Regarding value assumptions, CBTE model programs have taken the "redo" approach by packaging existing courses in behavioral objective form. This approach fails to reexamine the basic assumptions of traditional programs which the new programs are purportedly an attempt to change. To "redo" the same old thing may yield a more attractive package, but it will transform neither utility nor effects to students.

What must be grappled with is how best to meet the needs of culturally different children taught by cross-culturally deficient educators, to cite Aragón.[13] Related to the previous discussion of equal benefits, the issue becomes: How do we move toward equal education opportunity in an equal-benefits sense, along culturally pluralistic lines rather than along compensatory-education ones?

The negative consequences of compensatory-education approaches have been well researched by Arciniega and others.[14] The important point is that approaches which define the problem in terms of cultural and linguistic handicaps are doomed to failure. The problem is with schools, and it is schools that must be the focus for change. Both school districts and teacher training institutions must face up to that hard fact.

Implications which flow from accepting the culturally pluralistic paradigm alternative are extensive. In the case of the Chicano-Anglo school environment, schools would need to give equal status and prestige to both languages, both cultural heritages, and both histories on an equal basis. This would require the commitment and involvement of teachers, administrators, and counselors in developing curricula based on the use of both languages and cultures interchangeably in the classrooms, in school communications, and in cocurricular activities. Public school educators ideally would be bicultural and active promoters of cultural pluralism. Students graduating from such schools could anticipate being able to learn how to function, and function well, in two cultural modalities. This means that all students, upon completion of the school program, would be able to speak, read, and write in two languages and, more importantly, they would be able to learn academic conceptual material in either language. One of the most beautiful benefits to be derived from such a system is the creative ability to approach problem-solving activities with a built-in repertoire of bicultural perspectives. This is what's involved when we talk about eliminating incongruities between the cultural lifestyles of ethnic minority students and current schools. Even the best CBTE programs have incompletely addressed that issue. What is troublesome about this is not only the failure of such programs but, more seriously, the apparent lack of commitment to deal with these cultural pluralistic concerns in design and conceptual rhetoric. In the past, the enthusiasts of competency-based education have consistently dismissed the pleas of ethnic scholars and practitioners to account for their lack of commitment to cultural pluralism as simply being the "cries of anguish of those poor estranged disadvantaged."

Good CBTE programs have usually addressed program design from one of two approaches: (a) the assessment of student needs, or (b) the delineation of teacher roles. In the needs-assessment approach, attention is given first to the perceived needs of students in the schools. Once those needs are identified, then an attempt is made to organize a teacher training program in the university which can produce the type of teacher determined best able to meet those identified needs. The tasks of program design, resource allocation, and management implementation flow from the initial researching of target-client needs.

In identifying the teacher role approach, the first step is to examine the roles which effective teachers of target-school children will be required to play. The idea is to agree on what skills and competencies teachers need in order to function effectively in (a) the teacher-as-community-liaison role, (b) the teacher-as-ethnic-model role, (c) the teacher-as-subject-matter-specialist role, and (d) the teacher-as-multicultural-education-specialist role. University teacher training programs are then shaped to provide the training needed to produce teachers able to function well in these roles. Such programs and roles must of course be consistent with the perceived needs of the target community. The major problem with these conceptualizations is that without a commitment to cultural pluralism and changing schools to reflect what *should be* measured in culturally pluralistic terms, rather than *what is*, little will change. Until schools, universities, communities, and teacher organizations have established viable collaborative linkages in order to bring about a state of cultural pluralism in the schools, no authentic change can come about. Competency-based education will become another "significant" educational reform effort that failed to have any effect on the process of schooling in this country.

The reality of school business is that nothing really changes without major ideological reform. None of this should be interpreted to mean that the authors do not view CBE as a healthy and promising innovation. Our quarrel is with the nomenclature of the system being built to deliver on that promise.

A Design for Teacher Training in Multicultural Education

A teacher training model—Community, Home, Cultural Awareness and Language Training (CHCALT)—is one example of a competency-based program which attempts to work from basic assumptions regarding education for the culturally and linguistically different.[15] The CHCALT model was developed for Teacher Corps and will be implemented in the School of Education at San Diego State University as a program for the Specialist

Credential (an advanced California teaching credential which goes beyond an elementary or secondary credential) in Bilingual/Cross-Cultural Education. Program requirements are stated in terms of competencies and performance objectives. Competencies were identified and objectives developed after consultation with members from the various target communities to be addressed by the program. Students, professors, teachers, and administrators provided assistance in the programmatic aspects of the various components of the program. Implementation will involve strong emphasis on activities in the life of community members. The program will be offered for specialization in Mexican American, Afro American, Asian American and Native American cultures, as well as classroom activities in the community. Teaching competencies include developing performance criteria, teaching strategies, and measurement techniques which are culturally and linguistically appropriate. These classroom skills will be complemented by experiences in the community lifestyle. The components of the program are outlined below.

PROGRAM GOALS

The Bilingual/Cross-Cultural (BCC) Specialist candidate will be a teacher who has previously received training in educational philosophy and methods in order to obtain a single subject or multiple subject credential. In the specialist program, candidates will receive specialized training which will (a) enable them to accept the educational validity of a bilingual/bicultural pupil's home and community learning environment, and (b) provide them with strategies to build on that learning environment toward a meaningful and useful education for the pupils.

After completion of BCC Specialist Credential requirements, the candidate will value—

1. self-concept as a primary element in the education of the culturally and linguistically different,
2. language as a special dimension in the education of the culturally and linguistically different, and
3. language differences as representing valid means of communication, as opposed to the "language deficient" point of view.

The candidate will acquire—

1. a philosophy of education for the culturally and linguistically different,
2. sociocultural sensitivity which is home and community based,
3. assessment techniques for oral language as a diagnostic tool in the education of pupils,
4. language behavior objectives and instructional strategies to fulfill these objectives, and
5. strategies for (a) developing culturally and linguistically appropriate performance criteria, (b) diagnosing performance, (c) evaluating materials, and (d) adapting materials and strategies.

Community, Home, Cultural Awareness, and Language Training: An Outline of the Model

The CHCALT teacher training model is divided into four basic components:

1. Philosophy of education for the culturally and linguistically different
2. Sociocultural awareness—home and community based
3. Oral language and assessment techniques
4. Diagnostic and prescriptive strategies

The first phase of the CHCALT model introduces candidates to the study of culture from a multidisciplinary perspective—anthropological, sociological, psychological, aesthetic, linguistic, and historical. Phase two, the sociocultural awareness component, is completely community-based and provides candidates with the opportunity to observe and experience life in the community of the culture they select.

Equipped with a multidisciplinary perspective of culture and experience in the life of the community, candidates are prepared to approach phase three of the model, oral language and assessment techniques. This component involves a thorough understanding of the cultural and community context of children's language, and the role of language as a means of communication, transmittal of culture, and sociocultural identification. In phase four, diagnostic and prescriptive strategies, candidates acquire the skills to adapt and devise diagnostic tools and methods of prescription which are specifically suited to the needs of the community and culture of the children they will teach. The competencies which comprise each component of the model are listed below:

CHCALT PHASE ONE—PHILOSOPHY OF EDUCATION FOR THE CULTURALLY AND LINGUISTICALLY DIFFERENT

1. Anthropological perspective
   (a) The ability to apply a relativistic and holistic approach to the study of culture
   (b) A knowledge of the patterns and factors associated with cultural change and diversity
2. Sociological perspective
   (a) An understanding of the role and diversity of social, economic, and political patterns in culture
   (b) An understanding of the functions and effects of kinship and non-kinship associations in culture
3. Psychological perspective
   An awareness of the integrated nature of behavior and culture—the effect of cultural child-rearing practices on attitudes, and attitude's effect on cultural behavior and customs
4. Aesthetic and spiritual perspective

(a) An understanding of the spiritual and ethical values of people as they relate to religious beliefs and practices, social and political structure, and cultural behavior

(b) An understanding of aesthetic expression as a reflection of people's spiritual and ethical values

5. Linguistic perspective

An understanding of language as a tool in the transmittal of cultural behavior and attitudes

6. Historical perspective

A knowledge of the history of ethnic America, with special emphasis on social and cultural factors

This component forms the philosophical basis for professional preparation as a whole. It provides candidates with a multidisciplinary theoretical framework for understanding the dynamics of culture in general, so that they will be able to experience life in the target-community culture with an objective, relativistic, and holistic attitude. Candidates will be able to look at themselves as members of their own culture and at members of other cultures as each having learned a prescribed set of behaviors, roles, and values. Candidates will understand the magnitude of learning which any child has achieved and will achieve, independent of any school. Candidates will confront the need for integrating learning processes to be facilitated by the school with learning processes which are central to individual life within any given culture or cultures.

In order to achieve this understanding, candidates will look at culture from the perspectives of anthropology, sociology, psychology, aesthetics, linguistics, and history. They will learn the factors which determine the development of different cultural behaviors, beliefs, and feelings. Candidates will study the influence of political and economic structures and their implications for cultural patterning of behaviors.

An examination will be made of the effects of child-training practices on the behavior of individuals in a culture, and the factors which influence the choice of these practices. Candidates will understand the role of art in reflecting the spiritual, political, and social culture of people, and the role of language as a force of its own in holding and maintaining culture. In addition, candidates will establish for themselves a framework for studying the history of ethnic cultures in the U.S. through independent research and analysis.

CHCALT PHASE TWO—SOCIOCULTURAL AWARENESS

1. Home-family relations
   (a) A knowledge of influences and patterns of family structure and role definitions in the target-culture community
   (b) An awareness of how bilingual/bidialectal/bicultural influences affect and differentiate learning styles

(c) A knowledge of child-rearing practices in the target-culture community and their effects on behavior

2. Community culture
   (a) A knowledge of the structure of the community culture and the role groups within it
   (b) A knowledge of the functions and relationships among the schools and other institutions of the community
   (c) A knowledge of how home and community environment affect and differentiate learning styles

3. Cultural heritage/contemporary lifestyles
   (a) A knowledge of the cultural and historical development of the target culture, including influences of the generic culture
   (b) A knowledge of contemporary values, social and political activities, issues, and leaders in the target culture as they influence education

4. Personal awareness self-development
   (a) A knowledge of skills in interpersonal effectiveness and personal development
   (b) The ability to deal with conflict and confrontation
   (c) An awareness of self in relationship to one's own culture and to other cultures   169

The sociocultural awareness component is completely community based and incorporates field activities which will provide candidates with the opportunity to observe and directly experience life in the community of the culture they select. As the competencies listed above indicate, the candidates will become aware of the home and community context of culture. Candidates will also learn the cultural context of their own behavior.

Field experiences will provide opportunities for observation of and participation in current lifestyles of the target culture selected by candidates. Along with customs, attitudes, and values which are characteristic of the culture, candidates will observe family relationships and child-rearing practices.

The emphasis in this component is to provide skills that will enable candidates to communicate in a realistic manner with the target population and develop positive attitudes about people and their living styles.

Strong self-awareness in relation to one's own culture and to other cultures, combined with development of skills in interpersonal relations and communication, is also an important part of the sociocultural awareness component. Not only will these skills enable the candidate to communicate more effectively with the community, but they will provide a background for creating an environment in the classroom which will lead to pupils' achievement of improved skills in interpersonal relationships, self-development, and emergence of a positive self-concept.

Candidates will study the historical and cultural background of the target culture. Information gained about the cultural-historical heritage of the target culture will further enhance understanding of current community lifestyles and provide resources for selection of materials which will be culturally relevant to the children they will teach. In addition, candidates will learn about current values and issues in the target culture and will study them in terms of their relationship to education needs and policies.

CHCALT PHASE THREE—ORAL LANGUAGE AND ASSESSMENT TECHNIQUES

1. Communication and teaching vocabulary—The ability to conduct classroom and school activities in the target language and to communicate effectively with members of the community in the target language, as appropriate
2. Social function of language—A knowledge of the functions and variations of regional and social dialects within language systems and familiarity with dialect features
3. Linguistic characteristics—A knowledge of the linguistic features which comprise the target language and how they are contrasted with parallel features of Standard American English
4. Diagnosis of differences, dominance, and comprehension—The ability to diagnose and evaluate individual language learning needs and to utilize effective testing methods and procedures in a bilingual/bidialectal situation

Equipped with a multidisciplinary perspective of culture and actual experience in the life of the target community, candidates can achieve in phase three of the model a thorough understanding of the cultural and community context of pupils' language, and the role of language as a means of communication, transmittal of culture, and sociocultural identification.

Knowledge of the linguistic characteristics of the target language as compared to the characteristics of Standard American English (SAE) is a prerequisite to oral language assessment. As a further foundation for evaluation, candidates must know how to use the target language effectively and must be familiar with the form which that language takes in a given community. They must know the social characteristics of the language and be able to use the oral language of the target community in a manner which recognizes its sociolinguistic requirements.

These competencies will provide candidates with the ability to evaluate oral language performance of pupils in the target population, thereby determining dominance, degree of comprehension, and needs for language instruction. Candidates will then use these evaluations as a basis for classroom placement and individualized prescription. This component will further provide candidates with a positive attitude toward language differences and enable them to utilize the language children bring to school as a basis for expanding their pupils' linguistic ability and reinforcing a positive concept of self, home, and community through the children's language. Candidates will learn target-language vocabulary necessary for conducting class-room and school activities in the target language.

CHCALT PHASE FOUR—DIAGNOSTIC AND PRESCRIPTIVE STRATEGIES

1. Individualized instruction

   A knowledge of how individualized instruction accommodates different learning styles and how to use strategies of individualized instruction

2. Small groups and peer teaching

   (a) The ability to utilize paraprofessionals, community members, and community resources in the diversification of classroom strategies, the facilitation of individualized and group instruction, and other teaching

   (b) A knowledge of small group processes

3. Performance criteria

   The ability to establish realistic performance criteria in a bilingual/cross-cultural classroom

4. Relevant diagnosis

   The ability to use and devise criterion-referenced tests which are cul-turally and linguistically appropriate

5. Teaching strategies and relevant materials

   (a) The ability to use and devise instructional strategies which are cul-turally and linguistically appropriate for achievement of performance criteria

   (b) A comprehensive knowledge of recent research findings, available materials and curricula for bilingual/cross-cultural teaching tech-niques, and how to adapt and utilize these resources

6. Planning and program strategies

   (a) A knowledge of skills required to serve as a bilingual/cross-cultural resource agent

   (b) A knowledge of cross-cultural problems in educational measure-ment, educational research, use of educational research results to make policy decisions, and educational evaluation; and a knowledge of how to critique educational measurement and evaluation studies from an ethnoscientific point of view

This component allows candidates to translate knowledge and skills gained in the first three components into *specific* classroom strategies and activities. As the competencies listed above indicate, effective learning ex-periences for culturally and linguistically different children are based on individualized teaching strategies which can only be accomplished through a series of techniques designed for each individual child.

Individualized instruction is essential in providing learning experiences which will be meaningful for culturally and linguistically different children. Not only do these children come to school with a wide range of linguistic abilities and varying degrees of bilingualism or bidialectalism, but each individual child has his or her own set of learning styles which cannot be accommodated within a single method of instruction.

Candidates will apply their understandings of how home, community, and cultural and linguistic factors influence learning stages, abilities, and behaviors of children in order to gain skills in identifying these patterns in individual children.

In order to develop skills in adapting and devising materials for individualized instruction, candidates are provided with an opportunity to learn competency-based techniques in establishing performance criteria, designing diagnostic criterion-referenced tests, and developing instructional strategies based on these instruments which will provide meaningful and effective learning experiences for individual and group situations. Candidates will also become familiar with current research findings, and existing materials and curricula designed for the bilingual/cross-cultural classroom.

In addition to strategies for the classroom, candidates will learn about the components of bilingual/cross-cultural programs, skills needed to implement such programs, and how to involve community members in such programs. They will also acquire knowledge of educational measurement and research, and of cross-cultural problems in educational research. They will learn how to apply research information as well as how not to apply it in making their own educational decisions.

172

Conclusion

The model described above is, of course, not the only answer to multicultural education in teacher training. The salient features of the CHCALT model—strong emphasis on field-based activities, philosophical approach to the study of culture, sociocultural awareness, emphasis on oral language and assessment, and provision for culturally appropriate strategies for diagnosis and prescription—are offered as important areas to be reflected in any teacher-training program which is fully committed to providing a positive approach to culturally pluralistic education. In addition, the most important consideration in developing a program in multicultural education is taking steps to insure collaborative linkage among all sectors to be affected by the program.

REFERENCES

1 Rosner, Benjamin and Patricia M. Kay. "Will the Promise of C/PBTE Be Fulfilled?" *Phi Delta Kappan* 25, no. 5 (January 1974):290.

2 Ibid.

3 Engler, Robert. "Social Science and Social Conscience." In *The Dissenting Academy*, edited by Theodore Rozak. New York: Vintage Books, 1968, p. 186.

4 Smith, B. Othanel et al. *Teachers for the Real World.* Washington, D.C.: American Association of Colleges for Teacher Education, 1969.

5 Silberman, Charles. *Crisis in the Classroom*. New York: Random House, 1970.

6 Ibid., pp. 158-9.

7 Purpel, David E. and Maurice Belanger, eds. *Curriculum and the Cultural Revolution*. Berkeley, Calif.: McCutchan Publishing Corp., 1972 (No page given).

8 Arciniega, Tomás A. "The Myth of the Compensatory Education Model in Education of Chicanos." In *Chicanos and Native Americans. The Territorial Minorities*, edited by Rudolph O. de la Garza, Z. Anthony Kruszewski, and Tomás A. Arciniega. Englewood Cliffs, N.J.: Prentice-Hall, 1973, pp. 174-5.

9 Green, Thomas. *Educational Planning in Perspective*. Guilford, Surrey, England: Futures, Inc., IPC Science & Technology Press, Ltd., 1971, p. 27. Also referred to in Arciniega, "The Myth of the Compensatory Education Model," p. 174.

10 Coleman, James S. *The Concepts of Equal Educational Opportunity*. Washington, D.C.: U.S. Office of Education, U.S. Government Printing Office, 1966. Also referred to in Arciniega, p. 176.

11 Lau v. Nichols 414 U.S. 563 (1974); San Antonio Independent School District v. Rodriguez 411 U.S. 1 (1973); see also Serrano v. Priest 5 Cal 3rd 584, 487 P. 2nd 1241 (1971) for discussion of issues later decided in San Antonio School District v. Rodriguez.

12 Blosser, Dennis F. "Competency-Based Teacher Education and Principles of Evaluation." Unpublished manuscript. San Diego, Calif.: Institute for Cultural Pluralism, San Diego State University, 1973, p. 1.

13 Aragón, Juan. (Albuquerque: University of New Mexico) 1972: personal communication.

14 Arciniega, p. 180.

15 Mazón, M. Reyes. *CHCALT: A Design for Teacher Training in Multicultural Education*. Special Report, Institute for Cultural Pluralism. San Diego, Calif.: San Diego State University School of Education, 1974, pp. 4-10. The following discussion is based on a revised version of this paper.

173

BIBLIOGRAPHY

Carter, Thomas P. *Mexican Americans in School: A History of Educational Neglect*, New York: College Entrance Examination Board, 1970.

Jensen, Arthur R. "How Much Can We Boost I.Q. and Scholastic Achievement?" *Harvard Educational Review* 39. 1969.

Mazón, M. Reyes. *Oral Language Assessment: An Evaluation of a Modular Teacher Education Program*. A Teacher Corps Technical Assistance Project Report. San Diego, Calif.: Institute for Cultural Pluralism, San Diego State University, 1973.

Postman, Neal and Charles Weingartner. *The School Book*. New York: Delacourt Press, 1973.

CHAPTER 4

COMPETENCY-BASED TEACHER EDUCATION FOR MEXICAN AMERICAN STUDENTS

Ignacio Cordova
Professor, College of Education
University of New Mexico
Albuquerque, New Mexico

With Consultative Assistance from

Mari-Luci Jaramillo
Rupert Trujillo
College of Education
University of New Mexico
Albuquerque, New Mexico

174

A major responsibility of the American education system is to provide for all its citizens, regardless of ethnic or racial backgrounds, to share equally in the benefits of society. However, a recent Multilingual Assessment Project publication concludes: "public schools have not traditionally embodied the features of cultural democracy that would make this ideal a reality."[1]

Efforts to solve education problems related to minorities have left educators talking in circles. College and university administrators and faculty place the blame on public schools and teachers, teachers blame administrators and universities, parents fault public schools, and the general public blames parents.

Teacher preparation programs in the U.S. have traditionally been guided by certain common purposes which aim to help prospective teachers develop—

1. expertise in a teaching field,
2. an understanding of growth and development patterns of learners,
3. familiarity with learning processes,
4. knowledge of teaching strategies, and
5. a philosophy of education.

To achieve these objectives, prospective teachers usually must complete general education course requirements and pass a series of tests before admittance to a college of education. While completing the required arts and sciences courses, students take an introductory education course. Finally, their student teaching experience may be guided by views such as (a) teaching is an intuitive art and not a science that can be taught, or (b) inexperienced student teachers must be told exactly what to do.

This heretofore accepted paradigm has severe limitations and has come under heavy criticism. Critics of the education system have leveled charges of insensitivity to the needs of racial and ethnic minorities, of failure on the part of the profession to hold its membership accountable for the end product, of resistance to community inputs and needs, and of faculty assumptions upon which to base education.

Traditional Teacher Education and the Chicano

Traditionally, the dominant group has viewed the Chicano as an ahistoric people with a place in history reserved for them only when they have undergone some metamorphosis called "acculturation."[2] Schooling, as a subsystem of the larger society, has viewed the Chicano correspondingly.[3]

The melting pot view of equal education opportunities has meant that all children must be exposed to the same curriculum. Thus, culturally different learners usually found their training irrelevant because it was not based on needs or experiential background. In addition, culturally different learners had no alternative but to submit to the filtration process of acculturation. If they did not succeed in that process, typically the fault was placed on them for not taking advantage of the opportunity provided, rather than on the educational system for not *providing* equal opportunity.

Later, a second view assumed that individual learners would have different occupational futures and that equality of educational opportunity required provision of differential curricula for various careers. This conceptualization resulted largely in vocational training for minorities. Thus, equality of education could be achieved by channeling students into a vocational program which was expected to conform to their unique needs.

A third stage in the evolution of the concept of equal educational opportunity came with the Black challenge to the second notion. In *Plessy* v. *Ferguson* (1896) the Supreme Court announced a separate but equal doctrine predicated on the assumption that equality of treatment is accorded when the races are provided with substantially equal facilities.[4] Therefore, the notions of common curriculum and passive role for the school were reaffirmed. This meant that the acculturation posture of the school was reinforced and the culturally different learner was still not accorded any alternatives in obtaining an education.

The third stage ended in 1954 when the Supreme Court ruled that equal facilities and a common curriculum did not constitute equal educational opportunity.[5] In this case the Supreme Court articulated the "effects of schooling" concept. In essence, the court ruled that equality of educational opportunity depended on the effect of the school experience on the child.

One of the critical dysfunctions of traditional teacher education programs has been that they adhered to the pre-1954 view of educational opportunities. It has been 20 years since *Brown* v. *Board of Education*, yet only a handful of teacher education programs have been developed that systematically attempt to prepare teachers to provide specialized service to culturally different educational communities.

THE PATHOLOGICAL VIEW

Arciniega has taken another view of the school's response to culturally different learners with special emphasis on Mexican Americans. Arciniega contends that schools have wrongly viewed Mexican American group affiliation and the resultant lifestyle as pathological, presumably handicapping the students' educational achievement.[6] In that orientation, Chicanos are viewed as members of a distinct subcultural group, perpetuating handicapping deficiencies along generational lines. In sum, the student is seen as incompetent. The task of the school, then, is to eliminate cultural deficiencies. The general approach has been a values-dichotomy approach based on a culturally deterministic framework and posited in cultural-deficiency terms. Value dichotomies are seen as polar extremes, the Mexican American extreme being negative and the dominant culture being positive. The emphasis has been to move the culturally different learner from the negative to the positive extreme, generally through deliberate cultural impositions. Thus, compensatory education programs became important acculturation vehicles.[7]

As an alternative, the American Association of Colleges for Teacher Education (AACTE) has adopted a policy of recognizing cultural pluralism, enunciated in its position statement, *No One Model American,* based on a positive recognition of culturally different minorities. This statement poses an alternative to cultural homogenity—cultural pluralism.[8] It supports the notion that education should encourage qualitative expansion of existing cultures and their incorporation into the mainstream of American socioeconomic and political life.

One implication of such a statement for Chicanos is that it challenges the ahistoric view of Chicanos. It affords the opportunity to present an analysis, such as the following one developed by Romano:[9]

1. Chicanos do not view themselves as traditionally unchanging social entities, but rather as creators of sociocultural systems in their own right, including cooperatives, mutualist societies, political blocks, and international communication networks.
2. Chicanos view themselves as participants in the historical process of change and revolution, resulting in multiple mestizajes (racial mixtures), dialects, music, and personal interrelationships.

3. Chicano history is now seen as a continuous social engagement, the spurious concepts of resignation and fatalism notwithstanding.
4. The pervasive perception of the illiterate Mexican American is untenable, as illustrated by the fact that Mexican Americans have published over 500 newspapers in the Southwest from 1848 to 1950, as well as numerous other recent publications.
5. Chicanos have systems of rationality expressed in a viable sociocultural system.
6. Multiplicity of speech patterns, bilingualism, and a highly sophisticated humor that relies heavily upon metaphor and satire attest to the intellectual capabilities of Mexican Americans.

NEED FOR PLURALISTIC VIEW

A pluralistic view encourages exploration into the notion that Mexican American lifestyles are primarily functional adaptations to external conditions. Arciniega describes this as a "coper" type response to conditions imposed by the majority on the minority.[10] Thus, the focus has to be shifted from internal cultural or biological factors to *external* factors in order to understand minority-group social participation patterns and generally low achievement in school.

177

Culture has to be seen as both dynamic and adaptive. Lack of participation or development can then be better understood primarily by analyzing factors inherent in larger societal systems. Positive changes in the larger society should and would allow for positive changes in the adaptive structure of the culturally different group. In this view, Mexican Americans are capable of developing positive adaptations as more open conditions evolve. Public school systems organized according to this view differ significantly from the traditional acculturation orientation which attempts to correct nonexistent cultural deficiencies of Mexican American students. Public education then has the obligation to assist Mexican Americans and other culturally different learners. Such a system should concentrate on—

1. providing students with basic intellectual knowledge, skills, career guidance, and training; and
2. directly promoting changes in societal institutional structures in order to improve and secure opportunities for full participation by Mexican Americans and other culturally different groups in the society.

Educational programs which categorically give equal status to English and Spanish, along with the Mexican American and Anglo cultures, correspond to this view of the role of education. This view dictates structural and curricular changes which will promote bicultural programs to provide relevance for Mexican American and other culturally different learners, and equally benefit non-Chicano children. If Mexican American lifestyles and cultural contributions are to be accepted, and they *must* be if opportunities for equal education are to become reality, then attitudinal, normative, and cognitive changes in school and the dominant culture must take place.

Cultural differences must not only be legitimized but promoted as valuable human resources, much as we concern ourselves with preservation and cultivation of our natural resources. Ethnocentric educational viewpoints must be broadened to emphasize new alternatives and new learning behaviors. The task of multicultural education then becomes one of fashioning school environments where concepts of cultural differences do not become synonymous with differential status and inferiority. This means that educators and students must truly understand and genuinely accept cultural differences. Only under this condition will Mexican American and other culturally different learners feel they have a place in school, develop positive images of themselves, and acquire those skills previously outlined.

Competency-Based Teacher Education: An Overview

CBTE, coupled with the notion of cultural pluralism inherent in a multicultural education process, can have positive implications for the education of Chicanos. According to Weber and Cooper,[11] three criteria may be used to determine competency on the part of teacher candidates:

1. Knowledge criteria—to assess cognitive understanding
2. Performance criteria—to assess teaching behavior
3. Product criteria—to assess ability to teach by examining achievement of pupils already taught

CBTE can be successful if certain of its philosophical tenets are clearly developed—mainly cooperative development of a teacher education program, on-site appreciation, and extensive feedback. If programs are developed cooperatively by college of education faculty, community people knowledgeable about Chicano conditions, experienced teachers working with Chicanos, and students, effective performance criteria can be developed. Once students have demonstrated competency-based skills on campus for transfer to ongoing school situations, this cooperative process should be used to develop training packages for prospective teachers. With continuous professional feedback to student teachers, probabilities for effective classroom teaching are significantly improved. One approach to organizing these key elements involves defining the role of the effective teacher of Chicano children. Attention will be given to some of these elements in relation to implications for preparing teachers to work with Chicanos:

1. Competencies (knowledge, skills, behaviors) to be demonstrated are derived from conceptions of teacher roles. These are stated so as to make possible the assessment of teacher candidate behavior in relation to specific competencies, and are made public in advance. Through cooperative planning, available research, and ongoing research, teacher roles hypothesized to be effective with Chicanos need to be developed and made operational so that their effectiveness can be assessed and closely monitored. The feedback tenet promises continual modification, even beyond preservice preparation. The cooperative broad-based decision tenet promises inclusion of community/parental/student involvement in planning and programs.

2. CBTE uses candidate performance as primary evidence of competency. It takes into account evidence of candidate knowledge as relevant to planning for, analyzing, interpreting, and evaluating behavior. This philosophical tenet, coupled with that of individualized and personalized instruction, focus on exit competencies, and timeless progression, has positive implications for preparing teachers for service to Chicano communities. It promises an ideal opportunity for developing a more realistic and relevant base on which to build an effective teacher certification program. This implies that only prospective teachers who are effective with Chicano students would be certified. It also follows that as a result of their experience, prospective teachers would develop skills that would lead to more relevant evaluation procedures for Chicano students. Further, given that a training program focused on competencies, it seems logical to expect more relevant and effective training programs.

CBTE as a philosophy has great promise for increasing relevance in teacher preparation programs because it is closely allied to general notions inherent in emerging bilingual/bicultural programs. It provides an alternative to get us started on totally revamping teacher education, based on a positive cultural base. Furthermore, it can become a strong vehicle toward the development of hypotheses and action research so desperately needed in the field of Chicano education. The promise can be fulfilled, given a strong commitment to cultural pluralism.

179

A General CBTE Model for Training Teachers for Service to Chicano Communities

The model which follows is designed to take into consideration the points noted above. It would encompass two years to fit into a professional sequence and stresses the importance of collaboration. This model is built around several critical elements. First, we cannot stress strongly enough the necessity for representation and cooperation of personnel among the college of education, community, local school district, and student. This model promotes the active participation of the Chicano community, which historically has been excluded from participation in educational decisions affecting their lives. This exclusion has been the major cause for lack of relevance in programs. CBTE, and this model in particular, will be successful only if people knowledgeable about the Chicano community and committed to the notion of cultural pluralism are accepted as equal partners throughout the process. The role of community representatives will be to monitor preassessment, instruction, evaluation, and community activities for relevance and optimization. Local school district personnel will be primarily responsible for monitoring and advising the public schools. The instructional team will be responsible for planning and implementing the CBTE program. They must share the responsibility of supervision and remediation whenever this becomes necessary.

One other element critical to this model is preassessment. In the view of the authors, preassessment becomes the cornerstone for the instructional program. First, the criteria to be used both in preassessment and postassessment are developed by the instructional team, with careful attention to making sure that criteria are relevant and that a balanced program is developed in terms of skills levels and content areas. Preassessment is done by the instructional team, which makes sure that the student has ample input as to how assessment is accomplished and how it is used to develop an instructional program.

The five phases outlined in the model constitute the development of specified areas. These areas become strands that do not end with the completion of that phase, but continue to serve as an undergirth for subsequent phases.

PHASE I

Self-Awareness

Central Thematic: Value Clarification

1. What are values?
2. Why are values?
3. How are values developed?
4. What are *my values*?
5. What are my *value priorities*?
6. Why do I hold these values?
7. How did I develop these values?
8. What do these values make me do?

Preassessment (By instructional team)

1. Community input
2. Role-play situation
3. Locally made test
4. Locally made attitude scales
5. Preassessment interview

Activities

1. Readings in value development
2. Readings in attitude formation
3. Readings in attitude/value assessment
4. Readings in culture/socialization
5. Sensitivity group
6. Therapy groups (t-groups)
7. Encounter groups (counter groups)
8. Role playing
9. Value listing
10. Reality testing

Laboratory (Exit)

1. Sensitivity lab
2. T-groups
3. Resource
4. Simulation
5. Microteaching

Education Seminar
1. Culture-based instruction
2. Competencies for self-learning

PHASE I

The thematic thrust of Phase I is value clarification of the prospective teacher. One of the most significant factors related to teacher preparation worthy of consideration involves processes which will allow potential teachers to acquire the sensitivity to enable them to respect, understand, and appreciate others as well as themselves.

We spend a lot of time talking about understanding "those minorities," but the crux of the problem does not lie with the minorities. Rather it lies in the questions: "Who am I?, How did I get to be what I am?, and Where am I going?" In short, before we can understand others we must understand ourselves.

People hold values, most of them unconscious and unverbalized, and behave in certain ways because of them. Yet few of us are provided opportunities which allow us to consciously define our values and, therefore, many of us go through life without ever realizing exactly what our values are. If we know what values we hold, we seldom find it necessary to go through the process of examining what rationale, if any, undergirds them. Why do we value Standard American English (SAE) and classify the dialect spoken by Blacks as nonstandard? Children who speak a language other than English adhere to the unconsciously learned grammatical rules and logic of their language in the same way as children who speak SAE. Any educator who interferes with the child's language situation may create for that child, regardless of good intentions, painful social and psychological problems.

Phase I focuses on helping prospective teachers identify what their values are, recognize their priorities, realize how they develop their values, and identify patterns of behavior associated with these values. The general competencies to be developed during this phase follow. Through acquisition of these competencies, the prospective teacher will be able to—

1. identify ways of finding out what his/her values, attitudes, and feelings are (self-assessment techniques);
2. identify and explain what values, attitudes, and feelings are and how they are developed;
3. explain what roles values and attitudes play in determining behavior;
4. identify his/her values, attitudes, and feelings;
5. identify his/her value priorities and provide a rationale for them;
6. identify ways he/she expresses these values, attitudes, and feelings;
7. identify and explain what verbal and nonverbal behaviors he/she pursues in order to protect or promote these values and attitudes;
8. identify and explain how and why he/she developed these values, attitudes, and feelings; and

9. identify and explain the culture base of learning in his/her life experiences.

Preassessment. Preassessment for Phase I should be done by an instructional team that includes college of education personnel, community personnel, and local public school personnel. People involved in preassessment should focus on how these criteria relate to adequacy and fit into their particular domains. Suggested modes for preassessment are: role-playing situations, attitude scales, locally developed tests, and preassessment interviews. The prospective teachers, as well as the assessment team, must know the criteria in advance. They must also know that these will serve as exit criteria as well. The results of this assessment then become the basis for preparing learning activities for developing or strengthening inadequate competencies. The prospective teacher must be given ample opportunity to help design activities and formulate ways for demonstrating competency.

Activities. Possible activities that are appropriate as learning experiences and that can be developed as alternative modes are:

1. Readings in value development
2. Readings in attitude formation
3. Readings in attitude/value assessment
4. Readings in culture/socialization
5. Sensitivity groups
6. Therapy groups (t-groups)
7. Encounter groups
8. Role playing
9. Value listing
10. Reality testing—seeing how teacher candidate behaves in real situations
11. Force, field analysis
12. Formal lectures
13. Discussions

Opportunities to engage in these or other activities must be made available. One way would be a values laboratory where regularly scheduled activities could be held, such as lectures, films, t-groups, discussions, etc. Opportunities to develop these competencies and demonstrate them with/to peers before attempting to exit can be dealt with here.

When the student feels she/he is ready to demonstrate these capabilities she/he can appear before assembled examiners: college of education personnel, community personnel, practicing teachers, and other interns. These examiners should also be ready and able to give the student feedback and prescribe modifications and remediation.

Education Seminar. One large area of value clarification should deal with education. The self-awareness phase should deal with questions of self-conception of education as well as values, attitudes, and feelings about what education is, what it does, and how it happens. During this phase students should be able to identify—

1. what they think education is,
2. what the functions of education are—for society and from an individual perspective,
3. their own life experiences and what they learned from them (culture-based instruction),
4. how to assess their own learning competencies, and
5. what their learning competencies are.

PHASE II

Other-Awareness

Central Thematic: Identification of other groups, other indivduals, and other values or lifestyles

1. What other groups exist?
2. What are their values?
3. What priorities do they hold?
4. Why did they develop these values, attitudes, and feelings?
5. How did they develop them?
6. What behaviors do they engage in association to these values?

Preassessment (College of education [COE] personnel, public school personnel, community)

1. Locally made test
2. Formal presentation
3. Paper/study
4. Preassessment interview
5. Role playing (simulation)

Activities

1. Readings
2. Observations
3. Community service organization internships
4. Formal presentations
5. Foster homes
6. Study of community (action research)
7. Community activities

Laboratory (Cultural Center, on site)

1. Lectures
2. Guidance
3. Demonstration (cultural)
4. Assessment/prescription
5. Microtesting
6. Simulation
7. Sensitivity session
8. Discussions
9. Resource people

Education Seminar
1. Chicano education problem
2. Chicano culture-based instruction
3. Chicano learning styles/resources
4. Integrative activities

PHASE II

Phase II is an extension of Phase I. Its focus is on other groups, other individuals, and other value orientations, with the purpose of exposing prospective teachers to their clients—in this case, the Chicano community. The general competencies to be developed here are the abilities to—

1. identify other groups that exist in the community, including subgroups within the Chicano culture, prominent familiar organizations, religions, and groups such as the Brown Berets, LULAC,* etc.;
2. identify and be able to use models, techniques, and tools appropriate in analyzing or studying groups and communities;
3. identify and explain lifestyles of these groups;
4. identify and explain values, attitudes, and priorities of these groups;
5. identify and explain why and how these groups developed their lifestyles and values; and
6. identify and explain behavior associated with these values.

Preassessment. Preassessment should be a cooperative venture designed by college of education personnel, community people knowledgeable about the Chicano community, and public school people including Chicano students. Preassessment can be either formal or informal, consisting of a prepared presentation, written test, or interview.

Preassessment should serve primarily to find out what competencies the student already possesses, and to determine what competencies he/she needs to develop and/or strengthen. The assessment team then utilizes this knowledge to help the prospective teacher develop learning experiences for meeting the exit criteria.

Activities. Some activities appropriate for this phase include—

1. readings about the Chicano culture, including history, literature, sociological studies, anthropological studies, etc.;
2. observations—community analysis and studies about work in community organizations, youth clubs, school recreation programs, community centers, etc.;
3. work in social agencies—juvenile probation, social services, etc.;
4. formal lectures;
5. visits/discussions with community people;

184

*LULAC is an acronym for League of United Latin-American Citizens, with national headquarters at 400 1st St., N.W., Suite 716, Washington, D.C. 20001.

6. participation in community/familial activities—fiestas, bautismos, funerales, matanzas,* etc; and
7. living with a community family.

Cultural Center. The cultural center phase should be primarily field based in the Chicano community. A cultural center (laboratory) can be established on campus (but ideally it should be out in the community), where regularly scheduled activities are going on for students who might want to participate. The physical, social, and psychological arrangement should display and be oriented toward the Chicano lifestyle, culture, and talents of the local community. Local people should form an integral part of the instructional staff and activities during this phase. Local historians, artists, crafts specialists, and residents should provide prospective teachers with firsthand knowledge, feelings, and attitudes of the community lifestyle and culture. The center should be the focus for other activities that build on Phase I self-awareness competencies, activities that assist the teacher candidate to understand the lifestyles, values, attitudes, and feelings of the Chicano student and the Chicano community. Some possible activities and functions of the center might be—

1. lectures or presentations by staff and local people,
2. discussions,
3. films,
4. sensitivity sessions,
5. media laboratory, and
6. resource depository.

This center should also provide a laboratory for practice of competencies with peers and other local people before trying them out in a classroom or real community situation. Further, it can be used as a guidance center for the instructional team to assess competencies and provide feedback.

Chicano Education Seminar. An integrating seminar would be a constituent part of this model. Another large area of awareness prospective teachers should focus on is education. The general issues and competencies developed here are—

1. values, attitudes, feelings, and priorities about education within these groups;
2. experiences with schools, and education of these communities;
3. culturally based education, learning, modes, experiences;
4. alternative modes of learning and teaching; and
5. problem areas and issues in Chicano education.

---

*A *matanza* usually occurs at the time of important family celebrations and involves the killing and eating of a pig or other animal.

PHASE III

Learning Environments: Interaction

Central Thematic: Learning Environments

    1. Formal organizational structures
       (a) Self-contained, departmentalized
       (b) Open classrooms
       (c) Individualized instruction
       (d) Social-theory learning centers
       (e) Team teaching
       (f) Traditional
    2. Organizational climates
    3. Interaction skills: formal, informal
       (a) Teacher-child
       (b) Child-child
       (c) Adult-adult

Preassessment (Cooperative)

    1. Cognitive assessment—written/oral
    2. Analysis task
    3. Simulation
    4. Active participation

Activities

    1. Readings
    2. Observations
    3. Role playing
    4. Lectures
    5. Sensitivity groups
    6. Practicums

Laboratory

    1. Formal lectures
    2. Sensitivity groups
    3. Role playing
    4. Video/microteaching
    5. Reading materials
    6. Resources

Seminar

    1. Learning environments and Chicano lifestyles
    2. Learning environments and Chicano learning styles
    3. Learning environments and Chicano interaction styles
    4. Integrative activities

PHASE III

Phase III deals with development of interaction skills, both in a formal structure and in an informal setting. Now that student teachers know themselves and the Chicano community, they need to know the school structure and how these different organizational structures affect interaction. Phase

III should provide the opportunity to study interaction processes firsthand, in real classroms and schools. The following are competencies to be developed during this phase:

1. Teacher candidates are bilingual (Spanish-English) in order to carry out classroom instruction.
2. Teacher candidates will be able to analyze the organizational climate of schools (in terms of open-closed) and behaviors exhibited by organizational participants.
3. Teacher candidates will be able to identify and explain teacher classroom interaction patterns in traditional self-contained rooms, departmentalized rooms, open classrooms, individualized instruction, and social-theory learning centers.
4. Teacher candidates will be able to explain pupil interaction patterns in the classroom, both teacher-pupil and pupil-pupil.
5. Teacher candidates will be able to identify and utilize appropriate interaction assessment models, tools, and techniques (i.e., Flanders interaction technique, sociograms).
6. Teacher candidates will be able to use appropriate verbal interaction classroom skills, such as—
   (a) listen to their pupils,
   (b) give their pupils a chance to talk,
   (c) provide clear and explicit direction in both languages,
   (d) ask questions at all levels,
   (e) use appropriate community language,
   (f) select tone of voice appropriate to different settings,
   (g) guide their pupils to express feelings and emotions verbally,
   (h) guide their pupils to formulate appropriate questions,
   (i) formulate answers to pupil questions, and
   (j) understand morphology, structure, and meaning of their pupils' language.
7. Teacher candidates will be able to identify and respond appropriately to their pupils' nonverbal language, as in the—
   (a) use of appropriate gestures,
   (b) use of appropriate social distance,
   (c) use of appropriate eye contact,
   (d) use of appropriate facial expressions,
   (e) use of appropriate body expressions,
   (f) use of appropriate modes of dress,
   (g) use of appropriate greetings such as handshakes, and
   (h) knowledge of cultural history.
8. Teacher candidates will be able to establish social and physical settings to elicit desired appropriate responses from students.

Preassessment. Preassessment can be of three general types, depending on competencies being assessed. First, there can be a written/oral assessment, such as a pretest for knowledge of organizational climates, or identification of existing modes of assessing interaction. Second, a task performance can be used, such as an actual analysis of organizational climate. Third, preassessment can be accomplished by observation of the prospective teacher in actual situations, judging how well the candidate can read and respond to nonverbal language, or use appropriate language intonation. Preassessment must take all the cultural knowledge, both verbal and nonverbal, into consideration. Therefore, the community people familiar with these aspects of Chicano culture must be depended on for guidance in the assessment process. Focus on real situations is necessary, because in many cases it takes the physical and social setting to adequately elicit subconscious attitudes, values, and feelings. This is particularly true in the affective area where it is hard to measure and be suggestive.

Activities. Some suggested activities appropriate for this area are—

1. readings in language development;
2. readings in sociology of language focused on Chicano experiences;
3. participant observation for interaction activities in both schools, classrooms, and homes of Chicano children;
4. formal lectures and presentations;
5. discussions with teachers who are sensitive to Chicano students;
6. school experiences;
7. sensitivity groups utilizing Chicano students and Chicano parents; and
8. role playing.

Informal interaction skills are as important as formal language skills. Informal organizational structures are as important as formal organizational structures. Importance must be given to activities that promote developmental skills of interaction in informal settings and skills of analysis which cut through informal organizations.

Interaction Laboratory. An on-campus laboratory must be provided where ongoing activities are scheduled for students—lectures, t-groups, demonstrations, discussions. These need not be required, but resources should be available to students at their request. Opportunities must be made available for them to practice, discuss, and receive feedback for continual direction. Some exit performances may be tested out in this laboratory, others may be tested in real classroom situations.

188

PHASE IV

Assessment

Central Thematic: Assessment of pupil behavior-teacher behavior
1. Child growth and development
2. Learning theory

3. Learning styles
4. Assessment tools, techniques
5. Diagnostic evaluations
6. Research design
7. Data analysis/interpretation
8. Action research

Preassessment

1. Cognitive aspect—oral/written
2. Instrument development
3. Instrument application
4. Data interpretation
5. Remediation (data utilization)

Activities

1. Readings, learning modules
2. Observations
3. Peer teaching
4. Simulation
5. Test construction
6. Action research

Laboratory (assessment)

1. Formal presentations
2. Simulation
3. Microteaching
4. Reading materials
5. Skills practice

Seminar

1. Integrative ideas (application of Phase IV to Chicanos)
2. Modification of assessment instruments to Chicanos
3. Discussion of assessment and Chicanos

PHASE IV

Phase IV deals with pupil behavior in general, and as it relates to learning behavior specifically. Focal points of this phase are child growth and development, learning theories, and assessment of learning behavior. The general competencies to be developed during this phase will serve to help students—

1. identify and explain child growth and development characteristics and patterns as they apply to Chicano youngsters;
2. identify and explain various learning theories as they apply to Chicano youngsters;
3. identify and explain learning styles of Chicano youngsters;
4. design research activities to test hypotheses regarding Chicano pupil learning styles;

5. identify, select, and utilize appropriate evaluation instruments for Chicano students;
6. design appropriate instruments for diagnosis of Chicano learner behavior;
7. collect and qualify data from appropriate instruments; and
8. interpret data and utilize it as a diagnostic sequence.

Very little has been done in developing models, tools, and techniques for studying Chicano pupil behavior. Consequently, the authors feel that what is now available should be utilized primarily as hypotheses to be tested. Teachers must, therefore, possess adequate research skills to be able to interpret existing information to draw hypotheses, and to formulate appropriate activities to test these hypotheses.

Preassessment. Preassessment as well as assessment of exit performance can be achieved in a variety of ways, depending on the competency under review, such as formal written or oral examinations. Utilization of assessment instruments can be evaluated through actual development, application, and interpretation of such tools in either simulated or actual situations.

Activities. Activities appropriate for this phase are limitless. Some suggested activities are—

1. readings in the areas of child growth and development, learning theories, test development, assessment, etc.;
2. observations in actual classrooms and home settings;
3. lectures and formal presentations on germane subjects;
4. discussion groups;
5. peer teaching sessions;
6. simulated experiences;
7. actual experiences in test construction, test giving, interpretation of data, and diagnosis of learning behavior; and
8. design and implementation of activities research.

Activities must be formulated so that emphasis is given to field-based experiences. Opportunities for observation must be provided to test various learning theories, child-growth theories, and development theories in actual settings, both in the classroom and at home. Assessment techniques and tools must first be learned on site and then implemented in real situations. Feedback must be continuous and modifications ongoing.

Assessment Laboratory. A laboratory experience is included in this phase. This laboratory can be used to provide formal presentations, small-group sessions, activities in assessment, test construction, test-administered data interpretation, peer-learning activities, etc. Once activities are designed in this laboratory and a student practices the skill, it can then be moved on site. Microteaching with videotaping and feedback would be ongoing. Remediation sessions at student request or mutually agreed upon by teacher and student can occur here.

Organizing Teaching Skills—Delivery Modes

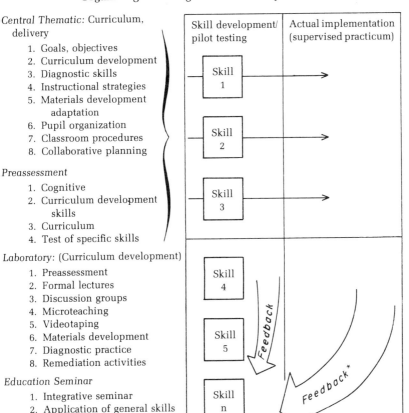

Central Thematic: Curriculum, delivery
  1. Goals, objectives
  2. Curriculum development
  3. Diagnostic skills
  4. Instructional strategies
  5. Materials development adaptation
  6. Pupil organization
  7. Classroom procedures
  8. Collaborative planning

Preassessment
  1. Cognitive
  2. Curriculum development skills
  3. Curriculum
  4. Test of specific skills

Laboratory: (Curriculum development)
  1. Preassessment
  2. Formal lectures
  3. Discussion groups
  4. Microteaching
  5. Videotaping
  6. Materials development
  7. Diagnostic practice
  8. Remediation activities

Education Seminar
  1. Integrative seminar
  2. Application of general skills to Chicano situation
  3. Remediation

PHASE V

Phase V is designed around organizational skills for teaching. The primary focus is curriculum assessment, curriculum development, and delivery modes. Competencies such as the following will be experienced during this phase:

1. Developing appropriate curriculum for Chicano students for whatever age level
2. Developing, selecting, and specifying goals and objectives appropriate to the needs, interests, and abilities of Chicano students

---

*Feedback into remediation activities occurs at both points.

3. Learning skills needed to diagnose the needs, interests, and capabilities of Chicano students as dictated by specified objectives
4. Developing and/or selecting appropriate instructional strategies based on teacher candidate's diagnosis to carry out specified objectives
5. Selecting and developing materials to carry out selected instructional strategies
6. Organizing pupils for implementing teacher candidate's instructional strategies
7. Developing classroom procedures and routines to carry out selected instructional strategies
8. Collaborating with students and other adults in planning

The first focus of Phase V is curriculum. We do not know what curriculum is best for the Chicano communities. We do not know what objectives will meet the needs of Chicano students. Chicano students and communities are highly pluralistic culturally. For these reasons prospective teachers must have the analytical and assessment skills to develop and modify objectives that are appropriate to the Chicano kids *they are working with.* Second, they must have enough subject knowledge and curriculum development skills to formulate learning packages to fulfill these objectives. Third, prospective teachers must develop delivery modes that are appropriate to the children they are working with.

The first part of Phase V deals with providing prospective teachers with knowledge of curriculum assessment and curriculum development skills. The second part of Phase V focuses on developing delivery or instructional skills. These are specifically isolated, extrapolated, and finally implemented in real settings. The third part deals with skills to bring these phases together, coordinate skills, and implement them in a real classroom.

Preassessment. Preassessment activities will be much like those detailed in the previous section. A member who is thoroughly knowledgeable about the Chicano community, culture, and lifestyle is necessary. This person should monitor activities in order to assure that prescribed criteria, skills, and learning packages are relevant to Chicano student school experiences, and that the activities will enhance the effectiveness of instruction for Chicano pupils.

Activities. The following are appropriate activities for this phase:

1. Readings related to curriculum, objectives, diagnosis, and instructional planning
2. Curricular analysis of existing curriculum in schools for Chicanos
3. Classroom observations in Chicano schools
4. Discussion with students, teachers, parents, and peers
5. Formal presentations by instructional team members and resource persons
6. Materials development workshops
7. Microteaching and peer learning activities

8. Actual classroom experience

Curriculum Laboratory. A curriculum laboratory must be provided where preassessment and exit performances can be evaluated. Activities and resources germane to this phase can be accomplished here as well. Microteaching and videotaping activities are a must to provide practice and feedback before actual on-site implementation.

Summary

The model presented in the previous pages is intended as a general one. Obviously it needs greater expansion and specificity. It is intended to be sufficiently flexible to incorporate cultural, organizational, and other factors consistent with the needs of Chicanos.

An extensive research component is needed to evaluate and monitor the workings of such a program. Continuous feedback from students, community people, local school-district people, and teacher trainers must be utilized to continuously formulate and test new hypotheses, in order to modify both competencies and the instructional program accordingly.

REFERENCES

1 Multi-Lingual Assessment Project. Riverside Component. *Culturally Democratic Learning Environments: A Cognitive Styles Approach.* Riverside, Calif.: Systems and Evaluation (No year or page given).

2 Romano, Octavio Ignacio. "The Anthropology and Sociology of the Mexican American: The Distortion of Mexican American History." *El Grito* 2, no. 1 (1963): 14.

3 Cordova, Ignacio R. "Cultural Differences and Implications for Education of the Spanish American." Santa Fe, N.M.: New Mexico State Department of Education, 1973, p. 11.

4 Ibid., and Plessy v. Ferguson 163 U.S. 537 (1896) .

5 Brown v. Board of Education 347 U.S. 483 (1954).

6 Arciniega, Tomás A. "The Myth of Compensatory Education in the Education of Chicanos." Unpublished manuscript. San Diego, Calif: School of Education, San Diego State University, 1973, p. 11.

7 Cordova, Ignacio R. "Cultural Differences and Implications," p. 13.

8 American Association of Colleges for Teacher Education, Commission on Multicultural Education. "No One Model American." *Journal of Teacher Education* 24, no. 4 (Winter 1973): 264-5. The statement has been printed separately and is available from AACTE.

9 Romano, Octavio Ignacio. "Social Science, Objectivity and the Chicanos." *El Grito* 4, no. 1 (1970): 13-14.

10 Arciniega, Tomás A. "The Myth of Compensatory Education," p. 13.

11 Weber, Wilford C., James Cooper, and Charles Johnson. "A Competency-based Systems Approach to Education." First chapter of *Designing Competency-based Teacher Education Programs. A Systems Approach.* Unpublished manuscript, 1971, as cited by Stanley Elam, *Performance-Based Teacher Education: What Is the State of the Art?* Washington, D.C.: American Association of Colleges for Teacher Education, 1971, p. 6.

PART IV

Prime Writer

Henrietta Whiteman (Southern Cheyenne)
Director, Native American Studies Program
University of Montana
Missoula, Montana

Associate Prime Writer

Rosella J. Covington
Project Director
Native American Cultural Institute
University of Montana
Missoula, Montana

Writer-Editors

Fount Holland
Director, Indian Intern Teacher Training Program
Northeastern Oklahoma State College
Tahlequah, Oklahoma

Donald Lemon
Director, Northern Plains Teacher Corps
University of North Dakota
Grand Forks, North Dakota

Patricia Locke
Director, Planning Resources in Minority Education
Western Interstate Commission on Higher Education
Boulder, Colorado

The Native American Perspective On Teacher Competencies:

"It is not necessary for necessary for eagles to be crows"

196

INTRODUCTION

Wisely observant of the world about them, the original proud possessors of this continent—tribal Native Americans—recognized diversity, not only of the winged peoples of the air, but, also, of the two leggeds—humankind. Furthermore, they recognized this diversity as an inalienable right, which they were ever ready to defend. The great Lakota leader, Sitting Bull, expressed sophisticated philosophy concerning diversity decades ago with this statement:

> I am a red man. If the Great Spirit had desired me to be a white man he would have made me so in the first place. He put in your heart certain wishes and plans, in my heart he put other and different desires. Each man is good in his sight. It is not necessary for eagles to be crows. Now we are poor, but we are free. No white man controls our footsteps. If we must die, we die defending our rights.[1]

It comes late to Indian thought for society today in the twentieth century to begin a thrust for diversity of cultural experience in the educational system of this nation, a nation built by peoples of differing national origins. This concept is couched in the terms of multicultural education, and educators are grappling with a beginning. What is that beginning?

We begin by recognizing that each individual is unique, has worth, has dignity, has integrity and the host of other qualities that make up his or her self in the point of beginning. Beyond this, we must explore the commonality of individual tribes of American Indians and of all peoples. It goes without saying that each individual and each of the expanding groups is evolving. Thus, to develop a complete and accurate list of competencies for teachers of Native Americans is a theoretic and practical impossibility. Nevertheless, a set of competencies can be suggested, appropriately alterable for individuals and groups, which will address itself to the needs of culturally diverse peoples and especially to the American Indian.

General Competencies for All Teachers

Approaching the task of developing competencies for teachers from the position thus stated permits teacher competencies to be categorized. The following categories and subcategories, developed for the Northern Plains Teacher Corps Program at the University of North Dakota, Grand Forks, directed by Don Lemon, are suggested as appropriate, in a general way, for all teachers:

1. Career Education
   a. Surveying and identifying local resources
   b. Career counseling
   c. Manual skill experience

      d. Application
  2. Clinical Experience
      a. Rapport with staff/children
      b. Management of the learning environment
      c. Motivation/reinforcement/feedback
      d. Professionalism
  3. Community-Based Education
      a. Utilization of community resources
      b. Community involvement
      c. Health
  4. Curriculum Content Areas
      a. Fine arts
      b. Language arts/reading
      c. Mathematics
      d. Physical education
      e. Practical arts
      f. Science
      g. Social studies

  5. Diagnostic/Prescriptive
      a. Instrument selection
      b. Assessment instrument development
      c. Learning styles assessment
      d. Special education diagnosis
  6. Individualization of Instruction
      a. Learning cycle
      b. Diversified learning activities
      c. Grouping patterns
  7. Interdisciplinary Approaches
      a. Human growth and development
      b. Philosophical development
      c. Self-actualization of the learner
  8. Multicultural dimensions
      a. Cultural self-awareness
      b. Cultural awareness of the child

Within each area of competency there will be competencies appropriate for every teacher competencies appropriate for each teacher who has an Indian child in his/her classroom, and competencies appropriate to specific tribal groups.

Thirteen Broad Concepts of Competencies

The development of competencies for the Indian world and for a tribal group would best be developed by Indian educators and Indian peoples. Without full access to those populations, it seems reasonable to develop a catalog of broad concepts with the understanding that the specific competencies will be developed by the Indian community. Thirteen broad concepts of competencies were thus developed by the writer-editors of this section, which it is believed are necessary for teachers of culturally diverse children. Those broad concepts of teacher competencies are as follows:

1. A teacher must develop skills to get families involved in the classroom.
2. A teacher must be able to identify teaching resources such as materials, community persons, career opportunities, historical information, and economic data which are appropriate for teaching children of the identified cultural group.
3. A teacher must be able to recognize cultural differences as strengths rather than weaknesses.
4. A teacher must develop skills in the language variances of the learner.
5. A teacher must be prepared to create and teach curricular materials that are determined to be important to the identified cultural group of the learner.
6. A teacher must develop the ability to teach with honesty and integrity in all curricular areas, particularly in the discipline of the history of an identified cultural group.
7. A teacher must demonstrate a knowledge of the pervasive contributions that diverse cultural groups have made and are making to present-day society.
8. A teacher must demonstrate a knowledge of the vast linguistic and cultural differences among the diverse cultures of the United States and what economic, philosophical, political, and sociological forces have brought about these vast differences.
9. A teacher must demonstrate an understanding of the Civil Rights Act as it pertains to all groups.
10. A teacher must demonstrate an understanding of the causes of minority resentment toward the dominant society.
11. A teacher must demonstrate a knowledge of why minority persons have found themselves locked into the cycle of poverty.
12. A teacher must understand that culturally different youth have respect for and respond to family authority; however, response by learners to school authorities tends to be fearful. The tendency is to withdraw when faced with school authority.
13. A teacher must be able to relate to the children and parents in terms of his/her understanding of the mores, customs, attitudes, values, and expectations of the home community.

Legislative Recognition of Diversity

Broad concepts of teacher competencies have been defined, but it is recognized that they serve as but a base for the development of specific competencies. It is expected that specific competencies will be defined at the local level by tribal peoples themselves to more fully implement the concept of Indian self-determination in the area of education. This approach is mandatory in view of the policy of the Bureau of Indian Affairs, (BIA), functioning for the United States Government as the trustee for the American Indian. BIA policies have vacillated between two extremes—paternalism and complete withdrawal of federal services, i.e. termination. This history of oppression has resulted in the psychological need for Native Americans to determine their immediate objectives and future goals. Succinctly, Native Americans must be allowed to determine their own destiny through the implementation of self-determination, affirmed to be the Indian policy of the Nixon administration. This stated policy of self-determination is crucial to generating effective programs in view of the heterogeneity of the approximately 300 tribes that comprise the group commonly referred to as Native Americans. Any program must, of necessity, involve local tribal communities, for it is only they who know their needs and concerns.

It is hereby emphasized that despite the obvious failure of the United States Government in exercising its trust responsibility to the American Indian, the federal-Indian relationships must be maintained. American Indians are unique in that they are the only group that functions in a semi-sovereign status to the United States Government, and are the only peoples specifically mentioned in the Constitution of the United States. This unique status should in no way be construed as indicating incompetence; rather it emphasizes the need for providing meaningful educational experiences specifically called for in many of the 400 treaties entered into with various American Indian tribes in return for land, which now comprises what is referred to as the United States of America.

200

The Indian Education Act of 1972 points to the need for alleviating the low quality of education for the indigenous peoples of this nation.[2] This type of legislation is a hallmark for Indian education at the federal level. This has been equalled by State of Montana legislation, which sets a precedent for other states in the union regarding Indian education. This Montana legislation requires—

> . . . . American Indian Studies to be part of the educational background of public school teaching personnel employed on or in public schools located in the vicinity of Indian reservations where the enrollment of Indian children qualifies the school for federal funds for Indian education programs, and . . . .[3]

encouraged American Indian studies as part of the educational background of all school personnel employed in the state.

The Montana 43rd Legislative Assembly also adopted a joint resolution of the Senate and the House of Representatives, instructing ". . . the Board of Public Education and the Board of Higher Education to devise a master plan for enriching the background of all public school teachers in American Indian culture."[4]

Legislative mandates, such as the preceding two, recognize the necessity of teacher competencies in the area of American Indian education. Cultural diversity has also been recognized. The progress made by Indian leaders in Montana is only a beginning, but the example stands as a beacon light for Native American educators in other states where significant numbers of American Indians reside. Achieving such legislative direction, however, is not the end of the struggle to accomplish desirable Indian education in our schools. Mandates must be fulfilled with teacher training programs designed to produce teachers adequately prepared to carry out the intent of the law, which is to provide Native American learners with the kind of education fought for by Indian education leaders.

Indian Designed Pre- and In-service Training Programs

Schools of education have had ample opportunity in the past to meet the educational needs of Indian people, but have either refused or neglected to accept the responsibility. Now the task has been assumed and must continue to be given to the Native Americans themselves. Already, Indian educators in various sections of the country have designed and made operational programs to help satisfy the great need for specially trained teachers for Native American students. These programs can be considered as potential models by Indian communities and tribal leaders concerned with effecting teacher training reform in their local areas.

Two examples of preservice training models for Indian teachers are presented in position papers by Milo Kalectaca (Hopi) and Louise Miller (Yurok) which are included in this report. In each of these papers, the respective author is concerned with training teachers for competencies needed to adequately teach Indian learners. Both training models have been developed around the concept of competency-based teacher education (CBTE) which permits the spelling out of competence to be developed by teacher trainees and which allows for a high degree of accountability.

Another dimension of teacher training which must be considered is the inservice training of teachers who are now teaching in Indian schools but who lack the competencies for effectively working with Native American students. Models for retraining the inservice teacher have also been designed by Indian educators. One model which includes training components for both the preservice teacher and the inservice teacher has been developed at the Northeastern State College, Tahlequah, Oklahoma, and is currently being used in preparing teachers for schools with large enrollments of Cherokee students. Another model dealing exclusively with preservice training is the Native American Cultural Institute (NACI) at the University of Montana, Missoula, Montana. Working in cooperation with the NACI at Missoula is the Native American Studies Program which serves as a core for preservice training efforts.

PRESERVICE AND INSERVICE MODEL FOR TRAINING INDIAN TEACHERS

Fount Holland
Director, Indian Intern Teacher Training Program
Northeastern State College
Tahlequah, Oklahoma

The Northeastern Oklahoma State University model for training teachers of Indian students is a preservice-inservice design prepared cooperatively by representatives of the Cherokee Nation of Oklahoma, the Bureau of Indian Affairs, the Indian Division of the Oklahoma State Department of Education, and the University. Both the preservice and inservice components of the model operate in concert. However, an emphasis is placed on the preservice phase, with priority for participating in the model given to education students of Indian descent. Funds needed to support the model come from a federal grant, a Johnson O'Malley (JOM) contract,[5] and the University. The preservice component are financed primarily by the Education Professions Development Act (Teachers for Indian Children Program), while funds for the inservice component are provided by the Bureau of Indian Affairs with a Johnson O'Malley contract through the Indian Division of the State Department of Education. The University provides facilities, teaching faculty, and part-time administrative supervision (See Figure 1).

Preservice Training Component

With the exception of the Indian Studies Program which falls under the Office of Continuing Education and Special Programs, preservice activities are conducted by the University's Division of Education and Psychology. The Indian Studies Program consists of courses in Indian history, culture, art, rhetoric, literature, etc. A major in Indian studies has been established at the University. Students with an interest in Indian education are advised to take at least a minor in Indian Studies. During the professional education sequence, which is competency based, all students are exposed to units on various aspects of Indian education and those with a particular interest in this area do in-depth individualized study projects. The special seminars are conducted in connection with the in-field phase of preservice and will be explained later.

The in-field phase consists of 16 weeks of intern teaching in one of the several Johnson O'Malley rural elementary and secondary schools in North-eastern Oklahoma or in the BIA high school located near Tahlequah, home of the University. All the rural public schools used as intern teaching centers have an Indian enrollment ranging from 50 to 97 percent. This particular phase of the model is open only to student interns of at least one-fourth Indian descent with an interest in teaching in Indian schools. During the intern experience, which is competency based, each participant is provided a $75 per week stipend from an Education and Professional Development Act (EPDA) grant. The program is limited to 40 participants per year (20 interns for the fall term and 20 for the spring term). While interning under the supervision of a Johnson O'Malley teacher or a BIA teacher, each intern is required to develop units of study on some phase of Indian history, culture, or literature and to design each academic unit taught (math, home economics, physical education, etc.) so that it will be relevant to the Indian learners in the class.

While participants in the program are interning, frequent on-site visits are made by project staff members including the two codirectors and the curriculum specialist. The purpose of these visits is to observe the intern and to provide on-site training for the intern and the supervising teacher. In addition, each participant is required to attend 10 seminars on Indian education. Consultants for the seminars are selected from the Bureau of Indian Affairs office in Muskogee, Oklahoma, the Cherokee Tribe, the Cherokee Bilingual Center in Tahlequah, members of the Cherokee Community Organizations, and the University. Seminars topics include:

1. Orientation to the program and to Indian schools
2. Indian history and culture
3. Learning patterns unique to Indian students
4. Development of units of study and teaching materials
5. Counseling techniques in career awareness
6. Behavior patterns of Indian students and classroom management
7. Techniques for evaluating the academic progress of Indian students
8. Problems Indian students have assimilating into the school environment

Inservice Training Component

The inservice training component contains three phases—one for supervising teachers, another for teachers in Johnson O'Malley-supported schools, and a third for all teachers interested in Indian education. Each phase is coordinated with the preservice component so that all efforts in preparing teachers of Indian students will have some degree of uniformity. For example, the same techniques used in training Indian interns are used during the inservice effort but are restructured to better suit the needs of the inservice teacher.

Inservice training for teachers who serve as supervisors for the Indian interns is conducted in the field by staff members of the EPDA project. In addition, supervising teachers are required to attend one seminar each semester which is designed to improve their skills in teaching Indian students to better prepare them to work with interns.

Each semester, inservice training is provided for a minimum of 40 teachers employed in Johnson O'Malley-supported schools. This effort is financed by the Bureau of Indian Affairs office in Muskogee with a contract through the Indian Division of the Oklahoma State Department of Education. By means of a subcontract with the University, the Indian Division coordinates these inservice sessions, utilizing the staff of the EPDA Indian Intern Program. Two eight-week evening training sessions are held after school hours in one of the rural JOM-supported schools. One session is for teachers who have received little or no special training in Indian education and the second is an advanced session for those teachers who participated in the beginning session the semester before. The beginning session is devoted primarily to Indian awareness, history, culture, and communication skills. The advanced session is designed to help teachers acquire and increase skills in developing special materials for teaching Indian students.

204   The third phase of the inservice component is a week-long summer workshop held on the University campus. This workshop, financed by the University and the Consultative Center for Equal Education Opportunity at Oklahoma University, is a human relations workshop with an emphasis on conflict problems between Indian students and non-Indian teachers. Exact workshop design varies depending upon the needs and experiences of participants.

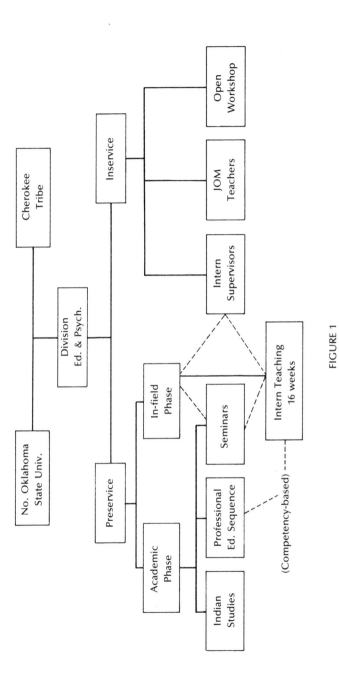

FIGURE 1

NORTHEASTERN OKLAHOMA STATE UNIVERSITY — CHEROKEE TRIBE
Preservice-Inservice Training Model
For Teachers of Indian Children

205

INSERVICE MODEL FOR TRAINING
PUBLIC SCHOOL TEACHERS
OF INDIAN STUDENTS

Rosella J. Covington
Project Director
Native American Cultural Institute
Native American Studies Program
University of Montana
Missoula, Montana

The Native American Cultural Institute (NACI) is a project federally funded by the Division of Equal Educational Opportunity, of the U.S. Office of Education.[6] The Native American Studies Program at the University of Montana, Missoula, has been the recipient of the Title IV teacher training program for the past three years and is funded for Fiscal Year 1975. The progam has four main objectives:

1. To sensitize school personnel in the service area, and to make them aware of the uniqueness of the American Indian student; to bring about an elimination of segregation; to bring about an awareness and recognition of the existing cultural gap; and to provide school personnel with some solutions and approaches to problems of Indian and non-Indian relationships by means of technical assistance and training

2. To develop new curricular techniques and materials for use in the desegregated classroom

3. To develop new administrative structures, counseling techniques, and bilingual/bicultural techniques for use in the desegregated school

4. To provide technical assistance for other school districts within the State of Montana relating to contents of the proposal or other desegregation processes

For Fiscal Year 1975, there are 15 participating school districts; 12 are located on or near the Blackfeet, Flathead, Fort Belknap, and Rocky Boy's Indian Reservations. Three urban school districts which have a large enrollment of Indian students are also participating.

A three-week Summer Institute is conducted each year for approximately 50 school personnel selected from the 15 school districts. The Institute is held on the University of Montana campus for two weeks, and one week is devoted to off-campus visits to four Indian Reservations—Blackfeet, Flathead, Fort Belknap, and Rocky Boy's. The Summer Institute concentrates on the first main objective previously stated. Any person who is employed by a target school district in the State of Montana could qualify for participation in the Summer Institute. This includes superintendents, principals, teachers, teacher aides, and school board members. During the Summer Institute, the staff of NACI conduct classes, small group discussions, and field trips. Consultants and several prominent Indian and non-Indian guest lecturers are utilized as instructors.

During the academic year, a follow-up program is implemented. The Institute participants and other school personnel in the target schools are involved in "on-site" inservice training. The follow-up activities include: (a) training in areas determined by project objectives and requests throughout the year; (b) workshops in the areas of counseling, school administration, curriculum development, and bilingual/bicultural education for participating schools; (c) observations of school personnel who participated in the three-week institute; (d) local education forums on areas of concern for specific schools; (e) training of local school staff on desegregation issues (by summer institute participants); (f) consultants being utilized as requested by participating schools; (g) development of curriculum materials for the schools in Montana by project staff and consultants; and (h) ongoing evaluation.

From past experience, it is anticipated that numerous school districts throughout the State of Montana, not included in this program proposal, may from time to time request assistance from the Native American Cultural Institute. This assistance is provided only during the follow-up phase of the project.

The failure to understand the Indian student has created a number of critical problems. These problems are found in areas such as cultural differences, psychology of the Indian student, the achievement gap, relevancy of the curriculum, bilingual problems, and the origin and expression of Indian conflict. The NACI staff recognizes that after one year's training of the school's personnel, all these problems will not be alleviated. However, an effort to alleviate them *is* being made.

REFERENCES

1 Armstrong, Virginia Irving. *I Have Spoken: American History Through the Voices of Indians.* Chicago: Swallow Press, 1971, p. 112.
2 Indian Education Act of 1972. Title IV of the Education Amendments of 1972 (Public Law 92-318).
3 State of Montana, 43rd Legislative Assembly, House Bill no. 342 (1973).
4 State of Montana, 43rd Legislative Assembly, Joint Resolution 60 (1973).

5 The Johnson O'Malley Act of Congress (1934) authorizes the Secretary of the Interior to enter into contracts with states to provide for the educational needs, medical attention, agricultural assistance and social welfare of American Indians. Since then, JOM contracts have come to be mainly concerned with Indian education. *(An Even Change,* Pamphlet [NAACP Legal Defense and Educational Fund, Inc., with the co-operation of the Center for Law and Education, Harvard University, 1971], p. 67.)

6 U.S. Civil Rights Act of 1964. Title IV, Section 404 (Public Law 88-352).

208

CHAPTER 1

HIGHER EDUCATION AND ITS IMPLICATIONS FOR AMERICAN INDIANS

Patricia Locke
Director, Planning Resources in Minority Education
Western Interstate Commission on Higher Education
Boulder, Colorado

I. Historical Background   209

Since 1930, the states have assumed increased responsibility for Indian education, aided by the provision of federal funds. The Indian people fear that the federal government may withdraw entirely from its special relationship to Indians. This fear continues to have a dominant influence on Indian reaction to changes in the extent, nature, and administration of federal programs.

In November 1966, two meetings were held in Denver, Colorado to discuss where responsibility for Indian education should be located within the federal government. Attending the first meeting were 18 tribal chairmen and members of tribal education committees. Attending the second meeting were college and university faculty who have conducted research on Indian problems, and teachers of Indian children. Indians expressed concern about the transfer of education from the Bureau of Indian Affairs (BIA) to the U.S. Office of Education. They were generally opposed to disruption of the traditional relationships and distrustful of fragmentation of Indian services within the federal government. Participants in the second meeting felt that educational programs should recognize the different problems of Indians in federal and public schools and should consider the readiness of local or state systems to provide educational services. The consensus at both meetings was that the BIA should be given time to carry out its new educational program before serious consideration would be given to a transfer of the educational function from one agency to another.

During the 1967 hearings on amendments to Public Law 89-10, the Elementary and Secondary Education Act of 1965, a report was prepared for the Subcommittee on Education of the Committee on Labor and Public Welfare. The report, called *Quality Education for American Indians: A Report on Organizational Location,* recommended that the BIA should retain the education function, working in close cooperation with the Office of Education (OE) of the Department of Health, Education and Welfare (HEW). It suggested that OE should review its programs to determine how to make these available to the greatest extent possible for the benefit of Indian children enrolled in federally operated schools. It recommended that education must be viewed as a single continuing process which ranges from preschool through adulthood. It stated that consideration should be given to supporting a center for graduate study of the languages, history, and culture of American Indians. The concept of Indian control and increased responsibility for education by Indian parents and tribal leaders was supported and recommended. The report also recommended that ways should be explored to encourage development of junior or community colleges on or near the larger reservations to facilitate opportunities for larger numbers of Indian children to receive higher education.

When Dillon S. Meyer became Commissioner of Indian Affairs, in May 1950, the BIA began a new epoch. As part of a great change in the basic organization of the Bureau, there was a further delegation of authority to area directors and an increase in their authority over superintendents. Commissioner Meyer stated that "the federal off-reservation education of Navajos is directed entirely toward the preparation of these children for permanent off-reservation employment. Indians are being provided . . . with adequate training programs to fit them for employment in skilled occupations off the reservations."

In 1955, the BIA launched a pilot program in adult education designed to make five tribal groups literate in English, and it supported legislation for a program of vocational training.* Yet, at the same time, it has eliminated or curtailed many activities which seem to involve vocational training. Arts and crafts projects were shut down or left to shift for themselves. Bureau guidance and support were stopped for the Qualla Cooperative at Cherokee, North Carolina; the Sequoyah weaving project in Oklahoma; and the pottery and weaving project at Pine Ridge, South Dakota.

II. American Indian Studies and Community Colleges

American Indians perceive education as a continuing process. Under optimum conditions, all parts of education should interrelate as the family and community interrelate. Education, from Head Start through elementary, secondary, and college levels, to adult and continuing education, is viewed as an interrelated instrument of social integration and mobility.

Under optimum conditions, elders and community leaders would help

---

*For statistics on BIA adult vocational grants, see Appendix E at the end of this chapter. Further data on BIA financial assistance appears in Appendices B and C.

college students from their tribes to prepare for the ultimate community service by defining group needs. College students would tutor and provide role models for secondary students. College students and secondary students would provide tutorial services and assume teacher aide roles in primary schools. Parents, family, and other adults would be involved in support roles at preschool and Head Start programs and would be supportive in community college programs. As involvement increases, commitment increases.

Perhaps the most immediate, pressing problem in the area of Indian education today is how to correct and reverse the discouraging history of failure in Indian postsecondary education. The attrition rate for Indian students during their first year of college stands at an astonishing 74 percent.** This figure points to a complete lack of success on the part of the nation's colleges in their educational programs for American Indians. Perhaps these Indian student push-outs are the symbolic miner's canary of the nation's educational system. Lack of financial support, inadequate counseling and guidance programs, and irrelevant curricula are due in part to a long-standing policy of coercive acculturation. The goals of American higher education to a very large degree are out of tune and in conflict with the Indian's psychological and philosophical frame of reference.

Postsecondary education for American Indians in the United States is education for displaced persons. That educational system is still a system devised for people who are non-Indian and who ascribe to the imported values and modes of behavior of European peoples. It is audacious to assume that this kind of majority education based on Judeo-Christian values will work for peoples of different value systems. It is audacious to assume that non-Judeo-Christian peoples should accept it or try to modify themselves to accommodate it.

There may be postsecondary education at Black colleges for Black students, taught and administered by Black people, but it is essentially the same kind of educational system that serves the dominant society.† There may be postsecondary education at American Indian community colleges for Indian students taught by Indian people, but even though some educational breakthroughs have been made, there is a pervading domination of accreditation by non-Indians who refuse to allow much variance in the sacrosanct European-imported educational system. Doesn't Indian postsecondary education at established and traditional colleges and universities usually mean that we are allowed some American Indian counselors to encourage us to hang in there so that we can compete with one another and with the majority society? Doesn't it mean that we are talent searched, upward bounded, and financial aided to learn to internalize and assimilate the "American" values of mercantilism, individualism, and acquisitiveness?

**For statistics on postsecondary Indian students, see Appendix D at the end of this chapter.

†Minority under-representation at the postsecondary level is detailed in Appendix A.

What does *innovative* mean in relation to minority postsecondary education? Should a whole new and different style of education be developed for those minority people who have been denied access but who aspire to traditional outcomes? Perhaps the need here is only for a wider door, and not for inconceivable new worlds of education.

Fundamental institutional changes have not been made. Institutions have only minutely expanded. A few Indian counselors and tutors have been hired. There has been some frantic activity to hire a few token Indian faculty members and to establish "Indian" programs by luring "scholastically qualified" students to the campus so that compliance in Affirmative Action Programs can be documented. As a result, we have fragmented Indian programs across the nation, with our few Indian faculty and students fighting lonely battles against the near impenetrable walls of majority educational systems.

The creative ferment now apparent in postsecondary education for American Indians may be the bravest step toward the inconceivable new world of education. American Indians can truly teach our guests on this continent ways of survival if we are to be allowed that opportunity.

This creative ferment that caused change in the Indian postsecondary education world occurred almost simultaneously in Alaska, Montana, Arizona, California, South Dakota, North Dakota, Wyoming, Oklahoma, New Mexico, Idaho, Minnesota, and Washington, D.C. Mini-repercussions have awakened tribes in neighboring areas.

AMERICAN INDIAN HIGHER EDUCATION CONSORTIUM

In October 1972, the Planning Resources in Minority Education Program of the Western Interstate Commission for Higher Education, in co-operation with the Office of American Indian Affairs of the U.S. Office of Education, convened the directors and presidents of the boards of regents of Indian community colleges in order to form a consortium.

Two months later at the Phoenix, Arizona office of the Navajo Community College, mutual agreements were made to form the American Indian Higher Education Consortium. Member institutions are: Turtle Mountain Community College on the Turtle Mountain Reservation in North Dakota; Standing Rock Community College on the Standing Rock Resevation that borders North and South Dakota; Lakota Higher Education Center on the Pine Ridge Reservation in South Dakota; Haskell Indian Junior College near Lawrence, Kansas; the Institute of American Indian Arts in Santa Fe, New Mexico; the Southwest Indian Polytechnic Institute in Albuquerque, New Mexico; the Navajo Community College on the Navajo Reservation in Arizona that also borders three other states; and the Hehaka Sapa College at D-Q University near Davis, California. Kuskokwim Community College at Bethel, Alaska, is considering membership. This momentum may soon include the Bannock and Shoshone of the Fort Hall Reservation in Idaho, the Arapaho and Shoshone of the Wind River Reservation in Wyoming, the Sisseton-Wahpeton in South Dakota, the Northern Cheyenne in Montana, and the Confederated tribes of the Warm Springs Reservation in Oregon.

The Consortium schools are unique in that they are governed by American Indian boards of regents, that they are served by predominantly American Indian administrators and faculty, and the student bodies are predominantly American Indian. They strive to meet the postsecondary educational needs of the tribal-specific reservation people. They reinforce tribal-specific value systems in their educational modalities. They are thwarted only to the extent that non-Indian accreditation systems enforce non-Indian educational prerequisites upon them. This latter reality may be why the Consortium members' first priority is to formulate an accreditation system that will be true Indian education accreditation by peer decision. There is no doubt that there will be violent resistance. Indian people concerned with Indian education for Indians are ready to fight that battle.

This is positive thrust by the tribes to reinforce their unique cultural traditions, which can be utilized by Indian students to prepare them for productive contemporary life. These kinds of developing on-reservation or near-reservation postsecondary educational facilities will increase. It can be expected that there will be at least three new such institutions developed each year in the forseeable future.

The member institutions differ in several ways—they are in different geographical areas, they are complex linguistically and speak different languages, they are tribal-specific, they are multi-tribal, some are on reservations, some are off reservations—in varying stages of dependence and autonomy. As such, their needs and expectations differ within the Consortium, but the ultimate goal of each is the same: the strengthening of their own and all other postsecondary Indian educational programs.

Consortium goals are to establish—

1. an American Indian higher education accreditation agency,
2. a financial and institutional resources office,
3. a human resources development program,
4. an American Indian education data bank, and
5. an American Indian curriculum development program.

A NEW INDIAN UNIVERSITY AND RESEARCH INSTITUTE

There is yet a new battle on the horizon. During the past few years, some Indian people have been planning for a National American Indian University and Research Institute. There is a cavernous gap after the two-year Indian community colleges. The tribes, as sovereign nations, have particular educational needs that are not now being met by the hundreds of colleges and universities in the United States. Research for and about Indians is being done to and on Indians, but not by Indians. The many Indian people who are planning tribal higher education have formulated some specific recommendations to present to the tribes:

1. The National American Indian University and Research Institute should be designed by American Indian architects, and it should be located near a sacred place.
2. Undergraduate and graduate curriculum should be designed by Indian educators and respected persons.

The Research Institute will relate to the following issues of American Indian survival: federal and state legislation endangering tribal sovereignty; federal legislation endangering tribal resources, including land and water rights; civil rights legislation and its adverse effect on American Indian people; state, federal, and foundation monies being spent and misspent on American Indian education; Indians in penal institutions; Indians in mental hospitals (who are there because they are diagnosed by proponents of foreign psychological systems); the 4,000 to 6,000 Indian children in non-Indian foster homes; American Indian biomedical research; economic development research for the several hundred reservations, villages, rancherías, and Indian communities; and the treaty responsibilities to the tribes of the United States Government, and its states, departments, offices, and agencies.

III. Discussion of Issues

The basic issues follow.
1. Are Indian studies programs in non-Indian colleges and universities providing quality education for American Indian students?
2. Are Indian community colleges on the reservations and in the Indian communities providing a viable alternative to other educational institutions?
3. Where does the primary authority rest for Indian postsecondary education—in the BIA or in the U.S. Office of Education? (Some tribes in the states of Alaska, Oklahoma, California, and eastern states may want to relate directly to the state departments of education. Other tribes in such states as Arizona, New Mexico, North Dakota, South Dakota, Minnesota, and Montana may want to relate exclusively to the BIA but with some affiliation to OE programs.) There must be tribal and regional agreement on relationships.
4. American Indian students lose out financially and programmatically in minority studies programs when they compete with Black and Chicano students. Indian students are usually outnumbered by other minority students and usually do not make demands in the same manner as other minorities.
5. There must be further office and agency (BIA-Interior and OE-HEW) agreements on higher education function and entitlements.

IV. Recommendations

GENERAL RECOMMENDATIONS

1. There should be at least one national Indian university with appropriate graduate schools in conjunction with the Research Institute.

2. Teacher training should take place at the nine selected regional non-Indian universities and at Indian community colleges as determined by the diverse tribal needs.

3. Vocational and educational needs should be met at the Indian reservation community colleges and the nine selected regional non-Indian universities.

4. Financial aid needs of Indian students should be met by education appropriation from the Congress through the BIA, based on demographic projection. It must be established through the Indian Attorneys Association, Indian law and treaty specialists, that education is a basic right of Indians and not a privilege as is now interpreted.

INDIAN STUDIES IN NON-INDIAN COLLEGES AND UNIVERSITIES

1. The National Tribal Chairmen's Association and the National Indian Education Association must determine where federal dollars should go. These monies (for instance, Fund for the Improvement of Post-Secondary Education (FIPE), Title III, Title IV-D, Educational Professions Development Act (EPDA), etc.) should be placed according to the following criteria:

1. The departments and capabilities
2. Indian tribal involvement and support
3. Curricula geared to Indian and community needs
4. Indian faculty and guidance counselors
5. Financial support and commitment
6. High Indian population impact

Possibly nine areas should be selected: Great Lakes, Central Plains, Northeast, Southeast, South, Southwest, Rocky Mountain, West Coast, and Alaska.

2. Proliferation of Indian programs should be controlled and/or curtailed. Proliferation results in the ineffective dispersal of the few Indian administrators, faculty, and guidance counselors. Continued proliferation should begin at a new undetermined date when reservations' postsecondary needs have been met by graduating Indian personnel that would be serving either at the nine selected non-Indian colleges and universities or at the various reservation postsecondary education centers.

COMMUNITY COLLEGES ON THE RESERVATIONS

1. Congress must appropriate comprehensive annual funding for postsecondary learning centers on the reservation for basic support, including operating costs, administration, faculty, and building costs as determined by the specific tribes.

2. Initial congressional appropriations must support existing postsecondary education, learning centers, or community colleges such as Kuskokwim Community College, Lakota Higher Education Center, Sinte Gleska Community College, Turtle Mountain Community College, Standing Rock Community College, and Navajo Community College.

215

3. Succeeding appropriations would support other developing community colleges on reservations that are projected at the rate of five each year. Reservations now in developmental stages are Bannock-Shoshone at Fort Hall, Idaho; Arapaho-Shoshone at Wind River, Wyoming; Northern Cheyenne at Lame Deer, Montana; and the Confederated Tribes at Warm Springs, Oregon.

RATIONALE

Individual tribes have different postsecondary educational goals. The alternative educational modes are required in order to increase enrollment retention and attainments that will meet tribal short-range and long-range goals. Congress has recognized the educational need to put community colleges on the reservations and has established precedent by appropriating $5 million for the establishment of Navajo Community College.

APPENDIX A

Minority Under-representation
at the Postsecondary Level

"The degree of under-representation of each of the four minority groups may be determined by computing the relationship between each minority's estimated enrollment and its estimated total population. The ratios (expressed as percentages) are as follows:

TABLE I	
PERCENT OF POPULATION	
Black Americans	2.0
Mexican Americans	1.0
Puerto Ricans	1.3
American Indians	0.6
Sub-total	1.8
All others	4.3
Total	3.9

"In order to achieve proportional representation, the enrollment of minorities would have to be increased to the point where their ratios were the same as that given for "all others" (4.3 percent). To reach that goal immediately—

1. the estimated Black enrollment in 1970 would have to be increased 543,000 (from 470,000 to 1,013,000)—an increase of *116 percent (all italics added)*;
2. the estimated Mexican American enrollment in 1970 would have to be increased by 165,000 (from 50,000 to 215,000)—*an increase of 330 percent;*

3. the estimated Puerto Rican enrollment in 1970 would have to be increased by 45,000 (from 20,000 to 65,000)—an increase of *225 percent*; and
4. the estimated American Indian enrollment in 1970 would have to be increased by 26,000 (from 4,000 to 30,000)—an increase of *650 percent.*"

Source: Fred E. Crossland, *Minority Access to College: A Ford Foundation Report* (New York: Schocken Books, 1971), pp. 15-16. Crossland developed these figures from his own interpretation of 1970 college enrollment estimates.

APPENDIX B

BIA Financial Assistance, 1972-73 Postsecondary Indian Education

In December 1972, a $2.5 million supplemental appropriation for the BIA made it possible for an additional 3,000 Indian youths to receive scholarship grants to begin or continue their education at the college level. Some 11,000 students are receiving higher education assistance under the BIA's regular appropriation.

Approximately 14,000 applications for scholarship grants were received in the summer of 1972. The 14,000 students now receiving assistance is almost 20 times the number receiving assistance 10 years ago and about five times the number assisted four years ago. More than 100 students receiving assistance are in law school and approximately 100 more are in other postgraduate programs.

The total monies provided through the BIA for higher education is $20.9 million for the fiscal year 1973.

Source: Report of Bureau of Indian Affairs, Higher Education Office, Albuquerque, New Mexico, 1973.

APPENDIX C

Federally recognized tribes	478
State recognized tribes	17
Tribal entities recognized by state or federal government	52
TOTAL	547

B.I.A. Indian Scholarship Fund for FY '73: $20,956,000
Request FY '74: $19,938,000

13,500 students have B.I.A. scholarships.

Data Source: Secretary of Interior Morton Reports on Indian Matters, Press Release, March 1973.

APPENDIX D

Postsecondary Indian Students

In 1957, an estimated 2,000 Indian students were in colleges and other postsecondary institutions. This number had increased to about 10,000 in 1970.

It is estimated that about 3,000 Indian high school graduates entered college in 1970 and that about one-fourth of this number will graduate from a four-year course. This indicates that approximately 18 percent of an age cohort are entering college, compared with about 40 percent of the age group of all American youth; and that 4 percent are graduating from a four-year course compared with about 22 percent of the total American age cohort.

Among postsecondary students, 42 percent are attending colleges and taking academic courses, while the other 58 percent are taking vocational-technical courses which require from one to three years of training.

The ratio of men to women among postsecondary students is approximately 55 to 45.

Source: Estelle Fuchs and Robert J. Havighurst, *To Live on This Earth: American Indian Education* (New York: Doubleday, 1972, no page given).

APPENDIX E

TABLE 2
BUREAU OF INDIAN AFFAIRS PROJECTIONS

	1971-72	1972-73	1973-74
Number of students funded	6,623	10,000	14,000
Adult vocational grants	907	14,000	1,150-1,957
Dropouts	953	1,521	1,974
Graduates	345	551	600
Total Expenditures	$6,098,000	$15,248,000	$16,148,000

COMPETENCIES FOR TEACHERS OF CULTURALLY DIFFERENT CHILDREN: TEACHER COMPETENCIES FOR TEACHING NATIVE AMERICAN CHILDREN

Milo Kalectaca
Associate Director of Teacher Corps
Northern Arizona University, Flagstaff

219

This is a culturally diverse nation. Many people have seen this as a divisive force within this country and have, thus, promulgated the "melting pot philosophy" in an attempt to obscure these differences. Today many of these culturally distinct groups have proclaimed nonacceptance of amalgamation. This practice of nonacceptance of cultural distinctions must terminate and society must be reeducated to the concept of the *tossed salad philosophy* from the melting pot theory (i.e. each element mixed with others while maintaining its own unique flavor, making a unique contribution to the total quality of the American experience with no element seen as worse or better than any other).[1]

Dealing with Cultural Diversity

"Having a diversity of cultures within a single country can be a threat, a problem, or an asset."[2] Thus steps must be taken to make it an asset. Just because a group of people look at and solve a problem differently doesn't mean they are any better or worse as people.

Traditional teacher education programs are not producing people equipped to teach minority children and youth effectively. If humanizing the curriculum is truly a value in the educational system in twentieth century America, then the people for whom the curriculum is designed must be involved.

The official position is that minority group children who are "culturally deprived" should be taught middle-class values, yet—"Individuality can only exist in a pluralistic society wherein differences are appreciated and protected."[3]

If we are to have relevancy in education and a democratic society, goals and objectives should be based on the cultural values and differences of the various socioeconomic groups of America and should be reflected in the goals of the total educational system. There should be programs in which the tribal-specific language and culture of the children are brought into the classroom as an integrated part of the school program. The child needs to learn the language and culture of the school, but the school needs to learn about and appreciate the language and culture of the child as well. Cultural differences involve alternative ways of looking at and doing things.

Teacher competencies have to be specified and must relate to *understanding cultural diversity*. A curriculum in order to be successful must represent several cultures, and the development of that curriculum must be handled by those who represent the diversity of cultures through which the learner must daily maneuver.

Definition of Teacher Competency

Perhaps it would be appropriate to define at this time what we mean by *teacher competency*. Competencies may be simply defined as behaviors which effectively satisfy their objectives. Teacher competencies are performances which have been judged to be effective in satisfying the objectives of the teaching profession. Statements of teacher competencies describe what the authorities who have specified them regard as adequate descriptions of a competent teacher. In most teacher education programs the comprehensive set of these statements provides a description of what the judges believe a teacher should be like when he or she is ready to teach.[4]

Knowing the Community

In order for the teacher to gain community support and maneuver within the students' environment outside the classroom, the teacher should have the ability to maneuver within the community. Often, little or no effort is made to visit the child's home and community to understand the child as a whole. A teacher should recognize and respect that a community also consists of a government, service agencies, history, language and culture, value system, religion, and education.[5] These elements should become part of the curriculum as well as influence the teacher's attitude toward his or her students.

A competent teacher of an Indian community, for example, should be able to—

1. describe the geography, home life, and economics of that Indian community;
2. describe the services offered by the various community agencies active in the school community; and

3. discuss the tribal government and name and describe the responsibilities of the officials.

In the area of language and culture, the competent teacher should be able to—

1. analyze the Indian language in comparison to English;
2. point out the difficulties that these children have in learning the English language; and
3. talk about the various arts and crafts of the Indian.

In history, the competent teacher should be able to—

1. give a brief history of that Indian group; and
2. name the great leaders of the past and present and be able to tell about them.

On other aspects of the community—value system, religion, and education—the teacher should be able to—

1. describe how a Navajo or Hopi views honesty, punishment, truth telling, rewards, sharing, competition, going against custom;
2. describe the religion;
3. differentiate between religious ceremonies that are private and those that are public;
4. tell the importance of each of the religious ceremonies;
5. describe the major educational systems on the reservation;
6. list the tribal education goals;
7. describe the feelings of community members about education; and
8. inform the parents on how they can be involved in the educational process of their children.

The primary purpose of our Navajo-Hopi Teacher Corps Program at Northern Arizona University is to draw more Indians into the field of Indian education, both on a professional basis and by direct community involvement. All too often the parents of children in reservation schools are not consulted about curriculum changes, staff changes, and other changes in school policy which affect their children daily. Indian interns can provide effective communication between the parents of the children and the educators and administrators of the school. Indian interns can provide those valuable links precisely because they are Indians, raised in the local culture and speaking the local language.

Preservice and Inservice Teacher Training

The Northern Arizona University preservice instructional program* focuses on giving a total picture of the Indian child in the home and school

---

*Portions of this program description are based on the Teacher Corps Proposal—Cycle 8 (Flagstaff: Northern Arizona University, February 15, 1973).

environment. Emphasis is on the individual in the educational process, and on emotional, social and cultural factors in the formation of the Indian child. The language section discusses (a) the problems of the bilingual child coming into an entirely new language situation; (b) how the native language depicts the culture; and (c) instruction in basic Navajo and Hopi languages (non-native speakers learn reading and writing, Indian interns study linguistic analysis). The sociocultural section deals with problems in "reaching" children. What are the cultural and social barriers in the way of the Indian child's education? The child development section includes testing and test interpretation with the non-Anglo child in mind.

COMPETENCIES EXPECTED OF INTERNS

We expect interns as a result of preservice training to understand reservation living conditions and cultures. The intern will—

1. know the history and role of minority groups in America;
2. become aware of values of Navajo and Hopi culture;
3. become proficient in culturally analyzing minority culture values;
4. discuss and analyze generally held stereotypes, fears, and misconceptions about minority groups;
5. understand how white cultural values penalize Indians for their cultural values through culture-biased tests;
6. compare values of white culture, Indian culture, with some other minority culture (e.g. Mexican American, Black); and
7. have experience in decoding an alien language to gain empathy for the problems of minority peoples.[6]

222

Competencies that Corps members will exhibit during their internship were developed by the Program. In the preparation of the evaluation criteria, several basic considerations were necessary. It was agreed that criteria for evaluation should be reflective of desired performance expected of a teacher —in other words, how teachers are expected to perform. The criteria for observation and evaluation have been placed under four general areas: *Preparation, Performance, Product* (the student), and *Personal and Professional Attitudes.*[7]

COMPETENCIES EXPECTED OF TEACHERS

The competencies selected from those in each area listed above are those needed to teach culturally diverse and/or culturally different children. These, then, become teacher competencies or behaviors expected of teachers:

Instructional Competencies

The teacher—

• involves students in a variety of relevant activities,
• presents alternate methods of instruction when required,

- utilizes a variety of resources,
- uses appropriate remedial material.

Community Competencies

The teacher—
- welcomes parental and community visitation,
- communicates with the community on school matters,
- participates in appropriate community activities and organizations,
- assesses and/or identifies community attitudes.

Student-Teacher Relationship Competencies

The teacher—
- exhibits an honest liking and sincere regard for students,
- encourages student respect for all cultures,
- encourages students to work cooperatively as well as individually.

Having resource persons in the classroom who are fluent in the children's language can increase language understanding and use in a way that encourages children to express themselves. Learning materials and experiences which reflect the positive social, family, and ethnic background of different child-groups within the classroom can do much to build positive self-concepts and individual strengths in children. A program that is sensitive to the cultural needs of the children, which incorporates important elements of cultural backgrounds of families being served—language, music, ceremonial days—can achieve continuity between the home and the school.

223

Teacher Competencies for a Multicultural Society

Multicultural education should develop teachers who will deeply respect cultural differences which can contribute *positively* to American education by providing cultural experiences and enrichment to other ethnic groups. The following are some competencies for teachers of culturally diverse children (some of these may be repetitive because they have been touched on in previous sections of the paper, others are additional). The competent teacher:

1. Recognizes that all cultures have the same human needs
2. Utilizes those materials and resources which promote positive self-concepts
3. Utilizes those aspects of a student's culture for planning and presenting instruction which will enhance student self-development
4. Helps students understand their values and attitudes
5. Recognizes the effects and expectancies of the dominant culture which stifle motivation and learning
6. Knows about the sociopolitical characteristics of American society and the local community

7. Participates with parents and students in designing and evaluating activities
8. Develops an atmosphere of shared decision making in the classroom
9. Encourages individuality and originality
10. Instills in students an appreciation of human diversity
11. Encourages student participation and divergent points of view
12. Incorporates community resources in the school program
13. Utilizes community resources in classroom instruction

Competency-Based Teacher Education—A Strategy

With this great diversity in culture and individual differences in children and their teachers, it is assumed that institutional resources as a primary basis for accreditation must be questioned. Further, we assume that knowledge of subject matter, some teaching methods, and a term of student teaching can no longer be acceptable as a primary basis to predict success of a prospective teacher and the granting of certification. Teacher education does necessitate continuing the combination of knowledge, theory, and practice; however, this education is believed most desirable and most effective when acquired in a clinical mode, with a flexible program focusing on the criteria of performance—performance of competencies expressed in general and specific behavioral objectives.

An ideal program would—

1. specify basic and specific competencies of teachers and teaching interns within and out of the classroom;
2. provide a training program to meet the specific needs of the students;
3. continue reevaluation of curriculum and teaching techniques;
4. expand practicum time, through either a longer regular internship or five-year program; and
5. provide a variety of student teaching (intern) laboratory experiences.

Competency-based teacher education has the potential as a strategy for preparing effective teachers mainly because of its basic characteristics:

1. Competencies are made public in advance.
2. The students' rate of progress through the program is determined by demonstrated competency rather than by time or course completion.
3. Instruction is individualized and personalized.
4. The emphasis is on exit, not on entrance, requirements.
5. Instruction is modularized which allows for self-pacing.
6. The program is field-centered.[8]

In CBTE the learner is the most important element. Flexibility in the scheduling of learning activities is paramount in importance. In this writer's approach, utilization of a variety of instructional activities is emphasized. Furthermore, alternate sets of performance activities are provided. Learning styles have been categorized into three areas: *visual, auditory,* and *psychomotor.* We have found through reevaluation that the first set of instructional activities, being more visually oriented, do not always satisfy all individual needs. It may be that through *auditory means* or *psychomotor means,* objectives can be better met. There are no fixed rules as to how, when, or where learning is to be accomplished. Opportunities are provided to acquire competencies in practical field experience or on the job.

This type of experience can be both practical and beneficial. Competencies that are already possessed by the individual can be recognized, and the person should be allowed to demonstrate these competencies. If competencies are performed to satisfaction, proper credits should be given and the individual allowed to bypass certain blocks of studies. The concern is for exit requirements, not entrance requirements. Continuous evaluation, feedback, and revision are integral parts of the program. Field-centered experiences which allow continuous evaluation can encompass a broad-based involvement in teacher training by university, community, school, and students themselves. Students can decide on their own if teaching is really what they want to do. Naturally, the community is given the opportunity to say which and what kind of teachers it wants for its schools and children.

Self-pacing allows for individualization and personalization of instruction. The slow learners are no longer frustrated because they cannot keep up with fast learners, while the fast learners are not held back by slow learners and can continue on to more challenging areas. Since emphasis is placed on exit rather than entrance requirements, training programs are open for a wide variety of persons entering the field. With continuous assessment of the progress of each student moving at his/her own rate, and with a variety of choices for a goal, many who would normally have been excluded because of educational assessment, cultural background, race, or previous interest can enter and successfully complete a teacher training program. The result can be a wholesome diversity of background in the teaching profession.

The goal of CBTE in relationship to multicultural education should be the training of competent educators who are able to relate to the diverse cultures of our society. This training should be designed to develop such unique competencies as an understanding of cultural pluralism, bilingualism, and dialects (in systems where needed, it will require bilingual personnel). Training should also include competencies in cross-cultural curriculum development, community-based education, and effective learning as it relates to minorities. The goal of CBTE should be to provide the kind of trainees for differentiated staff positions who are supportive of the innovative changes needed for effective educational development.[9]

REFERENCES

1 Sullivan, Allen K. "Issues on Assessing Multi-Cultured Youth: Its Implications for

Teachers." Paper prepared for Teacher Corps Associates Conference on CBTE: The Potential for Multi-cultural Education, Madison, Wisconsin, November 1-2, 1973, pp. 3-4.

2 Stent, Madelon et al., eds. *Cultural Pluralism in Education: A Mandate for Change.* New York: Appleton-Century-Crofts, 1973, p. 1.

3 Kalectaca, Milo, Gerald Knowles, and Robin Butterfield. "To Help—Not to Homogenize Native American Children." *Educational Leadership* 31, no. 7 (April 1974): 590-2.

4 Johnson, Charles E. *Competencies for Teachers: A Handbook for Specifying and Organizing Teaching Performances.* Teacher Corps. Washington, D.C.: U.S. Government Printing Office, August 1972, pp. 1, 4, 9.

5 Kalectaca, Milo. *Competencies for a Hopi Reservation Teacher: Hopi Background Competencies for Teachers.* Madison, Wisconsin: University of Wisconsin, Spring 1973.

6 Teacher Corps Proposal—Cycle 8. Flagstaff: Northern Arizona University, February 15, 1973.

7 Teacher Corps. *Navajo-Hopi Teacher Inservice Handbook.* Flagstaff: Northern Arizona University, Summer 1972, pp. 22-32.

8 Elam, Stanley. *Performance-Based Teacher Education: What Is the State of the Art?* Washington, D.C.: American Association of Colleges for Teacher Education, 1971, pp. 6-9.

9 Grant, Carl. "Implications for the Recruitment and Training of Minority Educators." *PBTE* 7. Newsletter of the Multi-State Consortium on Performance-Based Teacher Education, Syracuse, New York. January 1974, p. 4.

CHAPTER 3

A NEED FOR COMPETENCY-BASED TEACHER EDUCATION FOR NATIVE AMERICANS

Louise Miller
Education Specialist
Assistant Area Director, Education
Bureau of Indian Affairs
Sacramento, California

Education has borne the major thrust of the challenge which contemporary human issues have put to social institutions. Among various social concerns, it is the issue of the education of the Native American Indian which has leveled the most persistent and unresolved challenge. The challenge has not been completely ignored, as the records of the Bureau of Indian Affairs (BIA) and public school programs attest. However, as the statistics of Indian education failure testify, the challenge has yet gone unmet. 227

The answer to the unmet challenge has consistently eluded educators. An effective overall strategy for educating Indian children has not yet been found. This situation exists despite the implementation of a wide variety of programs and approaches. However, as we examine the philosophy which undergirds such programs, we may begin to discern the patently self-defeating structure on which they are founded. That philosophy, so forcefully projected onto the American Indian, is one of assimilation into the mainstream of American life and a ubiquitous denigration of Indianness that is perpetuated within American society and educational institutions.

In his poem, "The Lavender Kitten,"*Alonzo Lopez, a young Papago poet from Pima County, Arizona, eloquently brings into focus the feelings of American Indians and their abortive struggle to attain that elusive place that society dictates they must achieve.

> Miles and miles of pasture
> rolled on before me.
> Covered with grass and clover
> dyed pink, white and blue.

---

*"The Lavender Kitten" by Alonzo Lopez from THE WHISPERING WIND: Poetry by Young American Indians, edited by Terry Allen copyright 1972 by The Institute of American Indian Arts. Reprinted by permission of Doubleday & Co., Inc.

At the edge of the fluctuating
  sea of watercolors
Sat a lavender kitten.
Its fur glinted from an oscillating
  ray of pink,
Quivered gently at the touch of a
  swirling blue breeze.
Its emerald eyes glittered
And gazed blindly at the lighting
  and fading sky of hazy red,
Yellow, white, and blue.
My heart knocked within my chest.
I must have the lavender kitten!
I ran across the multi-colored field,
  my arms reaching forward.
Time slowed.
I tried to run faster
  but moved twice as slowly.
The blue breeze circled and tightened
  around me.
Holding me back.
The kitten rose and stretched
  sending lavender mist
Swimming in every direction.
It turned and started away
  in huge, slow strides.
I followed and,
  by a shimmering prism lake,
I came within reach of the kitten.
I offered my hand
  and the kitten edged away,
Farther and farther.
Then the lake turned from crystal
  to deep purple.
I looked around.
The colors began to melt.
The red sun turned to a dull grey.
The colored-filled sky turned to black.
The grass and clover began
  to wither and die.
I looked down into the pool before me.
There, at the bottom of
  the orchid glass cage,
Lay the lavender kitten.[1]

The scourge of Indianness addressed within these lines unsheathes a
deeper tragedy. Beautiful words betray obscene genocide; the lavender
kitten becomes the ultimate and unobtainable goal of assimilation to be
grasped after and made a personal coup; the prism lake—so like a well-
honed knife—surely, swiftly turns to the deep purple of blood, the edge
so sharp the Indian hardly knows that the kitten is really the Indian who

is dead. The deeper tragedy reflected in Lopez's words lies in its oppressive reality. American Indians have not, and cannot, cease to be what and who they are, because when they do, it means they are dead.

But to remain Indian is intricately woven into the American social context as somehow undesirable and evil. The disparaging connotation of being Indian is molded into our laws, our religions, our language, and our system of education. It is this latter condition which is here indicated as the source of Indian educational failure.

Why Indian Children Fail

Bruce Gaarder states in a report[2] that one of the underlying causes of the Indian child's failure in school is that the educational policy for American Indian children has been based on the principle that the Indians' salvation lies in their ceasing to be what and who they are. Essentially, the message communicated to Indian children is that their worth is contingent on the extent to which they can approximate whiteness. This same message is projected within the various programs which have been spawned to remediate the Indian educational failure which has been fostered by that very message.

The cycle of failure faced by Indian children in schools, whether federal or public, may well continue for years to come because, typically, the approach to Indian education has been consistently focused on compensatory education and the need for Indian children to assimilate into the larger and dominant society without regard to the children's rich cultural background and the learning styles which they have already acquired. Indian culture has been presumed to be, at best, irrelevant but more commonly dysfunctional vis-a-vis the education process.

When this orientation is carried to the extent of communicating to children that their adequacy is contingent upon diminishing that which is most natural to them, it cannot but have a profoundly crippling effect, if not indeed end in complete destruction of the child. Specifically, this negative valuation projected onto the Indian child develops feelings of anomie which are highly psychologically charged. To withdraw and fail academically remains the only recourse for personal survival left to the Indian child.

Education has not met the Indian child's educational needs and is being "called on the carpet" for its failure. Deutsch made this point quite cogently in stating, "Education is being asked to compensate not only for its own failure but for society's as well. Education's fault has been its inability to identify its own problems and its moral callousness in allowing massive failure and miserable educational conditions to exist for a substantial segment of the school population."[3]

Building a New Indian Self-Image

According to Spindler, the school is the chief vehicle of socialization;

within it are programs of study containing those areas of experience and content which are essential to the development of desired characteristics of behavior selected from the total range of possibilities existing in the culture. He suggests that intelligent selection can be based only on considerable cultural insight and understanding.[4] This is particularly true for the Native American child. The Special Subcommittee on Indian Education states that the Indian's image of himself or herself depends, in that last analysis, upon the image held by the dominant white society.[5]

Most theorists agree that feelings of self-worth and adequacy within an individual are largely a learned phenomenon, in which an individual develops a self-image or concept by incorporating sources of data from significant others in his or her environment. It is, as Sullivan puts it, a product of the "reflected appraisals" of the society within which the individual lives.[6]

Indeed, if this brand of discrimination and rejection has been fostered unwittingly by the educational system, then it must be admitted openly and new educational premises must be constructed. Fromm offers this reassurance: "As long as we can think of alternatives, we are not lost; as long as we can consult together and plan together, we can hope."[7] It is in effect what the Indian community is asking.

230

EDUCATION FOR INDIAN PRIDE

One of the most positive educational alternatives that must be considered by educational institutions, particularly on the university level, is the rapidly developing Indian ethic that began to emerge in the late 1960s. That ethic reflects the Indian pride movement and the search for self-determination. This emergence has the potential for reversing the Indian educational failure and the accompanying derogation of the Indian which has been promulgated within American social institutions in general and most grossly within American educational institutions. It is also the source of mounting pressure for the development and inclusion of Indian culture and history as a relevant and essential area for curriculum development. Most crucial in all of this is the reversal of the deficient orientation of education programs for Indian students.

Therein lies the potential for making school a positive learning experience for the Indian child and a viable process for enriching the curriculum for all children. For those schools of education which have a sincere interest in improving Indian education, there are existing workable programs which serve as models. These models are: The American Indian Survival Schools in Milwaukee and Chicago; Arapaho, Shoshone High School in Wyoming; Busby and Rocky Boy's Schools in Montana; Kuskokwim Valley in Alaska; and Ramah Navaho Day School and Rough Rock Demonstration School in New Mexico.

The educational challenge is clear. Educational institutions must respond to the challenge if they are to survive and continue to serve society. The emerging Indian cultural positives must be encompassed and used as a major defining theme for the development of successful Indian education programs and the establishment of clearly defined tasks. These programs and tasks will enable Indians to become part of and to utilize the school system as a meaningful resource to sustain the lifestyle that meets their social and economic needs.

Federal Report on Indian Education

To fully grasp the complexity and the enormity of the task involved in Indian educational change, it is necessary to review the past. The *First Annual Report to the Congress of the United States* by the National Advisory Council on Indian Education[8] gives a concise and accurate summary of historical findings from *Indian Education: National Tragedy – A National Challenge:*

I. POLICY FAILURE

The dominant policy of the Federal Government toward the American Indian has been one of coercive assimilation. The policy resulted in:

A. The destruction and disorganization of Indian communities and individuals.
B. A desperately severe and self-perpetuating cycle of poverty for most Indians.
C. The growth of a large, ineffective, and self-perpetuating bureaucracy which retards the elimination of Indian poverty.
D. A waste of Federal appropriations.

II. NATIONAL ATTITUDES

The coercive assimilation policy has had a strong negative influence on national attitudes. It has resulted in:

A. A nation that is massively uninformed and misinformed about the American Indian, and his past and present.
B. Prejudice, racial intolerance, and discrimination towards Indians far more widespread and serious than generally recognized.

III. EDUCATIONAL FAILURE

The coercive assimilation policy has had disastrous effect on the education of Indian children. It has resulted in:

A. The classroom and the school becoming a kind of battle-ground where the Indian child attempts to protect his integrity and identify as an individual by defeating the purposes of the school.

B. Schools which fail to understand or adapt to, and in fact often denigrate, cultural differences.

C. Schools which blame their own failure on the Indian student and reinforce his defensiveness.

D. Schools which fail to recognize the importance and validity of the Indian community. The community and child retaliate by treating the school as an alien institution.

E. A dismal record of absenteeism, dropouts, negative self-image, low achievement, and ultimately, academic failure for many Indian children.

F. A perpetuation of the cycle of poverty which undermines the success of all other Federal programs.

IV. CAUSES OF THE POLICY FAILURE

The coercive assimilation has two primary historical roots:

A. A continuous desire to exploit, and expropriate Indian land and physical resources.

B. A self-righteous intolerance of tribal communities and cultural differences.[9]

232

It is evident that an institution that has historically perpetuated such destructive racism against a group of people cannot of its own volition define the needs of that particular group. Rather, definition for change must emanate from that group that has been discriminated against, preyed upon, and robbed of much of its human dignity. Only then can there be a drawing into full focus of the historical events, the sociological and psychological forces of the past—those prime factors that are waiting to shape Indian students' behavior and attitudes that make them uniquely what they are.

The prime requisites for change must be generated in a climate of willingness on the part of educational institutions to assume the responsibility of their role as change agents and to validate the definition of educational expectations, needs, and priorities as defined by the Indian community. Those definitions of educational needs by the Indian community should then be processed into existing teacher training programs as viable and essential components in the teacher training process. To lack the knowledge of cultural, sociological, and historical perspectives of various peoples is to be without an understanding of how they are to be, without an understanding of how they behave and the rationale for such behavior; it is then that education becomes a process of trial and error classification of professional endeavor. This is particularly true when learning constructs insist on espousing a single majority cultural orientation. The teacher should be trained in the process of transposing the environment of the Indian child into principles and concepts that are necessary for that child to deal with the learning process and to be successful in it.

A Competency-Based Model for Training Teachers Of the Culturally Different Child

One of the most comprehensive models that deal with the training of teachers for the ethnically different child is being developed at the Institute for Cultural Pluralism, San Diego State University.[10] It is a competency-based teacher training program that parallels the positive Indian thrust for an effective educational intervention strategy.

The Community, Home, Cultural Awareness, and Language Training (CHCALT) model is composed of four basic components:

1. Philosophy of education for the culturally and linguistically different
2. Sociocultural awareness—home and community based
3. Oral language and assessment techniques
4. Diagnostic and prescriptive strategies[11]

The salient features of each of the four components of the CHCALT model are outlined in the chapter by Mazón in this book. A list of the specific competencies considered essential for achieving the goals of each component is followed by a rationale for the program component.

Before viewing teacher competencies specifically for the Native American segment, it must be remembered that one of the fallacies and the basic underlying assumption of Indian education has been to lump the needs of all Native Americans into one global definition. Rather, it must be understood that each Indian tribal group has its own language, its own economics, its own philosophy, its own psychology, its own religious base, and its own history of origin. These components inextricably become the base of any particular tribal culture. The conclusion must then be drawn that, if teaching competencies are to be defined, they must come from that target group. Communication is the vital link in the building of a workable teacher training program.

Teacher Attitudes Study

To explore further the need for implementation of a competency-based teacher education program, a yet unpublished study in California conducted in ten school districts statewide[12] revealed many of the reasons why the Native American student has not succeeded in the educational process of that state. The study was based upon 19 concerns that were identified by the Indian community at large as important factors in the education of the Indian child in the public school system. Those concerns were constructed into a questionnaire and administered in 10 school districts that serve a high Indian student population. Participating in that questionnaire, or F test, were 141 Indian students, 120 parents, and 402 non-Indian teachers and administrators.

From the point of view of Indian people, the following nine points reveal some negative attitudes of teachers:

1. Indian students should be regarded the same as all other students.
2. It is not important for school to identify Indian students as a group.
3. The child's Indian background was an influence in the child's success/failure in school.
4. It is not important for the Indian child to speak his/her native language.
5. If an Indian student is having difficulty in school, perhaps the Bureau choice would be a better choice.
6. There is lack of communication between teachers and Indian students.
7. There is even less communication between teachers and Indian parents.
8. There is little value in a home visit by the teacher if the student is having difficulty.
9. Teachers felt there was only a small degree of discrimination against the Indian student by other students, staff, or administration.

Conversely, teachers also felt that it is important for teachers—

1. to know local Indian tribal groups,
2. to know local Indian culture,
3. to have Indian clubs on campus,
4. to have Indian students participate in sports events and extra-curricular activities,
5. to have the Indian child retain his/her Indian culture.

Specific Competencies for Teachers of Native Americans

Based on the analysis of data such as this, the following competencies for teacher education are offered.

ANTHROPOLOGICAL PERSPECTIVES

1. Demonstrate knowledge of Indian tribalism, the vast linguistic and cultural differences among the Indian tribes of the United States, what forces (economic, political or other) brought about those vast differences.
2. Demonstrate a knowledge of the United States Indian Reservation System, their locations, and the historical and legal bases of the local reservations and communities in particular.
3. Demonstrate knowledge of the Indians' semi-sovereign status to the United States Government that no other group possesses.
4. Demonstrate knowledge of the diverse linguistic groups of the American Indian. (Nearly 200 tribal languages are spoken today.)

SOCIOLOGICAL PERSPECTIVES

1. Demonstrate an understanding of the nature of cooperative societies as opposed to a competitive society.

2. Demonstrate an understanding of internal controls imposed by the Indian community on its members.
3. Demonstrate an understanding of Indian civil rights that is different from the civil rights of other ethnic groups.
4. Demonstrate an understanding of the extended family as opposed to the nuclear family.
5. Demonstrate an understanding of why the Indian continues to adhere to Indian values, morals, and traditions.
6. Demonstrate an understanding of Indian resentment toward the overridingly oppressive social system.
7. Demonstrate a knowledge of the vast contributions the American Indian has made and is making to present-day society.
8. Demonstrate a knowledge of why the Indian is locked into the cycle of poverty.
9. Demonstrate a knowledge of the Indian's relationship to the state and federal government.

AESTHETIC AND RELIGIOUS PERSPECTIVES

1. Understand that aesthetic values and religious beliefs have a very close relationships many times being one and the same.
2. Understand that oral histories and lifeways are the basis for teaching the morality and laws of tribal groups.
3. Understand that leadership, both religious and secular, are intrically bound together.
4. Realize and understand that many American Indian groups already have ethically and morally valid belief systems.

235

LINGUISTIC PERSPECTIVE

Understand how language represents the functions and philosophies of a culture; and how impingement of alien languages forces those "speakers into two different images of reality."[13]

DIAGNOSTIC AND PRESCRIPTIVE STRATEGIES

A teacher must understand behavorial tendencies which may differ with geographic location, but which are usually present in some degree. The following are examples:

1. Understand that Indians and non-Indians have different referents and perceptions to humor. These are often antagonistic to each other. Indian humor may not be humorous to non-Indians. Indians' formalized joking relationships (teasing) and story-telling (make believe) are intrinsic to Indian culture. This perception of humor may be perceived as troublesome and disruptive to non-Indians. The teacher should be aware that this is a possible source of cultural misinterpretation and conflict.
2. Understand that Indian students have respect for and respond to family

authority; however, response by learners to school authorities tends to be fearful. Indians tend to withdraw when faced with school authority.

3. Understand that the Indian learner is taught at home to be independent and self-sufficient, generous, quiet, and dignified. The Indian child is taught to avoid boasting about achievements.

4. Understand that Indian students prefer to work at their own pace, and tend to resist group activities which are competitive in nature. Teachers must understand the standard group instructional mode in schools produces predictable academic failure for Indian learners.

5. Understand that Indian children are taught to be quiet and dignified. They find it difficult to respond to the non-Indian because of built-up distrust. Status and position does not impress the Indian; each person is judged on personal merits.

6. Understand that Indian students are very sensitive to personal dignification requirements. Negative remarks about clothes, home or anything pertaining to Indians produces withdrawal and negative feelings which become progressively more intense with age.

7. Understand that the Indian learner feels it is important to show what you are and what you can do, but not in a boastful way. Indians have special concerns with pride for being "an Indian." They have strong feelings about the superior culture of the Indian.

8. Understand that Indian pride is severely injured by the negative approach the school uses in dealing with the American Indian in history.

9. Understand the dislike of Indian learners for competition expected in group academic environments. They will resist and withdraw when pushed.

10. Understand why the Indian learner develops feelings of rejection starting at lower grades based on perceived rejection by non-Indian peers, by teachers, by authority figures, and by community.

It is imperative that such recommendations be implemented with all possible haste! It is unthinkable that we can allow further irreversible damage to occur to our Indian children as the result of current miseducation.

REFERENCES

1 Allen, Terry, ed. *The Whispering Wind: Poetry by Young American Indians*. Garden City, New York: Doubleday, 1973, pp. 11-12. Reprinted by permission.

2 Gaarder, Bruce. Education of American Indian Children. Report presented at the Annual Conference of Southwest Council of Foreign Language Teachers, El Paso, Texas, November 1967.

3 Deutsch, Martin. *The Disadvantaged Child*. New York: Basic Books, 1967, p. 372.

4 Spindler, George D. *Education and Anthropology*. Stanford, Calif.: University Press, 1955, p. 295.

5 U.S. Senate. Special Subcommittee on Indian Education. *Indian Education: A National Tragedy—A National Challenge*. Hearing, 91st Cong. 2nd Sess., Nov. 3, 1969. Washington, D.C.: Government Printing Office, 1969.

6 Sullivan, H.S. *Conceptions of Modern Psychiatry*. Washington, D.C.: William Danson White Psychiatric Foundation, 1947.

7 Fromm, Eric. *The Sane Society.* New York: Holt, Rinehart and Winston, 1955, p. 363.

8 National Advisory Council on Indian Education. *First Annual Report to the Congress of the United States.* Washington, D.C.: U.S. Government Printing Office, 1974.

9 Ibid., pp. 6-7.

10 Mazón, M. Reyes. *CHCALT: A Design for Teacher Training in Multicultural Education.* Special Report, Institute for Cultural Pluralism. San Diego, Calif.: San Diego State University School of Education, 1974, pp. 4-10.

11 Ibid., p. 4.

12 Miller, Louise, "The California Indian's Perception of School Failure." Unpublished dissertation, Arizona State University, 1974.

13 Hall, Edward T. *The Silent Language.* New York: Premier Books, 1965, p. 13.

237

CONCLUDING STATEMENT

By the Panel of Native American Writer-Editors

In summary, education must reorient itself toward encompassing the realities of a culturally diverse society. Thus, education must address itself to providing competencies and skills necessary for teachers of Native American students. Educators confront the task of apprising themselves of the spectrum of Indian education. In this regard, the paper of Patricia Locke provides comprehensive historical and legal background for Indian education. The preservice and inservice training programs of Fount Holland and Rosella J. Covington serve as ongoing tribal-specific and reservation teacher training models. The position papers of Milo Kalectaca and Louise Miller provide additional perspectives of competencies and training that can and do have impact on education. The teacher competency categories of the Northern Plains Teacher Corps Program under the direction of Donald Lemon can serve as a broad base for the definition of specific competencies to be developed in concert with the local tribal community.

In conclusion, there are red men, there are different races of men, but all are good in the sight of the Great Spirit. With the implementation of multicultural education, "It is not necessary for eagles to be crows."

238

Prime Writer

Harry N. Rivlin
John Mosler Professor of Urban Education
Dean, School of Education
Fordham University—Lincoln Center
New York, New York

Associate Prime Writer

Frank Sciara
Director, Institute for Evaluation
of Teachers of the Disadvantaged
Professor of Elementary Education
Teachers College,
Ball State University
Muncie, Indiana

Writer-Editors

PART V

Hansom P. Baptiste
Director of Multicultural Education
College of Education
University of Houston
Houston, Texas

Patricia Cabrera
Director, Center for New
Dimensions in Education
Resources Development
University of Southern California
Los Angeles, California

Ernest A. Holmes
Assistant Professor of Education
Federal City College
Washington, D.C.

John A. Masla
Associate Dean, College of Education
Professor of Curriculum and Instruction
Ohio University
Athens, Ohio

Grant Clothier
Director, Midwest Educational
Training and Research
Organization (METRO)
Shawnee Mission, Kansas

A Cross-Cultural Approach to Multicultural Teacher Education

242

A CROSS-CULTURAL APPROACH TO MULTICULTURAL EDUCATION

The U.S. has always been a multicultural society, but only recently have the implications and even advantages of this condition been recognized. Today, many ethnic groups are deeply concerned about their role in society and about society's attitude toward different ethnic groups. In the three preceding sections, Blacks, Spanish-speaking Americans, and Native Americans have presented their views. This section, building on contributions made by these groups, examines concerns common to other ethnic groups, concerns which are probably applicable even to ethnic groups not represented at this conference.

Early Settlers

As settlements were established in colonial times, the population in each colony tended to be English-speaking and culturally homogeneous. When there were minority groups within the colony, they were expected to either assimilate into the dominant Anglo group or remain forever outsiders. So far as Native Americans were concerned, the colonists regarded them as outsiders only rarely to be assimilated, and the colonists were regarded in turn as outsiders by the Native Americans.

With the independence of the U.S., territorial expansion, and consequent increase in size and diversity of the population, greater multicultural dimensions became apparent. In general, however, ethnic and cultural differences were either ignored or rejected by the majority culture. Except when ethnic or cultural minorities were willing to surrender their distinctive values, customs, language, and dress, no attempt was made to merge the minority with the majority culture. It was assumed by both that the dominant group was the ruling group, and that minorities could either surrender and be assimilated, or else remain outsiders. As the controlling group, the dominant society decided, moreover, either deliberately or by an unwritten common understanding, which groups were eligible for assimilation. A caste system thus developed which rigidly excluded such ethnic groups as Blacks, Native Americans, and Spanish-speakers from ever assimilating, except in rare instances, with the dominant group.

The Melting Pot

The concept of the *melting pot* seemed at first to be a promising attempt to fuse peoples from various new and old immigrant groups into a new multicultural American society. While the concept was attractive to some late nineteenth-century immigrants, it never really worked. For one thing, it rejected as unmeltable many ethnic groups, including Native Americans, Blacks, Spanish-speakers, and Orientals. The concept assumed that only the dominant white Anglo-Saxon Protestant culture was worth saving, and it was expected that those who wished to be absorbed by the melting pot had to surrender their own cultural heritage as the price of admission.

Postwar Developments

Though sociologists had long questioned the soundness of the melting pot theory, it was not until after World War II that popular objection became powerful enough to end its being hailed as the keystone of race relations. For various social, political, and economic reasons, including desegregation of the armed forces, race relations became too important to be ignored. For example, the movement of Blacks to the North led to heavy concentrations of Blacks in northern cities for the first time. The extension of voting rights to people previously disenfranchised, and other aspects of the civil rights movement encouraged minority groups to protest the inferior role assigned them. Minority ethnic groups became increasingly powerful, politically and socially, and no longer tolerated being ignored by the dominant white middle-class power structures.

While there has long been polarization in American society between a powerful white dominant group and powerless nonwhite minority groups, today we see the polarization between two more or less equally powerful groups. Stressing cultural pluralism and encouraging multicultural education are attempts to reduce this polarization, and to work for the development of an American society in which many ethnic groups can live in a symbiotic relationship, where cultural differences are respected, without the implication that one culture is better or worse than another. Cultural pluralism does not deny the existence of differences in culture, but it sees no justification for asking anyone to reject his or her cultural identity and background in order to have a meaningful life in a multicultural society.

If cultural pluralism is to be achieved, it is essential to have the school's full participation in conducting educational programs that exemplify what life in a multicultural society should be. It is also true that the school's efforts alone will not produce the desired social effect. The goal of a multicultural society is so important, however, that we cannot afford to ignore the school simply because it is not the single, all-powerful change agent in so important and complex a problem as race relations.

As we work for multicultural education, we must be wary of committing an error analogous to that involved in acceptance of the melting pot ideology. This ideology assumed that the dominant social group remained unchanged while the minority groups melted in. It is equally invalid to assume that with multicultural education the minority ethnic group will remain unchanged while the dominant middle class does the adjusting. The goals of multicultural education will be realized only when *both* minority and majority ethnic groups recognize and accept the advantages and responsibilities of living in a multicultural society. No longer is it feasible for any one ethnic group to remain fixed in its ways while expecting other groups to adjust to their standard.

Multicultural education in the U.S. is more important today than ever before, because our population mobility and nationwide communication media eliminate the possibility that there are any ethnic enclaves that will long remain isolated from the tensions and resources of the rest of the country. Population movements from the rural South and Puerto Rico to northern cities, and the middle-class exodus to city suburbs illustrate current population shifts. Every American must now be made aware of the multicultural aspects of everyday life, and every teacher, regardless of where born or educated, must be prepared to work effectively with children and communities of different ethnic origins.

Role of CBTE

The three ethnic groups represented in this conference have rightly focused on their unique needs. The question remains as to whether there

are any needs that are common to the three groups as well as to other groups not represented here, such as the Filipino or Haitian children in our schools. The question is also asked whether competency-based teacher education is an effective means of developing cross-cultural teaching competencies in order to achieve multicultural education in our schools.

We regard competency-based teacher education as a promising means of achieving multicultural education. The end, to us, is more important than the means. If competency-based teacher education is more effective in achieving multicultural education than other procedures currently used, we are ardent advocates of competency-based teacher education, wisely planned and skillfully executed. We are equally ready to ignore or reject competency-based teacher education if it has no special value for our purposes.

Because the preceding sections include treatment of CBTE activities needed to achieve the objectives discussed, this section will not include discussion of activities necessary to achieve objectives important to all ethnic groups.

One of the reasons why paths of educational purpose are often far from smooth is that the road is strewn with abandoned bandwagons. We are not eager to add another bandwagon labeled CBTE. It is important, therefore, to study the contribution CBTE can make to multicultural education, not merely to see whether it can be rephrased or distorted only to *seem* to serve multicultural purposes.

When Knute Rockne was the Notre Dame football coach, he was asked by a friend why he permitted his opponents' scouts to attend Notre Dame's football practice sessions. Wasn't he afraid they would steal his plays? Rockne answered, "It's not the play but the execution that wins games." We want to see CBTE so executed as to achieve multicultural education for a culturally pluralistic society. If it cannot be so executed, we are ready to consider other procedures to achieve the goals of multicultural education.

Need to Eliminate Stereotypes

If we are to achieve multicultural education, we must reexamine the shortcomings of current education programs designed for children from minority ethnic groups. We must insure proper concern for understanding our students' cultural heritage, value systems, and the other economic, political, and social forces which affect them.

Teachers may overemphasize poverty and low socioeconomic class membership as stereotypes for children from minority ethnic groups. While there are certain cultural practices, including folklore and values, transmitted from elders which are integral to ethnic culture by choice, there are also lifestyles forced upon members of a social group because of poverty and economic deprivation, which are *not* voluntarily integral to the ethnic culture.

Most teachers do not have adequate knowledge of the various cultural systems from which their pupils come. It has been assumed for too long that good teachers can teach everyone, and that such teachers can provide for the necessary emotional and learning needs of children from diverse cultural backgrounds. However, as evidenced in low student achievement rates, there is an impelling need for reform.

Emphasis on intercultural acceptance among all groups is badly needed if we expect to enable new generations to reduce ethnocentrism and understand the world through the eyes of other people. Cognitive learning about the contributions of each other's culture is only the first step. Acceptance, as a value, must pass beyond mere toleration of others and provide for internalization of such an affective value. In this way we can arrive at the stage of working and living together without the obstacles of scapegoating, stereotyping, discrimination, and prejudice that prevent effective human interrelationships.

WHAT THE TEACHER CAN DO

Achievement of this grand plan calls forth from each of us the most penetrating scrutiny of ourselves as teachers and humans. We each view the other through perceptual screens that are as old as we are. We have learned all our lives about how it's "supposed to be." The thin veneer of four to six years of professional education is not enough to allow us to be other than we are.

We all have biases and prejudices which affect how we view the world and people in it. But if we would accept the role of teacher of children from diverse groups, we must accept the responsibility of discovering and controlling those patterns in our behavior which would interfere with the learners' free and uninhibited access to knowledge and self-development. Teacher education has the responsibility to search out, evaluate, and organize programs which will help teachers become competent in this dimension of human development, thereby giving teachers power over themselves and their behavior as they offer every child an equal education opportunity.

Identifying a culture can give the teacher insight into common values and attitudes. Teachers must acknowledge that there are often more differences within a single cultural group than between various cultural groups. Individual differences as well as degree of acculturation and assimilation produce a wide range of in-group differences. Thus, if one indulges in stereotyped thinking, one may believe that all Mexican Americans speak Spanish as their primary language, which is not necessarily true. While many may speak Spanish at home, others speak English.

Another example is that of stereotyping the authority of the father in Mexican American culture. In those families which tend to be traditional in their values, customs, and habits, the father is the chief authority figure. However, democratic sharing of authority between husband and wife is common in other Mexican American homes.

Teachers who are aware of and sensitive to a range of values within a culture avoid stereotyping. Instead, they assume the role of learner and attempt to learn more about each child, relating to him or her on the basis of that child's cultural framework. Learning each child's orientation is a continuous process which can assist the teacher in deciding which aspects of the child's culture can be best utilized in the learning process.

In a truly multicultural classroom, the teacher recognizes, encourages, and values the bicultural development of students. Rather than forcing all students into the majority culture mold, the teacher, with great care and sensitivity, can help children live in two cultures.

Since language is a great factor which unites or separates people within a culture, special attention should be given to it. While much attention should be paid to the development of the majority language of our American culture, the language of culturally different children should be included in the curriculum and not be ignored. The degree to which a teacher can do this will be limited by the teacher's own facility in the language of culturally different children. Obviously, a teacher who speaks Spanish and has Spanish-speaking youngsters in class can conduct learning activities in Spanish when appropriate.

The teacher who understands children who speak nonstandard English can encourage culturally different youth in creative writing, creative drama, and other learning activities. If students are allowed and encouraged to utilize their native language, their creative efforts, whether in writing or drama, can be enhanced greatly.

Both minority and majority ethnic groups can be helped to appreciate the contributions of culturally different groups to the enrichment of colloquial language. Popular songs, contemporary poems, and stories are often outlets for new expressions. A study of such contemporary art forms can help both groups develop a greater understanding and appreciation of the variety of language created by culturally different groups.

The study of holidays, customs, and foods offers a cross-cultural perspective as yet another avenue to be utilized in achieving the objectives of appreciation and acceptance of various cultures.

The identification and acceptance of multiculturalism as a desirable goal should assist diverse ethnic groups to value it as an important outcome of American education.

WHAT TEACHER EDUCATION CAN DO

In order to prepare and retool teachers for their roles in developing effective school settings, we must restructure the academic and pedagogical programs which have become entrenched as part of the traditional mode of teacher education. General education requirements, for example, ordinarily do not allow concentration in such disciplines as cultural anthropology, linguistics, and ethnography. Teacher education has failed to utilize and maximize the contributions of these academic areas in the preparation of teachers.

Teacher education programs must recognize and capitalize on ethnic diversity. They must change in response to the objectives of multicultural education advocated throughout this paper. If we accept cultural pluralism as our goal, with its recognition that cultures can be different without being better or worse, we should be prepared to expect diverse communication styles and cultural values, and to accept a multiplicity of languages and lifestyles.

Teacher education has not taken into account the fact that individuals of one culture have little understanding, appreciation, or acceptance of the pervading values and lifestyles of other cultures. Teachers must recognize that all cultures are dynamic, but that they vary considerably in their rate of change. For example, language styles in cultural groups are in a constant state of evolution. Another reflection of cultures' innate dynamics is the often rapid change in dress resulting from movies and television programs.

A program derived from an anthropological, linguistic, or sociological base would develop those teaching competencies regarded by the various ethnic groups as important and basic to developing philosophical values in the teacher. The restructuring of teacher education must consider the knowledge a prospective teacher can gain from a diversity of experiences afforded by a multidisciplinary teacher education program. The importance of this approach must not be sidetracked, since intercultural conflicts frequently surface in value and perceptions.

These culturally derived teaching competencies seem to be hinged to concepts of personalized (individualized) learning, which demand that the child be accepted as an individual with specific learning needs. It follows, then, that a diagnostic/prescriptive approach to teaching would take into account the individual needs of students. Diagnosis, a skill performed by most professionals, calls for determination of student interests, needs, learning styles, and strengths. Diagnosis should not be confused with scores derived from norm-referenced standardized testing and other modes of assessment which have a high cultural bias. The promise of CBTE is that it is an individualized teacher education program consisting of specific competencies to be demonstrated, alternative learning strategies, and criterion-referenced measurement.

If the adage "teachers teach as they were taught" is true, then a program of teacher education which reflects the type of teacher behavior *desired* in professional teaching is more likely to be relevant. In addition, the transferability of such behavior from professor to student is enhanced to a much greater degree, in contrast to a traditional credit-accumulation program steeped in lecture approaches to teaching and learning.

249

Teacher education programs, if they are to facilitate generic multicultural teaching competencies (i.e., cross-cultural teaching competencies), must allow opportunities for total, or at least partial, immersion into other cultures. This can be accommodated by establishing long-term internships rather than short-term student-teaching experiences. Internships call for experiences by teacher candidates where, with the aid of anthropologists, linguists, and educators, competencies identified as relating to particular cultural settings can be identified and developed. The culture of the school itself has a profound influence on student behavior as well as on that of teachers. With total immersion, or immersion within the limits of the teacher education program, prospective teachers would sharpen their perception of themselves and of how others perceive them. Such an internship would provide prospective teachers the experiences necessary for examining their own cultural biases and how these biases relate to other cultures.

Another strategy for the accommodation of cross-cultural competency development is to include and involve minority ethnic community members as adjunct program-developers and instructional staff. Collaborative organizational structures (teacher centers, personnel development centers) which can put aside credential requirements for preparing teachers may facilitate the immediate involvment of the community in the professional development of teachers!

If total immersion into another culture seems impossible now, it is vitally important to include community representatives of target cultures in all aspects of the teacher education program.

An equally important aspect of cross-cultural training is the acquisition of language skills. Potential teachers should not only be masters of standard American English (SAE), but must acquire those linguistic competencies which enable them, as teachers, to understand, accept, and analyze other language patterns and dialects. Linguistics and language competency will not only enable teachers to diagnose problems and prescribe activities for the learner, but will also enable them to communicate with the community of parents.

Some Necessary First Steps

Traditionally, teachers have focused their attention on instilling middle-class values of the dominant culture into their pupils. The demands for conformity to the school world are frequently at variance with pressures generated by family and community. As a result the child becomes a pawn in the contest of competing lifestyles. In this competition, everyone becomes a loser.

Some recent educational advocates have suggested that teachers should glorify and inculcate the values only of the particular culture in which the child lives, saying that "children should be taught to do better the things they are going to do anyway." Although this approach would obviously reduce the conflict between values taught in school and those found in the child's environment, it ignores the realities of American life and obviates the potential for enhanced living in a multicultural society.

Another purpose in keeping with the concepts of a truly multicultural society is discussed by Bayles, who concludes that education should promote positive development of student outlooks on life, and the capacity to construct such outlooks independently.[1] Such a purpose is a realistic goal for teachers in a multicultural society. It would result in increasing the options of *all* pupils. It would help children understand that there are different ways of behaving which may be appropriate in different situations, and that one's goals affect vitally the choices one makes. Thus, our aim is neither to glorify the status quo, nor to force acceptance or rejection of values upon which the children's world is presently based, but to promote both teachers' and children's ability to understand and cope with an environment which can and will change.

To accomplish this purpose, teachers should help pupils find answers to problems which confront them now or may confront them in the future. Instead of merely memorizing facts, pupils will investigate alternatives and propose solutions to their problems. This approach does not lessen the necessity for intensive study of society's accumulated knowledge. However, it does mean that knowledge is not an end in itself, but has a broader use. It is the basis for making decisions and solving problems. Pupils, instead of accepting passively the pronouncements of teachers, will be encouraged to question, search, reflect, and perceive relationships. In short, they will become increasingly responsible for their own intellectual, social, and emotional development. The teacher's importance is in no way diminished, for the teacher is responsible for continuously raising new questions, presenting information, probing for further knowledge, and helping pupils reach conclusions in harmony with the judgmental criteria that are taken to be applicable. The teacher thus becomes the director of a continuing research effort in which pupils share a progressively increasing responsibility.

It is important that all segments of majority ethnic groups, as well as the minorities, recognize the need for developing a multicultural teacher education program so that schools, in turn, may provide a sound multicultural education program for youngsters. The values sought by minority ethnic groups are equally important for the majority, and minority views of necessary multicultural competencies show us the directions in which teacher education must move.

REFERENCES

1 Bayles, Ernest E. *Pragmatism in Education*. New York: Harper & Row, 1966 (No page given).

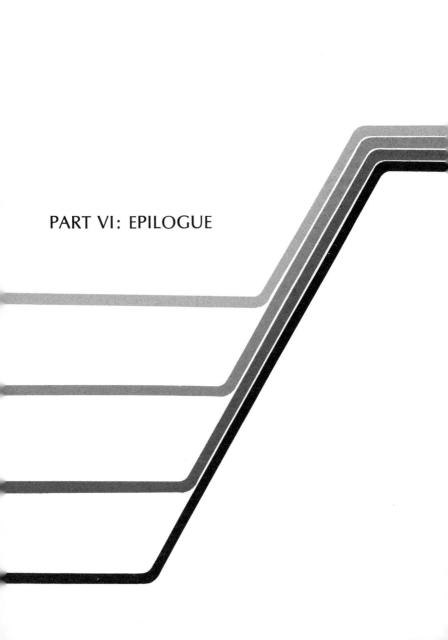

PART VI: EPILOGUE

NEXT STEPS—WHERE DO WE GO FROM HERE?

William A. Hunter

The case for multicultural education in America will have to be made for some years to come. Although inroads have been made, and efforts are gaining momentum in establishing the meaning, value, and virtue of multicultural education, it must become a continuing national mandate threading through all facets of education—dreams, plans, and practices. The inequities in American education did not develop overnight—nor will they be removed in a short time or as the result of a single effort. What is necessary, above and beyond commitment to this new multifaceted-society approach, is advocacy of multicultural education as an inherent part of the democratic way of life we teach.

253

Continuous commitment to multicultural education can be effected in at least two ways: (a) multiculturalism must be practiced; it must permeate policies, activities, and procedures; and (b) multiculturalism must be made a part of formal learning. All children and students should have multicultural perspectives in their subject learnings, where such perspectives would occupy their appropriate and rightful places, making all learning rich and alive. It is well documented in this book that the true mosaic of cultural contributions to this nation's heritage are not reflected in its current practices or teachings.

Moreover, through the channel of formal learning, multicultural education is a legitimate and fertile area for research; since it is a concentration of applied subjects, it forms a subject area in its own right. Substantive knowledge is available for a composite study of multicultural education as a whole, as well as a study of its contributing cultures.

A national program meaningfully conceptualized with multicultural values and responsive to multicultural needs, with input from the entire mosaic of ethnic communities, must begin. Such a program should recognize the diversity of needs to be accommodated and administered. We begin with the realization that such an effort must be substantial and of long duration in order to eradicate inequities which have existed in our country for at least three centuries.

What the States Should Do

The education profession and the states should set a pattern in the public schools requiring a minimum of bilingual or bidialectal communications. In states and regions where specific languages and language patterns are part of the contributing culture, those languages should also be taught and used in the schools. Teaching materials, teaching styles, and educational content should also be revised in terms of bilingual, bicultural, and multicultural considerations.

In order to be certified, teachers should meet multicultural requirements. Before a teacher gains full certification for teaching in public schools, that teacher should be required to live in the local school community. After at least a year of working and teaching in the local school and living in the community, and before full certification is granted, an assessment should be made of the teacher's effectiveness and potential. This assessment can be accomplished by a state department of education representative, a school administrator, a college or university representative, a master teacher, and others as the setting might dictate, including possibly the uncertified candidate.

There is supportive evidence of the success which can be achieved in making teachers more effective in multicultural settings, such as the Cooperative Urban Teacher Education (CUTE) Program.*

States would need to revise their required courses of study, not only to include necessary studies in contributing cultures but also to include multicultural content in all subject areas. The cooperation of colleges and universities, the academic profession, and agencies and organizations, as well as teachers, schools, communities, and businesses (particularly the publications industry) would be needed in the revision and development of instructional materials.

Education centers, cooperatively established by the state, universities and colleges, schools, the education profession, and the educationally sensitive community leadership, could establish continuing inservice teacher education programs as one of their major efforts. Such center programs would not only enable inservice personnel to continually upgrade them-

*The Cooperative Urban Teacher Education (CUTE) program is a unique inner-city teacher education program designed by the Mid-continent Regional Educational Laboratory (McREL), Kansas City, Mo. A pilot program established relationships between McREL and 13 liberal arts colleges in Missouri and Kansas, and the public school systems of Kansas City, Mo. and Kansas City, Ks. After testing and refining by the McREL staff, the program was expanded to include 68 public and private higher education institutions, 13 public and 2 parochial school systems, and presently provides field experience for prospective teachers of 12 urban centers across the nation. New installations include a wide spectrum of old and new physical plants and target populations. Most of the communities involved have more than one racial minority, including Spanish-speaking Americans, Orientals, Blacks, Native Americans, and whites. So far, about 2,000 prospective teachers have participated in this program. AACTE has had a long and cooperative association with the CUTE program, including joint publication of a quarterly newsletter, Target, which disseminated CUTE activities. This program is the only one which has twice received the AACTE Distinguished Achievement Award (DAA) for Excellence in Teacher Education.

254

selves, but would also provide a vehicle and forum for dealing with new problems and concerns.

What Colleges and Universities Should Do

The teacher training programs of colleges and universities need to gear up to handle (a) the new responsibilities of continuing inservice professional education, (b) research and preparation of an expanded phalanx of instructional materials and procedures for handling those materials, and (c) reorientation of preservice programs so that they will prepare education personnel to appreciate America's multicultural richness and incorporate it in their teachings. Among the specific competencies generic to all teacher capabilities is *sensitivity* to the cultural needs and integrities of all learners.

Teachers must become competent in multicultural *communication*. They must appreciate the power of communication and the logic of mental processes which accompany such communication. All teachers will need to be aware of different linguistic styles and appreciate the need to become conversant in the language of their students, both in thought and verbalization. Minimally, teachers will be bilingually competent, including knowledge of the local dialect where appropriate. This will mean that teacher education programs must reconstitute the communication component for appreciation purposes as well as for specialization. Prospective teachers may not be ready to choose their second language until they approach certification, unless they wish to specialize in a specific cultural setting.

255

THE ROLES OF THE SOCIAL SCIENCES AND HUMANITIES

The social science component of the general teacher education program would provide an appreciation of the essential nature of the multicultural heritage of our society, as well as the special applied aspects of the social sciences to problems and circumstances of various cultural groups.

The history of the country would be rewritten to reflect the presence, role, participation, and contributions of all peoples in the events which built our nation. This effort may need initial subsidies for at least two reasons: (a) research is needed in some significant areas because records concerning minority groups were either destroyed or by legal ruling not kept; and (b) the publishing industry has had a long history of resistance to publishing materials describing minority group contributions. Some have alleged that such publications would not have a market and would be offensive to majority group readers. All learning materials, including textbooks, must accurately portray the multicultural aspects of our heritage.

Additionally, the sociological, anthropological, economic, political, and business aspects of the social sciences require appropriate correction of the omissions which have characterized these studies, especially relating to ethnic aspects of the culture. The cumulative ethnic stereotype myths need to be dispelled.

The humanities in general education should likewise develop a greater general appreciation for art, music, drama, architecture, literature, and other cultural forms and their influence on our lives. This study should include the diverse contributions of all our ethnic groups. Especially, the humanities should offer the opportunity to specialize, study, and work in any one of these areas as it relates to a particular minority culture.

Next Steps

Further steps must be taken to have multicultural education recognized as an essential entity in American education. These steps include the following:

1. It is hoped that personnel selected for federal policy-making roles would be sympathetic to the multicultural view. Such officials must have representative, responsible, and responsive input at all program planning and implementation levels, particularly at the U.S. Office of Education (USOE). This view should apply to state and local government personnel as well. Finally, community representatives who take into account the diversity of the community must be allowed responsible input into decision-making and leadership roles, particularly as they affect multicultural education.

2. Responsive and knowledgeable consultative services must be organized to deal with problems concerning multicultural education, and made available to higher education associations, academic institutions, and state, local, and federal agencies.

3. Research must be undertaken to develop better evaluation measures of all kinds for instructional diagnosis, assessment, and improvement. Tests standardized against norms not reflective of true learning circumstances should be used for information purposes only. Such tests should not be used to categorize children in order to exclude them from education experiences. Tests and diagnostic tools need to be devised to communicate in the language and in terms of the cultural experience of those being tested. Performance criteria lend themselves to the development of such assessment procedures.

4. The capabilities of PBTE and multicultural education must be synthesized and realized in a comprehensive program which is applicable both individually and collectively to our multicultural youth. For specific recommendations on PBTE, see *Achieving the Potential of Performance-Based Teacher Education: Recommendations*, PBTE Series No. 16, by the AACTE Committee on Performance-Based Teacher Education, February 1974, available from AACTE.

Multicultural education through competency-based teacher education recognizes that there are positive differences among cultures. In the mosaic of our society, the whole is greater than the sum of its parts, for there is *No One Model American.*

256

WRITING CONFERENCE ON COMPETENCIES FOR TEACHERS OF DIFFERENT CULTURAL AND CROSS-CULTURAL GROUPS

Conference Site: Oklahoma Center for Continuing Education
Location: Norman, Oklahoma
Date: June 16-22, 1974

Sponsored by the
AMERICAN ASSOCIATION OF COLLEGES
FOR TEACHER EDUCATION

through its
MULTICULTURAL EDUCATION/COMPETENCY-BASED
TEACHER EDUCATION PROJECT

THE TEACHER CORPS through
THE UNIVERSITY OF TOLEDO

and in cooperation with the
AACTE Performance-Based Teacher Education Project

*The following pages are excerpted from the Conference program. Position titles of participants are listed as they were at the time of the Writing Conference, June 1974.

Program Schedule

SUNDAY, JUNE 16, 1974

3-5 p.m.	Registration	Forum Room A-6
6-8 p.m.	Get-acquainted Dinner	Dining Room-Commons Restaurant
8:30-9:30 p.m.	Briefing Session: William A. Hunter Prime Writers and Associate Prime Writers	

MONDAY, JUNE 17, 1974

8-9 a.m.	Registration (continued)	Forum Room A-6
8:30-9 a.m.	Welcome: Edward C. Pomeroy Conference Orientation: William A. Hunter	Forum Conf. Room A
9 a.m.-Noon	Interaction between Consultants and Position Paper Writers	

1. Summary Critique and Consultant Interaction with Position Paper Writers—Black Americans

2. Summary Critique and Consultant Interaction, Position Paper Writers—Spanish-speaking Americans

3. Summary Critique and Consultant Interaction, Position Paper Writers—Native Americans

12-1:55 p.m.	Luncheon Session
2-6 p.m.	Interaction Sessions of Position Paper Writers with Writer Editors

I. Teacher Competencies Effective for Teaching Black American Youth — Forum Room A-5

Position Paper Writers
L. Eudora Pettigrew
Allen R. Sullivan
Cordell Wynn
Asa G. Hilliard
Helen V. Foster

Panel of Writer-Editors
Richard L. James, Chairman
Paul B. Mohr, Cochairman
Anne R. Gayles
Gwendolyn C. Baker
Asa G. Hilliard
Charles Payne

II. Teacher Competencies　　　　　　　Forum Room C-1
    Effective for Teaching
    Spanish-speaking
    American Youth

Position Paper Writers	**Panel of Writer-Editors**
Ernest Garcia	Atilano A. Valencia,
M. Reyes Mazón	Chairman
Norma E. Hernandez	Tomás A. Arciniega, Co-
Luis M. Laosa	chairman
Ignacio Cordova	Ida Santos Stewart
Rupert Trujillo	Thomas Lopez
	Rudy Cordova

III. Teacher Competencies　　　　　　Forum Room C-2
    Effective for Teaching
    Native American Youth

Position Paper Writers	**Panel of Writer-Editors**
Will Antell	Henrietta Whiteman,
Milo Kalectaca	Chairman
Louise Miller	Rosella Covington, Co-
Ava F. Doty	chairman
	Fount Holland
	Eugene Sekaquaptewa
	Patricia Locke
	Michael Dorris

IV. Cross-Cultural Teacher　　　　　　Forum Room C-3
    Competencies Effective
    for teaching Youth in a
    Culturally Diverse Society

Panel of Writer-Editors
Harry N. Rivlin, Chairman
Frank J. Sciara, Cochairman
Patricia Cabrera
Hansom P. Baptiste
John A. Masla
Daniel Levine
Ernest A. Holmes
Grant Clothier

TUESDAY, JUNE 18, 1974
GROUP WRITING SESSIONS

9 a.m.-Noon 2-5 p.m.	I Black American Writer-Editors	Forum Room A-5
Extended	II Spanish-speaking American Writer-Editors	Forum Room C-1
writing sessions	III Native American Writer-Editors	Forum Room C-2
arranged by group chair-man	IV Cross-Cultural Writer-Editors will work with the several groups to identify common competencies	Forum Room C-3

WEDNESDAY, JUNE 19, 1974
GROUP WRITING SESSIONS (continued)

9 a.m.-Noon 2-5 p.m.	I Black American Writer-Editors	Forum Room A-5
Extended	II Spanish-speaking American Writer-Editors	Forum Room C-1
writing sessions	III Native American Writer-Editors	Forum Room C-2
arranged by group chair-man	IV Cross-Cultural Writer-Editors will work with the several groups to identify common competencies	Forum Room C-3

THURSDAY, JUNE 20, 1974

9-10 a.m.	Meeting of Prime Writers, Associate Prime Writers, and Editor	Joel L. Burdin, Associate Director, AACTE; Editor, *Journal of Teacher Education*

10 a.m.-Noon Work on Final Report

Lunch

2-5 p.m. Completion of Final Report

FRIDAY, JUNE 21, 1974

9 a.m.-Noon	Meeting of Steering Committee MCE/CBTE Project; Review of First Draft of Report Manuscript	Forum Room A-5

Lunch

Manuscript Reactions and Revisions; Designation and Approval of Publication Format

Roster of Participants

M. Reyes Mazón
Director, Institute for Cultural
Pluralism and Professor,
School of Education
San Diego State University
San Diego, California 92115

"Competency-Based Education
and the Culturally Different:
A Ray of Hope or More of the Same?"

Norma G. Hernandez, Chairperson
Curriculum and Instruction
    Department
The University of Texas at El Paso
El Paso, Texas 79968

"Multicultural Education and CBTE:
A Vehicle for Reform"

Luis M. Laosa
Assistant Professor
Graduate School of Education
College of Education
University of California, Los Angeles
Los Angeles, California 90024

"Toward a Research Model of Multicultural Competency-Based
Teacher Education"

Ignacio Cordova, Professor, and
Mari-Luci Jaramillo
Rupert Trujillo
College of Education
University of New Mexico
Albuquerque, New Mexico 87106

"CBTE for Mexican American
Students"

Native Americans

Titles of Papers

Will Antell
Graduate School of Education
Harvard University
Cambridge, Massachusetts 02138

Milo Kalectaca
Teacher Corps Associate
Northern Arizona University
Flagstaff, Arizona 86001

"Competencies for Teachers of
Culturally Different Children:
Teacher Competencies for Teaching
Native American Children"

Louise Miller
Education Specialist
Assistant Area Director, Education
Bureau of Indian Affairs
Sacramento, California 95825

"A Need for Competency-Based
Teacher Education for Native
Americans"

Ava F. Doty
Ft. Sill Indian School
Bureau of Indian Affairs
Lawton, Oklahoma 73504

"A Position Paper on Teacher
Competencies for Cultural Diversity"

PANELS OF WRITER-EDITORS

Black Writer-Editors

Richard James
Chairman, Department of Education
Morgan State College
Baltimore, Maryland 21212

Paul B. Mohr, Sr., Dean,
College of Education
Florida A & M University
Tallahassee, Florida 34307

Anne R. Gayles, Chairperson
Department of Secondary Education
and Foundations
Florida A & M University
Tallahassee, Florida 32307

Gwendolyn C. Baker, Assistant
Professor
Chairperson, Multicultural Program
School of Education
University of Michigan
Ann Arbor, Michigan 48104

Asa G. Hilliard, Dean
School of Education
San Francisco State University
San Francisco, California 94132

Charles R. Payne, Director
Multicultural Department of
Secondary, Adult and Higher
Education
Teachers College
Ball State University
Muncie, Indiana 47306

Native American Writer-Editors

Henrietta Whiteman (Southern
Cheyenne)
Director of the Native American
Studies Program
University of Montana
Missoula, Montana 59801

Fount Holland, Coeducator
Indian Intern Teacher Training Program
Northeastern Oklahoma State College
Tahlequah, Oklahoma 74464

Eugene Sekaquaptewa
Assistant Professor of Education
Arizona State University
Tempe, Arizona 85281

Patricia Locke, Director
Planning Resources in Minority
Education
Western Interstate Commission on
Higher Education
Boulder, Colorado 80302

Rosella J. Covington
Project Director
Native American Cultural Institute
University of Montana
Missoula, Montana 59801

Michael Dorris, Chairman
Native American Studies
Dartmouth College
Hanover, New Hampshire 03755

Donald Lemon, Director
Northern Plains Teacher Corps
University of North Dakota
Grand Forks, North Dakota 58201

263

264

Advisory and Policy Groups

MULTICULTURAL EDUCATION/COMPETENCY-BASED EDUCATION
PROJECT STEERING COMMITTEE

Tomás Arciniega, Chairman, Steering Committee, Dean, San Diego State University, San Diego, California 92115

Mary Hatwood, Classroom Teacher, Alexandria City School System, Alexandria, Virginia 22309

James Kelly, Jr., Dean, School of Education, University of Pittsburgh, Pittsburgh, Pa. 15213

Richard W. Saxe, Associate Dean, College of Education, The University of Toledo, Toledo, Ohio 43606

Atilano A. Valencia, Chairman, Department of Education, New Mexico Highlands University, Las Vegas, New Mexico 87701

Elaine Witty, Chairman, Department of Elementary Education, Norfolk State College, Norfolk, Virginia 23504

Henrietta Whiteman, Director of Native American Studies Program, University of Montana, Missoula, Montana 59801

MCE/CBTE Project Staff

William A. Hunter, Principal Investigator, Multicultural/CBTE Project, American Association of Colleges for Teacher Education, One Dupont Circle, Suite 610, Washington, D.C. 20036

Geneva F. Watkins, Program Assistant, Multicultural/CBTE Project

Iran Khan, Secretary

MEMBERS OF THE COMMISSION ON MULTICULTURAL EDUCATION

James Kelly, Jr., Dean, School of Education, University of Pittsburgh, Pittsburgh, Pennsylvania 15213

Richard H. Davis, Dean, School of Education, University of Wisconsin—Milwaukee, Milwaukee, Wisconsin 53201

Carl J. Dolce, Dean, School of Education, North Carolina State University, Raleigh, North Carolina 27607

Hilda Hidalgo, Chairman, Department of Urban Studies and Community Development, Livingston College, Rutgers University, New Brunswick, New Jersey 08903

Charles F. Leyba, Associate Professor, California State University, Los Angeles, Los Angeles, California 90020

Elaine Witty, Chairman, Department of Elementary Education, Norfolk State College, Norfolk, Virginia 23504

Henrietta Whiteman, Director of Native American Studies Program, University of Montana, Missoula, Montana 59801

Liaison Members:

Dave Darland, Associate Director, Instruction and Professional Development, National Education Association, 1201 16th Street, N.W., Washington, D.C. 20036

Rolf W. Larson, Director, National Council for Accreditation of Teacher Education, 1950 Pennsylvania Ave., N.W., Washington, D.C. 20006

AACTE TODAY

The American Association of Colleges for Teacher Education is a national voluntary professional association of more than 865 colleges and universities which prepare 90 percent of the nation's teachers. The Association is organized as a means for member institutions to work cooperatively for the improvement of programs preparing educational personnel.

268

The Association addresses itself to current issues facing education and the important role which well prepared school personnel play in American and world societies. The AACTE has, since 1970, provided national leadership in the study and encouragement of multicultural education. Through the efforts of a Commission on Multicultural Education, it has effectively called for greater attention to the preservation and enhancement of cultural pluralism in teacher education. The statement *No One Model American* and the Winter 1973 issue of the *Journal of Teacher Education* (vol. XXIV, no. 4), with multicultural education as its theme, are typical of the Commission's leadership efforts.

A committee currently studying performance-based teacher education is another example of AACTE's national leadership role. Additional key concerns include accreditation of teacher education, international education, and government relations. The Association's Washington, D.C. location gives it strong visibility and influence over public education policy.

AACTE is governed by official representatives appointed by each member institution. These representatives, who include both administrators and faculty members, elect the AACTE leadership and determine major policy direction of the organization.

Publications include the monthly *AACTE Bulletin,* the *Yearbook,* the *Directory,* and the *Journal of Teacher Education*. Books, periodicals, and monographs are regularly published for the membership. The AACTE is the administrative agency for the ERIC Clearinghouse on Teacher Education.

AACTE activities include an annual meeting, workshops, seminars, and other special programs. Its national office includes an executive director, four associate directors and more than 30 supporting personnel.

APPENDIX II

RECOMMENDATIONS FOR IMPROVING MINORITY-GROUP EDUCATION: A CASE STUDY ON CHICANOS*

I. CURRICULUM

1. State departments of education[1] in each of the five Southwestern States should establish requirements aimed at assuring that the individual interests, language, and learning skills of Mexican American children are given adequate attention and consideration in the curriculum and instructional materials used by local school districts. These requirements should include:

    (a) All curriculum and instructional materials must incorporate the history, language, and culture of Chicanos in the Southwest, in the State, and in the local community.

    (b) Courses of special interest to Chicano students, such as Mexican American history and Chicano studies, must be offered on a regular basis to all students.

    (c) Formal and informal rules prohibiting the speaking of Spanish in the classroom or on school grounds must be eliminated.

    (d) Mechanisms must be established to facilitate participation of Chicano pupils, parents, and community members in development of curriculum and instructional materials.

    (e) School districts with substantial numbers of Spanish speaking parents must provide concurrent translations of PTA and school board meetings so as to facilitate full participation of all parents in discussions and decisions.

    (f) Schools and school districts with substantial numbers of children of Spanish speaking parents must send notices home in Spanish as well as English.

    (g) School districts must establish numerical goals and timetables for securing equitable Chicano representation in staff positions involving the selection and implementation of curriculum.

    (h) Textbooks must reflect representative and accurate portrayals of Chicanos.

2. State departments of education should impose sanctions, including the cutoff of funds, against school districts which have violated the above requirements.

3. State departments of education should establish numerical goals and timetables for securing equitable representation in (a) staff positions

269

*SOURCE: U.S. Commission on Civil Rights, *Toward Quality Education for Mexican Americans, Report VI: Mexican-American Education Study* (Washington, D.C.: Government Printing Office, February 1974), pp. 76-82.

involving the selection and development of curriculum and (b) on State textbook committees.

4. State legislatures should enact legislation requiring districts to establish bilingual education or other curricular approaches designed to impart English language skills to non-English speaking students while incorporating into the curriculum the children's native language, culture, and history. These programs should be instituted for each group of students whose primary language is other than English, and who constitute five percent of the enrollment or number more than 20 in a given school.

5. State legislators should enact legislation prohibiting at-large elections of school board members in all communities and require instead election from single member districts.

6. Congress should increase its support for Bilingual Education by increasing Federal appropriations for the program and by providing special funds specifically for needed research and development in this area.

7. The National Institute of Education (NIE) should fund research to develop curricular programs designed to meet the educational needs of Chicano students.

STUDENT ASSIGNMENT

A. *Grade Retention*

1. State departments of education should develop requirements dealing with the two principal reasons given by schools for the practice of grade retention—academic failure and emotional immaturity of students. These requirements should prohibit grade retention unless the following conditions are met:

For academic failure

(a) Resources are available to determine thoroughly why the previous educational program was ineffective for the student.

(b) Resources are available to provide the retained student with full-time programs specifically tailored to meet his or her needs, interests, and existing skills and knowledge.

(c) There is substantial evidence that the student will benefit more from these special programs on a full-time basis than from being promoted to the next grade and receiving special help only during the preceding summer or on a part-time basis during the regular school year.

For emotional immaturity

(a) A State-licensed counselor, psychologist, or psychiatrist has recommended grade repetition after assessing the student's behavior in school, at home, and in the community.

(b) In the case of a student who is Mexican American, the official making the recommendation must be knowledgeable about the Chicano culture.

(c) In the case of a student or parents who are primarily Spanish speaking, the professional making the recommendation must be fluent in the Spanish language.
2. State departments of education should impose appropriate sanctions, including fund cutoffs, against school districts in violation of these requirements.
3. The Office for Civil Rights (OCR), HEW, should use substantial differences in the rate of grade retention of various racial or ethnic groups of students as an indicator of unequal educational services.

B. *Ability Grouping*
1. State departments of education should prohibit the use of long-term ability grouping.
2. State departments of education should develop requirements for the use of short-term groups for specific learning needs. At a minimum they should require:
    (a) That the size of classes be limited so that all pupils can receive individualized attention.
    (b) That there be bilingual instruction for students whose primary language is not English, taught by a bilingual teacher who is also familiar with the cultural background of these students.   271
    (c) That a definite time limit for these groups be established, not to exceed half the academic school year. Any extension must first be approved by the State department of education, based on a clear showing that additional time will directly benefit the students.
    (d) That both students and parents know and understand the purpose for a student's placement in a particular group and the proposed time a student will remain in the group.
    (e) That teachers who instruct a particular short-term group be specially trained in diagnosing and meeting the learning needs of students placed in these groups.
3. State departments of education should impose sanctions, including fund cutoff, on districts which are in violation of the requirements set forth in 1 and 2 above.

C. *Placement in EMR Classes*
1. Schools and districts should maintain Educable Mentally Retarded classes only for those children diagnosed as being severely deficient in both intellectual functioning *and* adaptation to home and school environments (adaptive behavior).
2. State departments of education should issue requirements for the placement of students in EMR classes, including:
    (a) That evaluation of a student include behavioral observation, home visitation, and interviews with parents and other community people so as to measure the student's ability to adapt to his or her environment.

(b) That in the case of Spanish speaking students or parents, this evaluation be made by a school psychologist who speaks their language and is familiar with their cultural background.

(c) That where there is no school psychologist who fulfills these requirements, another school staff member or community person who speaks the language and is familiar with the cultural background be used as an interpreter.

(d) That any test which is used for Chicanos or other minorities be validated for that group of students.

(e) That before placement occurs, a panel consisting of the school psychologist, other school personnel, and persons representing various segments of the community, including Chicanos, recommend placement for a student only after a thorough analysis of the evaluation by the school psychologist and other pertinent data.

(f) That parents understand the reasons for the possibility of the placement of their child in an EMR class, that these reasons be in writing in the language most familiar to the parents, and that parents give their written approval for such placement prior to placement.

3. State departments of education should issue requirements for the operation of EMR classes, including:

(a) That there be bilingual instruction for students whose first language is not English, taught by bilingual teachers.

(b) That students in EMR classes be thoroughly reevaluated twice during the academic year to determine whether they need to remain in such a class.

(c) That transitional classes be provided for those students who have been evaluated as no longer needing instruction in EMR classes. These classes should emphasize the basic skills of regular instruction and not last more than one year.

4. State departments of education should impose appropriate sanctions, including fund cutoff, on those districts which violate the above requirements.

5. State departments of education should set up a monitoring mechanism to determine, on a regular basis, whether school districts are in compliance with the above requirements.

6. State departments of education should require districts to report the number of students who are placed in EMR classes by ethnic group.

7. State departments of education should conduct compliance reviews of all districts which have an overrepresentation of Chicanos or other minorities in EMR classes for possible violations of the above requirements.

8. The National Institute of Education should provide funds for development of tests of adaptive behavior appropriate for different minority ethnic groups, including Chicanos.

III. TEACHER EDUCATION RECOMMENDATIONS

1. Teacher education institutions in the Southwest should incorporate information about Chicanos in each of their foundation courses and modify their methods courses to include the use of materials and techniques specifically designed for the background, interests, and life experiences of Chicanos. These courses should develop in all trainees:
   - (a) An understanding and appreciation of the history, language, culture, and individual differences of Chicanos.
   - (b) The ability to facilitate the fullest possible development of Chicano students' potential.
   - (c) Skill in interacting positively with Chicano students and adults.
2. Teacher education institutions in the Southwest should assure that trainees perform a portion of their practice teaching in schools with Chicano students, and under the supervision of teachers and professors who have demonstrated skill in teaching Chicano as well as Anglo students.
3. Teacher education institutions should actively recruit additional Chicano trainees, establishing numerical goals and timetables for securing equitable Chicano representation.
4. Teacher education institutions should actively recruit more Chicano staff, establishing numerical goals and timetables for securing equitable Chicano representation.
5. School districts in the Southwest should establish a preference for the hiring of teachers who have had the type of preparation specified in recommendations 1 and 2.
6. School districts in the Southwest should update the teaching skills of present instructional staff by providing in-service training that incorporates the elements specified in recommendations 1 and 2.
7. State departments of education should modify teacher certification standards to require the type of teacher preparation specified in recommendations 1 and 2.
8. State departments of education should establish procedures to assess the language skills and cultural understanding of applicants for teaching certificates and should indicate on all certificates which linguistically and culturally different groups of students the certificate holder is qualified to teach.
9. State departments of education should issue requirements that districts with students whose primary language is not English must provide teachers who speak the students' language and understand their cultural background.
10. State departments of education should actively recruit more Chicanos, establishing numerical goals and timetables for securing equitable Chicano representation.
11. The U.S. Office of Education should actively recruit more Chicanos, establishing numerical goals and timetables for securing equitable Chicano representation.

IV. COUNSELING

1. Institutions which train counselors should actively recruit Chicanos as trainees and staff members, establishing numerical goals and timetables for securing equitable Chicano representation.
2. Institutions which train counselors should maintain data on the trainees' ethnic background to determine the representation of various ethnic groups and to provide needed information to school districts seeking increased minority representation on the counseling staffs of their schools.
3. Institutions which train counselors should actively recruit candidates who have previous experience in working with youth, community organizations, and social or welfare agencies.
4. Institutions which train counselors should emphasize the teaching of counseling techniques and methods other than the traditional one-to-one methods, such as group methods, and alternative forms of counseling, including peer group guidance and the use of paraprofessionals.
5. School districts should encourage counselors to use the above recommended techniques, new methods, and other promising alternative forms of counseling.
6. State departments of education should require school districts actively to recruit additional Chicano counselors, establishing numerical goals and timetables for securing equitable Chicano representation.
7. State departments of education should require school districts to recruit additional counselors to lower the pupil-counselor ratio to 250 to 1 in secondary schools, as recommended by the American School Counselor Association (ASCA).
8. ASCA should inform school officials and the public in general of the need and importance of counseling at the elementary level.
9. State departments of education should require all school districts that have an elementary enrollment to provide at least one counselor, on a half-time basis, in each elementary school.
10. State departments of education in all five Southwestern States should modify State certification requirements for counselors to insure that all counselors, before they are certified, receive instruction in the history, language, and culture of Chicanos.
11. State departments of education should issue regulations that require school districts and schools to provide counselors with sufficient clerical assistance to relieve them of time-consuming paperwork.
12. State departments of education should require that school districts with students whose primary language is not English provide counselors who speak the students' language and understand their cultural background.
    (a) State departments of education should establish procedures for assessing the language skills and cultural understanding of applicants for counseling certificates.

    (b) State departments of education should indicate on all counselors' certificates the cultural and linguistic groups of students the certificate holder is qualified to counsel.

13. The National Institute of Education should fund research to develop techniques which are specifically aimed at meeting the counseling and guidance needs of Chicano pupils. Findings from such research should be disseminated in all areas where Chicanos attend school.

V. TITLE VI

1. OCR should take the steps necessary to increase substantially the number of districts reviewed annually regarding the denial of equal educational services to Mexican American students.
    (a) HEW should increase the educational staff of each OCR regional office so as to facilitate prompt investigation of complaints alleging a denial of equal educational services and to make it possible to conduct routine reviews of all districts included under Title VI.
    (b) To reduce time-consuming delays in negotiations resulting from the districts' lack of expertise, HEW should provide funds for technical assistance to districts which have been found in noncompliance and which need help in developing compliance plans to provide equal educational services. OCR should require that all consultants who are to be paid with these funds must be approved by OCR.

2. OCR should expand the scope of data collection in its annual school surveys so to have a broad set of indicators of likely denial of equal educational services to minority students. At a minimum, the additional data collected should include *for each school:*
    (a) The race or ethnicity of students placed in EMR classes.
    (b) Percentage of students entering school by race or ethnicity whose home language is not English.
    (c) Estimates of student achievement levels by race or ethnicity for the third and sixth grades.
    (d) The number of student hours per week in each grade spent on instruction other than English (excluding the specific teaching of foreign languages).

3. OCR should establish specific standards for evaluating the survey data collected to determine which districts should be subject to compliance reviews.

4. OCR should make greater use of the sanction of fund termination against districts which fail to negotiate or implement a voluntary compliance within specified time limits.

5. OCR should provide for prompt follow-up reviews of each district whose compliance plan has been accepted and subsequent regular monitoring to assure that the plan is being fully implemented.

6. OCR should produce updated printed materials on its official policies

275

for compliance with the equal educational services provisions of Title VI and disseminate these to all districts and to the general public. OCR should require districts to make these official OCR policy materials available to the public upon request.

---

1 Some recommendations in this report which are directed to State departments of education may, in specific States, more directly involve the jurisdiction of the State board of education. In such cases, the recommendations should be construed as directed to those Boards.

276

2-109